The Right Skills for the Job?

The Right Skills for the Job?

Rethinking Training Policies for Workers

Rita Almeida, Jere Behrman, and David Robalino
Editors

THE WORLD BANK
Washington, D.C.

ISBN (paper): 978-0-8213-8714-6
ISBN (electronic): 978-0-8213-8715-3
DOI: 10.1596/978-0-8213-8714-6

Library of Congress Cataloging-in-Publication Data
The right skills for the job? : rethinking training policies for workers / Rita Almeida ... [et al.], editors.
    p. cm. -- (Human development perspectives)
  Includes bibliographical references.
  ISBN 978-0-8213-8714-6 (alk. paper) -- ISBN 978-0-8213-8715-3
  1. Occupational training. 2. Employees--Training of. 3. Vocational education.
4. Manpower policy. I. Almeida, Rita. II. World Bank.
  HD5715.R54 2012
  658.3'124--dc23

                                                                                    2012011906

Cover painting: "Best Way" (2007) by Louis Epee Mbounja, Cameroon; World Bank Art Collection.
Cover design: Naylor Design.

Contents

Boxes

Figures

Tables

Foreword

As the world's economies struggle to create more and better jobs for all, skills development and training policies are at the center of the response. Workers are trying to acquire the right skills to become employable and well remunerated. Firms, in turn, are seeking workers with specific types of skills that—even in many countries with high unemployment—they are unable to find.

The problems are particularly acute in developing countries. First, many workers in these countries have very low levels of education and lack the basic cognitive skills to succeed in the labor market. Second, training programs in these countries often provide skills that are not in demand. The programs also underprovide the analytical and behavioral skills that firms demand and that are critical for enabling innovation and creating high-productivity jobs.

This book discusses how current training policies and programs in developing countries need to change to improve education levels and skills development. It uses the evidence from recent rigorous evaluations to provide a comprehensive review of technical vocational education and training (TVET) policies, incentives for on-the-job-training (OJT), and training-related active labor market programs (ALMPs). These interventions tend to fall short when based on insufficient understanding of the market failures they are trying to solve and/or the government failures that constrain their implementation. The book argues that the key to more productive investments in training and a better alignment between the supply and demand of technical, cognitive, and noncognitive skills lies in better functioning product, capital, and labor markets. Following on this diagnosis, the book presents several new ideas about how to improve the design and implementation of skills-related programs to make them more effective and relevant.

The Human Development Perspectives series seeks to present thorough research findings on issues of critical importance for developing countries. Well-designed and evidence-based public policy interventions, such as those discussed in this volume, are critical to improving living standards and eradicating poverty. *The Right Skills for the Job* are essential for achieving better incomes and higher productivity for all those who work in the developing world.

Arup Banerji   Ariel Fiszbein
Director   Chief Economist
Social Protection and Labor   Human Development
The World Bank   The World Bank

Acknowledgments

This report is part of an emerging program at the Human Development Network (HDN) of the World Bank to support work on skills development, employability, and productivity growth. The book was edited (in alphabetical order) by Rita Almeida (Human Development Network Social Protection [HDNSP], World Bank), Jere Behrman (University of Pennsylvania), and David Robalino (HDNSP, World Bank). Chapter authors include Rita Almeida, Jere Behrman, and David Robalino (chapter 2, Policy Framework); Jee-Peng Tan and Yoo-Jeung Joy Nam (chapter 3, Pre-Employment Technical and Vocational Education and Training); Rita Almeida and Yoonyoung Cho (chapter 4, Employer-Provided Training); and Jochen Kluve of Humboldt-Universität zu Berlin and RWI, and Friederike Rother and María Laura Sánchez Puerta of the World Bank (chapter 5, Training Programs).

We are extremely grateful for the continuous support provided by Arup Banerji (Director, HDNSP), Ariel Fiszbein (Chief Economist, Human Development Network [HDN]), and Mamta Murthi (Advisor, Europe and Central Asia Vice Presidency [ECAVP]). Detailed and insightful comments were also provided by Amit Dar (Sector Manager, South Asia Sector for Human Development [SASHD]), Wendy Cunningham (Sector Leader, Social Protection, Human Development Network [LCSHD]), and P. Zafiris Tzannatos (Consultant, Middle East & North Africa Human Development Sector Unit [MNSHD]). The report also greatly benefitted from comments by Peter Darvas (Senior Education Economist, Africa Education Sector Unit [AFTED]), Bruno Laporte (Director, World Bank Institute [WBI]), Helen Abadzi (Senior Education Specialist, Education for All Fast Track Initiative), Adriana Jaramillo (Senior Education Specialist, Education, Middle East and North Africa Region [MNSHE]), Mamta Murthi (Sector Manager, Education, Europe and Central Asia [ECAED]), Deon Filmer (Lead Economist, Development Research Group [DECHD]), Ian Walker (Lead Economist, Latin America and the Caribbean [LAC]), Christian Aedo (Senior Education Economist, Latin America and the Caribbean [LAC], Human Development, Education Unit [LCSHE]), Peter N. Materu (Lead Education Specialist, AFTED), and David Kaplan (Senior Economist, Inter-American Development Bank [IADB]). We also thank the participants of the Human Resource Development (HRD) Conference in the Republic of Korea (September 2010), as well as the participants of the Mini Labor Market Core Course (March 2011) and the Labor Market Core Course (April 2011) at the World Bank. Special thanks go to Yoo-Jeung Joy Nam for her outstanding editing and contributions to the overall coordination of the report.

This report builds partly on a series of background papers produced jointly by HDNSP and Korean partners at the Ministry of Labor, Korea Labor Institute (KLI) and Korea Research Institute for Vocational Education & Training (KRIVET). The background papers were developed under the project "Skills Development Strategies: Lessons from the Korean Experience and Global Trends." Special thanks go to Kyung Woo Shim, Kye Woo Lee, Young-Sun Ra, ChangKyun Chae, JooSeop Kim, Hye-Won Ko, Jaeho Chung, and Hyung-Jai Choi, who authored and provided very important inputs to these papers. We are also very thankful to Dug-ho Kim for his support in the dissemination of the project in Korea.

Abbreviations

ADB	Asian Development Bank
AFTED	Africa Education Sector Unit
ALMPs	Active Labor Market Programs
CIMO	*Calidad Integral y Modernización* (Integrated Quality and Modernization)
CSTI	Construction Skills Training Institute
DECHD	Development Research Group
ECA	Europe and Central Asia
ECAED	Education, Europe and Central Asia
ECAVP	Europe and Central Asia Vice Presidency
EDB	Economic Development Board, Singapore
EPAG	Economic Empowerment of Adolescent Girls
EPB	Economic Planning Board, Republic of Korea
EPT	Employer-Provided Training
EPWP	Expanded Public Work Program, South Africa
FDFP	*Fonds de Developpement de la Formation Professionnelle*
GAIN	Greater Avenues to Independence
GDP	Gross Domestic Product
GED	General Educational Development
HDN	Human Development Network
HDNCY	Human Development Network Children and Youth Department
HDNSP	Human Development Network Social Protection
HRDF	Human Resource Development Fund, Malaysia
IADB	Inter-American Development Bank
ICT	Information and Communications Technology
ILO	International Labour Organization
ISCED	International Standard Classification of Education

ISKUR	Turkish Public Employment Agency
IT	Information Technology
ITB	Investment Training Boards
ITE	Institute for Technical Education, Singapore
ITES	Information Technology-Enabled Services
LAC	Latin America and the Caribbean
L&T	Larsen and Toubro
LCSHE	Latin America and the Caribbean Region, Human Development, Education Unit
M&E	Monitoring and Evaluation
MENA	Middle East and North Africa
MNSHD	Middle East & North Africa Human Development Sector Unit
MNSHE	Education, Middle East and North Africa Region
NAC	NASSCOM Assessment of Competence
NASSCOM	National Association of Software and Service Companies
NDYP	New Deal for Young People, United Kingdom
NGO	Nongovernmental Organization
OECD	Organisation for Economic Co-operation and Development
OJT	On-the-Job Training
PAC	*Programa de Apoyo a la Capacitación* (Training Support Program), Mexico
PATI	*Programa de Apoyo Temporal al Ingreso* (Temporary Income Support Program), El Salvador
PMP	Policy-Making Process
QYSTI	Qing Yuan Senior Technical Institute, China
RMP	Rural Maintenance Program, Bangladesh
SABER	System Assessment and Benchmarking for Education Results
SASHD	South Asia Sector for Human Development
SENAI	*Serviço Nacional de Aprendizagem Industrial* (National Service for Industrial Training), Brazil
SENCE	*Servicio Nacional de Capacitación y Empleo* (National Training and Employment Service), Chile
SME	Small and Medium Enterprise
StEP	Skills toward Employability and Productivity
TC	Training Consortium
TISP	Temporary Income Support Program, El Salvador
TVET	Technical and Vocational Education and Training
UISA	Unemployment Insurance Savings Accounts
UNESCO	United Nations Educational, Scientific and Cultural Organization
VET	Vocational Education and Training
WBI	World Bank Institute

Introduction

The accumulation of human capital through the acquisition of knowledge and skills is recognized as central for economic development. More-educated workers not only have better employment opportunities, earn more, and have more stable and rewarding jobs, but they are also more adaptable and mobile.[1] Workers who acquire more skills make other workers and capital more productive and, within the firm, they facilitate the adaptation, adoption, and ultimately invention of new technologies. This is crucial to enable economic diversification, productivity growth, and ultimately raise the standards of living of the population.[2]

In the developing world, however, the majority of the labor force has very low levels of education. Even those with higher degrees might not have acquired the skills necessary to succeed in the labor market—particularly high-level analytical and interactive skills. Middle-high-income countries have the best indicators and yet the average number of years of schooling is only 8.5—primary plus some years of secondary education. Only 30 percent of the working age population has successfully finished high school and less than 7 percent have a university diploma.[3] In low-income countries, up to 73 percent of the labor force is illiterate (Niger) and average years of education can be as low as 1.2 (Mozambique).[4] Even those who have had the opportunity to attend school and obtain a university or vocational training diploma are today struggling. Across countries, a very small share of graduates attends top-level schools and gets access to the best jobs either in their country of origin or abroad. Compensation for these lucky few has been on the rise, but for others school to work transitions can be difficult and earnings have remained stagnant. Thus, wage premiums for high skills in certain occupations coincide with poor labor market indicators, including unemployment and inactivity.[5] At the same time, employers frequently complain that workers' lack of skills is a constraint to their business. This mismatch between the skills individuals have and those which are needed seems pervasive across countries. In India, for instance, 50 percent of university graduates obtain a diploma in arts, far exceeding employer demands.[6] In Tunisia, more than 50 percent of university graduates are in jobs that do not use the skills they acquired in university.[7] In Cambodia, employers also complain about skill mismatches, especially among out-of-school youth. More recent evidence from Lebanon shows that 40 percent of wage earners and the self-employed are in occupations that do not use their skills.[8]

The situation is further complicated by the diversity of skills that seem to matter. Indeed, recent empirical analyses show that success in the labor market does not only depend on the acquisition of technical skills.[9] Cognitive and noncognitive skills, in part acquired in early childhood and during basic and secondary schooling, are also important determinants of employment dynamics and earnings later in life.[10] A pattern that seems to emerge is that as economies develop and diversify, the demand for higher-level cognitive skills increases relative to the demands for manual job-specific skills. Yet, the few studies looking at the distribution of cognitive and noncognitive skills in the labor force in developing countries suggest that certain vulnerable groups, such as the unemployed (and first time job seekers) tend to have low cognitive scores or lack the behavioral skills that predict success as a self-employed worker or entrepreneur.[11]

There are, of course, no easy solutions to these problems. Any strategy to address them would need to consider interventions at different levels, starting with the creation of conditions for adequate early childhood development, laying a strong foundation in basic and secondary education, and building and upgrading job skills in response to labor market signals. Improving productivity and labor market outcomes would also require coordinated training and labor policies to promote entrepreneurship and innovation, facilitate the mobility of the labor force, and improve the matching of skills to jobs.[12] Clearly, the implementation of this cumulative and more comprehensive approach will mainly bring results over the medium and long terms.[13] Over the short term, countries still face the challenge of improving the skills of those who are already in the labor force.

This report brings new ideas about how to build and upgrade job relevant skills, focusing on three types of training programs relevant for individuals who are leaving the formal general schooling system or are already in the labor market: pre-employment technical and vocational education and training (TVET); on-the-job training (OJT); and training-related active labor market programs (ALMPs). Several previous studies have discussed some of the flaws in current systems and outlined options for reform.[14] Training centers had grown disconnected from market demands and investments in training within the firms did not increase as expected. Training related ALMPs, on the other hand, remained largely underdeveloped and focused more on formal than informal sector workers. As a consequence, there has been a shift away from the investment in pre-vocational training courses to programs to improve access to and the quality of general secondary education.[15] There have also been calls to encourage a stronger involvement of the private sector in the provision of training, together with increased emphasis in the quality and relevance of the content. One result has been a push to rethink the governance and financing arrangements of training institutions. But overall policies at these three levels of the training systems remain disconnected and there has not been an integrated framework linking them to specific market and government failures that need to be addressed.[16]

The contributions of the current report are twofold. First, the report takes an in-depth look at the types of market and government failures that can result in underinvestment in training or the supply of skills that are not immediately relevant to the labor market (see Chapter 2). Regarding markets, the discussion goes beyond the classic problem of individuals not taking into account the social benefits of their investments in education, and focuses instead on imperfections in labor and capital markets, as well as decision-making problems facing individuals. The second contribution focuses on policies. Building on the analysis of the limitations of both markets and governments and the results of case studies and recent impact evaluations, the report develops new ideas to improve the design and performance of current training programs, which often involve interventions outside the education and training systems (see Chapters 3 to 5).

Market Failures, OJT, and Training-Related ALMPs

An important message from the policy framework is that the design of training policies needs to be based on a better understanding of the problems facing the private sector to produce a socially desirable level and distribution of skills. One of the issues raised is *imperfections in labor markets,* which can reduce incentives to invest in skills, both among employers and employees. When there is no perfect competition in the markets for different skills, employers might invest less in training their workers who can be poached by others (poaching externalities). Workers are also less likely to invest in their own training if employers have market power and are able to keep wages down (bargaining externalities). There can also be coordination failures if, for instance, employers do not create high-productivity jobs because there are no skilled workers, and workers do not invest in skills because there are no jobs (innovation and vacancy externalities). Standard *problems with credit markets* can also affect the supply of skills, if either individuals or firms are not able to finance their investment in training. Finally, the lack of information—"myopia"—and the lack of the necessary cognitive and noncognitive skills can bias individuals' decisions regarding training: they can underinvest and stop their studies, choose the wrong specialization or provider, or simply fail to complete a given course or set of courses.

Solutions to all these problems do not necessarily include subsidizing training or taxing firms to finance OJT—two of the most common interventions. The focus, instead, can be in identifying and addressing the market failures at hand. This could be accomplished, for instance, by increasing the bargaining power of workers, reducing barriers to entry in product markets, facilitating the diffusion of new technologies that will create demands for skilled labor, designing contracts that reduce the likelihood of poaching, opening credit lines for specific types of training, and providing information about labor market conditions and the quality of various training providers. If, ultimately, subsidies are needed to address coordination failures or improve incentives to invest in training, then they should be targeted to individuals and firms that would not otherwise invest but that can benefit from training. Subsidies should be explicit and preferably financed out of general revenues instead of payroll taxes, which increase labor costs and eventually decrease the demand for labor.

The report also suggests that a special set of training programs could target vulnerable groups without access to formal programs—either because of low skill levels or because they operate in the informal sector where the access to training funds is more difficult. Besides providing job-specific skills, these programs could help address some of the decision-making and communication problems facing individuals with interventions such as training in life skills and counseling. Ideally, the programs would link individuals to internships or programs that support transitions into self-employment. International experience suggests that these types of integrated programs can have a positive impact on labor markets. An important feature of their design is to outsource the provision of services to private companies with contracting and payment systems based on specific outcomes (for example, the number of job placements).

Government Failures and TVET

Clearly, for years to come, a large share of the supply of training across countries will continue to come from the public sector through TVET programs. Improving the relevance of the skills that individuals acquire will require addressing failures in current institutional arrangements in order to improve accountability and strengthen links with the private sector. Part of the problem, as previously identified, is current financing mechanisms that directly allocate funds to training centers on a historical basis. The review of international experiences shows the importance of linking the disbursement of funds to performance and/or relying on voucher systems that allow individuals to choose and directly pay training providers. To set the stage for more direct financing of training, training centers should be given independence in the management of curricula, the selection of students, and human resource policies.

However, given the market failures described above, relying on pure market mechanisms might not be enough. To start with, there should be arrangements in place to provide information to potential students about career prospects and the quality of different providers. This requires certifying training centers and probably the different diplomas that are provided. Provided that institutional capacity exists, countries would also need to consider setting up independent apex training authorities to better organize and manage the oversight of training provision. Key components of success include ensuring that the training authorities enjoy strong partnerships with employers and other stakeholders, have decision-making power, and have the authority to oversee (without direct involvement in) the operations of individual TVET institutions.[17] Singapore's Institute for Technical Education (ITE) and Pakistan's Sindh Technical and Vocational Training Authority are two examples of such increasingly common apex training authorities. With clearly defined oversight functions, these entities have the capacity to encourage participation of nonstate providers while improving the service delivery capacity of public training providers. By fostering competition in the training market and effectively liaising between training institutions and stakeholders, these apex institutions are able to ensure more optimal TVET provision.

The government might also have a role in addressing coordination externalities that affect the development of strategic sectors. The successful experiences of the Republic of Korea; Taiwan, China; and Singapore illustrate how countries can incorporate demand-driven TVET into their national industrialization strategies.[18] These Asian tigers understood the type of coordination failures that can emerge in training markets in the early stages of development. In response, they pursued strategic government-led coordination that encouraged more effective alignment of skills demand and supply as well as sustainable investments in higher-level skills. Key institutional mechanisms for coordinating economic and training policy ensured that TVET programs were effectively linked to the overall strategy for industrialization. Singapore's Economic Development Board (EDB) is one such coordinating mechanism that is credited for leading successful skills development schemes during the agency's first three decades (1961–91).

An Agenda for Research and Policy Analysis

The various chapters in the report identify areas for future research and policy analysis. An important question is *how to define and measure the set of skills that determine individuals' employability and labor market outcomes in developing countries*. One of the main avenues for further research is the development of sound, regularly administered surveys of workers and firms at the country level that measure the supply and demand of technical, cognitive, and noncognitive skills. These surveys can then be used to assess how different skills affect labor outcomes, and to study issues related to mismatches between the supply and demand of skills.

Another important challenge is to improve our understanding of market failures that potentially affect skills supply both at the level of the firm and the individual. For instance, there should be a better understanding of why firms are not training: is it because there are poaching externalities or financing constraints or simply because, given the product and the markets where it is sold, it does not pay to invest in training? Similarly, failures at the individual level should be studied: how severe are information problems and myopia for different groups of workers? Only through a better understanding of the causes that affect the supply of skills can policy makers devise the right set of interventions.

Finally, with all levels of training—TVET, OJT, or training-related ALMPs—there are open questions about design and implementation. Most evaluations that exist today provide information on whether a given program or intervention is having an impact, but not why. It is important to gradually move to a second generation of impact evaluations that will focus less on the impact of programs and more on features of their design. For example, evaluations should be able to identify the best types of contracting and payment systems for providers or the best ways to finance and allocate training funds. Gradually, the knowledge generated across countries can be used to design blueprints for the implementation of the various programs.

Notes

1. There is a vast literature empirically supporting the value of investing in education to develop human capital and on the contribution of education to growth and development (see, for example, Vandenbussche, Aghion, and Meghir 2006; Aghion 2008; Helpman, 2004; Hanushek and Kimko 2000; Krueger and Lindahl 2000; Hanushek and Woessmann 2007).
2. See Helpman (2004).
3. See Cho et al. (2011).
4. See Cho et al. (2012).

5. The trends in skills premia have been very diverse across the world. Di Gropello and Sakellariou (2010) show that the more advanced countries in East Asia (for example, Indonesia, the Philippines, and Thailand) have experienced stagnating returns, while countries with faster growth but less-developed economies (for example, Vietnam, China, Mongolia, and Cambodia) are still experiencing strong increases in skill premia. In Latin America, Aedo and Walker (2012) show that the region experienced rising relative wages for people with tertiary education in the 1990s but that around 2002 the trend was reversed.

6. See World Bank (2012).

7. Skills toward Employability and Productivity (StEP) framework in Banerji et al. (2010).

8. See Pierre and Robalino (forthcoming).

9. For example, skills include the knowledge, expertise, and behaviors that the job holder needs in order to execute his or her responsibilities competently. They include mastery of a body of knowledge relevant to the job; familiarity with the tools and technologies used to perform the tasks associated with the job; understanding of the materials that are worked with; and the fostering and use of interpersonal relationships and interactions to accomplish the tasks required in the job.

10. Heckman, Stixrud, and Urzua (2006) show that both cognitive and noncognitive skills are important in explaining a diverse array of labor market outcomes. Although there are important gender differences in the effects of these skills, for most behaviors, both factors play an important role for both men and women. Carneiro and Heckman (2003), Heckman and Masterov (2004), Cunha et al. (2006), and numerous other papers establish that parents play an important role in producing both the cognitive and noncognitive skills of their children.

11. See Pierre and Robalino (forthcoming).

12. See the Skills toward Employability and Productivity (StEP) framework in Banerji et al. (2010).

13. The importance of creating the conditions for adequate early childhood development and of laying a strong foundation in basic and secondary schooling has been well established in multiple World Bank reports and publications (see, for example, Murnane and Levy (1996)).

14. For a discussion see Middleton, Ziderman, and Adams (1991, 1993). They discuss training policies that may help governments make the transition to a more dynamic and efficient use of public resources, ensure that the skills needed to meet the challenges of economic change are developed, and that equity objectives for the poor and the socially disadvantaged are effectively addressed. Their findings highlight that the design of training programs can be advanced by encouraging private sector training, improving the effectiveness and efficiency of public training, and using training as a complementary input in programs designed to improve the incomes of the poor and socially disadvantaged.

15. Sondergaard and Murthi (2012) show that, for Eastern Europe, reducing the skills shortage requires fundamental change in a country's education system. Such change should aim to deliver higher-quality education for the vast majority of students ("not just diplomas but skills"). Furthermore, the methods of

improved student learning should be more widely studied and used by education institutions and at the policy-making level.

16. See Canagarajah et al. (2002).
17. See ADB (2008).
18. See Ashton et al. 2002 and Kuruvilla et al. 2002.

References

Aedo, Cristián, and Ian Walker. 2012. *Skills for the 21st Century in Latin America and the Caribbean.* Washington, DC: World Bank.

Aghion, Philippe. 2008 "Growth and Education." Commission on Growth and Development, Working Paper 56. World Bank, Washington, DC.

Ashton, David, Francis Green, Johnny Sung, and Donna James. 2002. "The Evolution of Education and Training Strategies in Singapore, Taiwan and S. Korea: A Development Model of Skill Formation." *Journal of Education and Work* 15(1): 5–30.

Asian Development Bank (ADB). 2008. *Education and Skills: Strategies for Accelerated Development in Asia and the Pacific.* Manila: ADB.

Banerji, Arup, Wendy Cunningham, Ariel Fiszbein, Elizabeth King, Harry Patrinos, David Robalino, and Jee-Peng Tan. 2010. "Stepping Up Skills for More Jobs and Higher Productivity." World Bank, Washington, DC.

Canagarajah, Roy S., Amit Dar, Rikke Nording, and Dhushyanth Raju. 2002. "Effectiveness of Lending for Vocational Education and Training: Lessons from World Bank Experience." Social Protection Discussion Paper Series, No. 0222. Social Protection Unit, Human Development Network, World Bank, Washington, DC.

Carneiro, Pedro, and James J. Heckman. 2003. "Human Capital Policy." In James J. Heckman, Alan B. Krueger, and Benjamin M. Friedman, eds., *Inequality in America: What Role for Human Capital Policies?* Cambridge, MA: MIT Press.

Cho, Yoon, David Margolis, David Newhouse, and David Robalino. 2011. "Labor Markets in Middle and Low Income Countries: Challenges and Implications for the Social Protection Strategy." Background paper to the New Social Protection and Labor Strategy. Human Development Social Protection Discussion Paper Series. World Bank, Washington, DC.

———. 2012. "Labor Market in Middle and Low Income Countries: Implications for Social Protection and Labor Policies." Human Development Social Protection Discussion Paper Series. World Bank, Washington, DC.

Cunha, Flavio, James J. Heckman, Lance J. Lochner, and Dimitriy V. Masterov. 2006. "Interpreting the Evidence on Life Cycle Skill Formation." In Eric A. Hanushek and Frank Welch, eds., *Handbook of the Economics of Education.* Amsterdam: North Holland.

Di Gropello, Emanuela, and Chris Sakellariou. 2010. "Industry and Skill Wage Premiums in East Asia." Policy Research Working Paper 5379. World Bank, Washington, DC.

Gill, Indermit S., Amit Dar, and Fred Fluitman. 1998. *Skills and Change: Constraints and Innovation in the Reform of Vocational Education and Training.* Washington, DC and Geneva: World Bank and International Labour Office.

Hanushek, Eric A., and Dennis D. Kimko. 2000. "Schooling, Labor-Force Quality, and the Growth of Nations." *American Economic Review* 90(5): 1184–1208.

Hanushek, Eric A., and Ludger Woessmann. 2007. "The Role of Education Quality for Economic Growth." Policy Research Working Paper No. 4122. World Bank, Washington, DC.

Heckman, James J., and Dimitriy V. Masterov. 2004. "The Productivity Argument for Investing in Young Children." Technical Report Working Paper No. 5. Committee for Economic Development, Washington, DC.

Heckman, James J., Jora Stixrud, and Sergio Urzua. 2006. "The Effects of Cognitive and Noncognitive Abilities on Labor Market Outcomes and Social Behavior." *Journal of Labor Economics* 24: 411–82.

Helpman, Elhanan. 2004. *The Mystery of Economic Growth*. Cambridge, MA: Belknap Press of Harvard University Press.

Johanson, Richard K., and Arvil V. Adams. 2004. *Skills Development in Sub-Saharan Africa*. World Bank Regional and Sectoral Studies. Washington, DC: World Bank.

Krueger, Alan B., and Mikael Lindahl. 2000. "Education for Growth: Why and For Whom?" National Bureau of Economic Research (NBER) Working Paper 7591. NBER, Cambridge, MA.

Kuruvilla, Sarosh, Christopher L. Erickson, and Alvin Hwang. 2002. "An Assessment of the Singapore Skills Development System: Does It Constitute a Viable Model for Other Developing Countries?" *World Development* 30(8): 1461–76.

Levy, Frank, and Richard J. Murnane. 2005. *The New Division of Labor: How Computers Are Creating the Next Job Market*. Princeton, NJ: Princeton University Press.

Middleton, John, and Terri Demsky. 1989. "Vocational Education and Training: A Review of World Bank Investments." World Bank Discussion Paper 51. World Bank, Washington, DC.

Middleton, John, Adrian Ziderman, and Arvil V. Adams. 1991. "Vocational and Technical Education and Training." World Bank Policy Paper. World Bank, Washington, DC.

———. 1993. *Skills for Productivity: Vocational Education and Training in Developing Countries*. Washington, DC: Oxford University Press for the World Bank.

Murnane, Richard J., and Frank Levy. 1996. *Teaching the New Basic Skills: Principles for Educating Children to Thrive in a Changing Economy*. New York, NY: The Free Press.

Pierre, Gaëlle, and David Robalino. 2012. "Skills Mismatch: A Comprehensive Analysis of the Skills that Matter in the Lebanese Labor Market." Unpublished paper. World Bank, Washington, DC.

———. Forthcoming. "The Role of Technical, Cognitive, and Non-Cognitive Skills in Labor Markets in Lebanon." IZA Working Paper Series, Bonn, Germany.

Rigolini, Jamele, Laura Pabon, Mariana Infante, Andrew Jones, and Maria Laura Sanchez-Puerta. 2010. "Providing Skills for Equity and Growth: Preparing Cambodia's Youth for the Labor Market." Working Paper. Human Development Department, East Asia and Pacific Region. World Bank, Washington, DC.

Robalino, David A., Mario Di Filippo, Tanja Lohmann, and David N. Margolis. 2010. "Skills toward Employment and Productivity." Unpublished paper, Social Protection and Labor. World Bank, Washington, DC.

Sondergaard, Lars, and Mamta Murthi. 2012. *Skills, Not Just Diplomas: Managing Education for Results in Eastern Europe and Central Asia.* Directions in Development Series. Washington, DC: World Bank.

Vandenbussche, Jérôme, Philippe Aghion, and Costas Meghir. 2006. "Growth, Distance to Frontier and Composition of Human Capital." *Journal of Economic Growth* 11(2): 97–127.

World Bank. 2006. *World Development Report 2007: Development and the Next Generation.* Washington, DC: World Bank.

World Bank. 2012. *More and Better Jobs in South Asia.* Washington, DC: World Bank.

1

Overview

David Robalino and Rita Almeida

Introduction

Creating jobs and increasing productivity are at the top of the social and economic agendas of governments around the world. Skills development is an essential component of these agendas. Too many workers are simply unprepared to meet the needs of current and future jobs, which will involve a growing content of nonroutine analytical and/or interactive tasks. At the same time, the systems to provide training are often plagued by weak governance and poor incentives that make them unreliable or ineffective.

Thus even workers with higher levels of education might not have the skills necessary to succeed in the labor market. In India, for instance, 50 percent of university graduates obtain a diploma in arts, far exceeding employer demands.[1] In Tunisia, more than 50 percent of university graduates are in jobs that do not use the skills they acquired in university.[2] Furthermore, in Cambodia, employers in the construction, garment, and hospitality sectors identify soft employee skills, especially among out-of-school youth.[3]

Evidence from the World Bank's Enterprise Surveys[4] in more than 100 countries shows that lack of workers with the right skills affects firm performance. For example, the share of firms worried about inadequate worker education and skills averages about 25 percent in the Organisation for Economic Co-operation and Development (OECD) and in Europe and Central Asia (ECA), 40 percent in Sub-Saharan Africa, and 50 percent in East Asia and the Pacific. Even in the ECA region, where countries have enjoyed a legacy of high skill endowments, the great majority of firms surveyed in

2008 considered deficits in education and skills to be a major or severe constraint. Furthermore, skills bottlenecks are likely to worsen in the coming years. The employer complaints about skills are more often voiced by firms that are newer, faster-growing, more outwardly oriented, and more eager to move up the technology ladder.[5]

The problem is complicated by the diversity of skills that matter. Recent empirical analyses show that success in the labor market does not only depend on the acquisition of technical skills.[6] Cognitive and noncognitive skills, which are in part acquired in early childhood and during basic and secondary schooling, are also important determinants of employment dynamics and earnings later in life.[7,8] A pattern that seems to emerge is that as economies develop and diversify, the demand for higher-level cognitive skills increases relative to the demands for manual job-specific skills (see figure 1.1 and box 1.1). The importance of behavioral or noncognitive skills should not be underestimated. In many economies, employers are searching for workers who possess behavioral skills such as teamwork, diligence, creativity, and entrepreneurship. Skill-building systems will also need the capacity to improve behavioral attributes.

Policy making is complicated by the multiplicity of channels through which skills are acquired. These channels include parents and families in the early years of life; later through schools, universities, and vocational

Figure 1.1   Demand for Different Types of Skills in the United States, 1960–2002

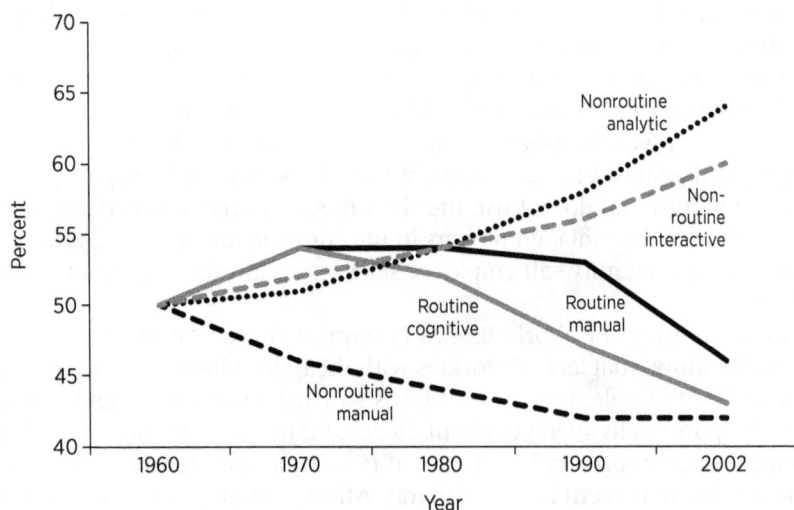

Source: Levy and Murnane (2005).

> **BOX 1.1**
>
> ## Defining Job-Relevant Skills and Acknowledging the Boundaries of Job Training Policies
>
> Job-relevant skills refer to a set of competencies or abilities valued by employers and useful for self-employment. They include technical skills relevant to the specific job of the worker, as well as other cognitive and noncognitive skills that enhance his or her productivity more generally. These other skills include:
>
> - problem-solving skills or the capacity to think critically and analyze
> - learning skills or the ability to acquire new knowledge ("learning to learn"), distill lessons from experience, and apply them in search of innovations
> - communication skills, including writing skills, collecting and using information to communicate with others, fluency in foreign languages, and use of information and communications technology (ICT)
> - personal skills for self-management, making sound judgments, and managing risks
> - social skills to collaborate with and motivate others in a team, manage client relations, exercise leadership, resolve conflicts, and develop social networks
>
> *Source:* Banerji et al. (2010).

centers; and, ultimately, on-the-job training and learning through experience. Whereas general skills like literacy and numeracy accumulate from early childhood and are reinforced through general basic education, job-relevant skills tend to be acquired later on, either prior to entry into the labor market or through on-the-job and building on the earlier skill foundations. In addition, whether the formation and accumulation of the right skills translates into higher employment and productivity growth depends on how well labor markets function. Labor markets where information is lacking or where the labor force cannot move freely may fail to match job seekers with the right jobs.

This book addresses the question of how to build and upgrade job relevant skills. Specifically, we focus on three types of training programs relevant for individuals who are leaving formal general schooling or are already in the labor market: pre-employment technical and vocational education and training (TVET); on-the-job training (OJT); and training-related active labor market programs (ALMPs). ALMPs are usually of shorter duration and target individuals who are seeking a second chance and who do not have access to TVET or OJT; these are often low-skilled unemployed or informal workers. Contrary to training-related ALMPs, pre-employment TVET is usually offered within the formal schooling track and tends to be administered by the ministries of education.[9]

The book discusses the main justifications for these programs and how they relate to market failures that can lead to underinvestment in training and misalignment between supply and demand for skills. These failures go beyond the classic problem of individuals not taking into account the social benefits of their investments in education. They reflect problems in product, labor, and capital markets that manifest themselves, for example, in the following ways:

- reduce incentives for firms to offer training because trained employees can be poached by other firms
- limit the information and knowledge that individuals have to make efficient decisions about investments in training
- make it difficult for firms and individuals to finance investments in training
- lead to situations where workers do not invest in training because there are no jobs for skilled workers and firms do not create these jobs because there are no skilled workers.

Unfortunately, governments are also prone to failure and many of the programs that countries have adopted today are part of the problem and not the solution. This book proposes options to improve the design and implementation of current skills development systems. Clearly, we cannot cover all issues in detail. Training methods among TVET, OJT, and ALMP programs are quite different, ranging from classroom instruction, laboratory research, TVET workshops, and apprenticeship arrangements and internships in firms. All have different challenges and specificities. The report highlights the most important design features of the different programs and points to the main knowledge gaps and areas for future research and analysis.

The book is organized into five chapters. Following this overview, Chapter 2 introduces the policy framework that guides the analysis in the book. This framework describes the main market and government failures that require attention and identifies potential interventions to address them. Chapters 3 to 5 then discuss the main challenges facing, respectively, TVET, OJT, and training-related ALMP programs and outlines recommendations to address them. The rest of this overview summarizes the main messages from each of the chapters and in the last section outlines the main knowledge gaps and proposes an agenda for future research and policy analysis.

Linking Market and Government Failures to the Design of Training-Related Interventions

Frequently, public interventions—including those related to TVET, OJT, and training-related ALMP programs—are designed and implemented without a full understanding of the reasons why markets alone do not generate an efficient distribution of skills. We argue that there are four potential reasons for failed interventions: imperfections in labor markets, imperfections in capital markets, coordination failures, and limited information and individual "myopia" (see figure 1.2). Below we discuss each of these reasons.

Matching and Poaching Externalities in the Labor Market

In perfectly competitive labor markets there would not be a need for government intervention. Employees would have incentives to invest in their training and acquire skills that were in demand, knowing they would receive fair remuneration for those investments (since there are many employers demanding these skills). Governments would simply need to make sure that individuals had the means to finance these investments. But perfectly competitive labor markets are more likely to be the exception than the rule for many reasons. These include barriers to entry that limit the number of firms competing for given skills; workers not having sufficient information about where the jobs are and/or not being able to move to where they are; or employers not having sufficient information about

Figure 1.2 Reasons for Market Failures

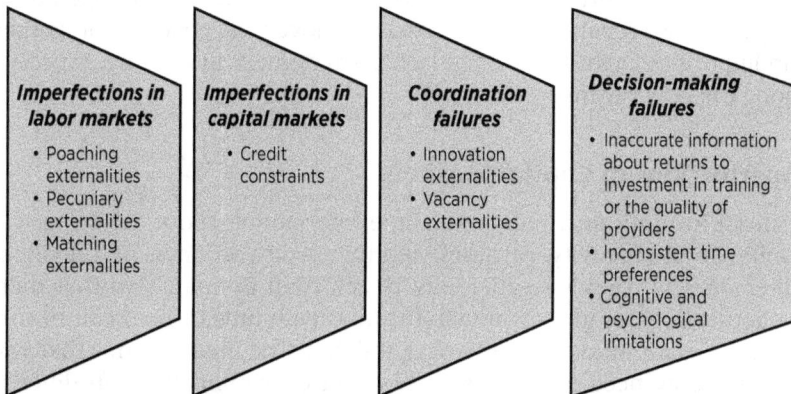

Imperfections in labor markets
- Poaching externalities
- Pecuniary externalities
- Matching externalities

Imperfections in capital markets
- Credit constraints

Coordination failures
- Innovation externalities
- Vacancy externalities

Decision-making failures
- Inaccurate information about returns to investment in training or the quality of providers
- Inconsistent time preferences
- Cognitive and psychological limitations

Source: World Bank.

the skills that workers have. In labor markets that are not perfectly competitive both firms and employees can underinvest in training. Firms underinvest because they cannot fully appropriate the returns to investment in training, since employees can be poached by other firms (we refer to these as poaching externalities);[10] employees underinvest because they would not receive fair remuneration for their higher productivity (we refer to these as matching externalities). The higher the bargaining power of employers the lower the investment in training by employees.

The discussion above has a few policy implications. The first is that the type of intervention that a given country implements needs to be consistent with labor market conditions. For instance, policy makers should not automatically assume that firms face poaching externalities and that something needs to be done to incentivize training. On the one hand, innovative firms that are entering new markets and presumably enjoy some level of market power may have considerable incentives to invest in training and most probably will. One example is India's Infosys, a software technology giant that completed a new 300-faculty Global Education Center in 2009 with a training capacity of 14,000 seats dedicated to enhancing the competency of their staff. On the other hand, when labor markets are reasonably competitive, the focus could be on ensuring that workers have the means to finance investments in job-related training themselves. Poaching externalities and matching externalities are more relevant in labor markets that are "in between" and could require a range of interventions. Examples might include improving the bargaining power of workers and designing contracts where OJT is linked to a given commitment to work for the firm (these would reduce poaching externalities). Recent cross-sectional evidence from the World Bank's Enterprise Surveys[11] shows that while most firms consider informal training sufficient for their regular operations, many firms also report that high worker turnover and poaching of workers is an important factor behind the lack of investment in training, especially among the larger firms.

Imperfections in Capital Markets

Financial institutions usually have little information about the impacts of training on productivity, earnings, and the creditworthiness of individuals and employers. They may therefore be reluctant to finance worker training, particularly for low-income individuals with little or no credit history. This may lead to underinvestment in training. The implication is that governments may need to address these credit constraints through different instruments such as guarantees, student loans, and better information for financial institutions.

Coordination Failures

Often, the success of a given investment depends on the coordinated actions of various agents. At the high end of the skills spectrum, innovation externalities may occur when workers do not invest enough in training because there are not enough jobs for highly qualified professionals. But the reason there are not more of these jobs is that there are not enough qualified professionals in the first place. Economies may thus end up in a low-level equilibrium where firms do not innovate enough and do not pay high enough wages, and workers do not invest in training because of a low skill premia. Similarly, at the low end of the skills spectrum, vacancy externalities may occur where firms do not hire skilled workers because there are not many of them and therefore their wages are high. This reduces low-skilled workers' incentives to invest in training resulting in a low-skills/low-productivity trap. This trap can occur, for example, in the construction or the tourism sector, where firms often operate with low-skilled labor and choose not to fill vacancies for more skilled job because of the higher labor costs.

Here also there are important policy implications. First, there is a need to try to measure and understand coordination problems. Second, interventions would need to include large investments in training for particular segments of the labor force in partnership with the private sector.

Decision-Making Failures

Even with perfect labor and capital markets and no coordination failures, individuals might not make the right decisions when it comes to investments in training. The main reasons are lack of information (knowledge), limited cognitive capacity to process complex problems, and psychological factors that make it difficult to commit to a given decision.[12] For example, quite often individuals have inaccurate information on returns to training that may lead to under- or overinvestment. Individuals also often lack reliable information on the quality of training providers and future employment prospects, and may invest in the wrong training. Even with the necessary information, investments in training and career choices are complex problems and individuals may not always make the right choice. Finally, high discount rates or the lack of noncognitive skills that predict success in school (such as discipline and perseverance) can lead many individuals to procrastinate and fail to get enough education.

Here too governments may need to intervene by improving information about the prospects of different diplomas and specializations, rating and certifying training providers, defining qualification frameworks, providing counseling, and providing incentives to invest in training.

Government Failures

The market failures discussed above may be partially offset by government interventions. Unfortunately, government interventions do not always lead to improvements over markets. They may lead to distortions from the point of view of efficiency and distributional objectives.[13] Chapter 2 reviews the three most common types of government failures associated with government interventions: inappropriate governance structures to design policies, lack of proper institutional arrangements for services delivery, and imperfect information. These failures are briefly discussed below.

Lack of adequate governance structures to design policies

Policy makers often lack the incentives or means to devise policies in the best interest of their citizens. Skills-development policies, for instance, may not be enacted until governments are under election pressures and need the support of politically powerful groups (for example, teachers), or need to lock in short-term achievements, possibly realized before the end of a political cycle. Addressing this problem is not easy. The emerging consensus is that much depends on the quality of the policy-making process (PMP), understood as the process of discussing, approving, and implementing public policies.[14] The quality of PMP depends on the set of political actors and the incentives that they face. These, in turn, are determined, at least in part, by political institutions (such as the legislature, the party system, and the judiciary) and institutional rules (for example, electoral rules). What countries that have introduced successful reforms have in common is a PMP in which political actors cooperate and are able to reach and enforce agreements. Cooperation is more likely to exist where (i) leadership is strong; (ii) there are good "aggregators" to reduce the number of actors with direct influence on policy making; (iii) the key actors plan for the long term and interact repeatedly; (iv) there are institutionalized arenas for political exchange; (v) there are credible institutions to enforce agreements and prevent corruption (like an independent judiciary); and (vi) there is a strong bureaucracy to which the analysis and implementation of policies can be delegated. Some fundamentals of a good PMP are a transparent process to discuss and design policies involving different stakeholders; a clear strategic vision for skills development; and more reliance on technical staff within ministries who can ensure continuity in the policy dialogue.

Lack of proper institutional arrangements for service delivery

Even when the political process is right, policies will fail if they do not provide the right set of incentives and margin of maneuver to those involved in the delivery of training. For instance, the quality and relevance of training in public centers is unlikely to improve if teachers' remuneration and career prospects are unrelated to their performance, or if budgets are delinked from the level of demand for the center's services. At the same time, the right incentives will not result in better services delivery if managers have their hands tied by excessive centralization or inappropriate regulations. Governments are therefore advised to develop sound institutional arrangements for the implementation agencies, and award them with sufficient autonomy. Measures such as individual vouchers for increased choice over training providers may also contribute to improving issues of incentives and accountability.

Imperfect information

Governments are at times assumed incorrectly to have more and better information than private parties regarding training programs. But government interventions are less warranted or differ in type when the government actually does not have more knowledge than private parties about present and future developments in training. The general advice is that governments should not be involved in the design of manpower plans that set targets for different types of training. They should focus instead on collecting and disseminating data about labor market trends. In addition, governments should carefully monitor and evaluate the policies and programs they implement. It is important to have proper monitoring and evaluation (M&E) systems in place that can ensure regular data collection and continuous evaluation that feeds into program design and managerial decision-making.

Implications for Training Programs

Chapters 3 to 5 look at the main issues facing TVET programs, initiatives to promote OJT, and training-related ALMPs. Based on the framework summarized above and reviews of international experiences and impact evaluations, the authors present recommendations for reform and outline issues for further research and policy analysis.

Pre-Employment Technical and Vocational Education and Training (TVET)

Pre-employment TVET continues to garner the interest of developed and developing countries alike as a critical pathway toward gainful employment. With the objective of imparting readily applicable, job-relevant skills, it focuses mainly on young people nearing the end of their initial formal schooling and entering the labor market. The surge in basic education graduates worldwide, as well as TVET's perceived role in fostering East Asia's industrialization, has further increased the attention on TVET in recent years. Nonetheless, developing countries face a multitude of issues in the provision of job-relevant TVET. The challenges range from the lack of adequate resources and provision for the agricultural and informal sectors, to the skills mismatches against constantly evolving labor market demands in the more modern sectors.[15] Chapter 3 begins with an overview of the global trends in pre-employment TVET and the evidence on its impact on labor market outcomes. The chapter then discusses three policy challenges that all systems confront: fostering economic relevance, responding to social and equity concerns, and ensuring effectiveness and efficiency. Successful country examples illustrate how these issues are prioritized and addressed in various contexts.

Even though comparing TVET enrollments across countries poses special difficulties due to cross-country differences in the structures of the systems and in the instructional content of programs, several trends emerge. First, enrollment in TVET programs is more common at the upper secondary (ISCED 3) level than at the lower secondary (ISCED 2) level.[16] In a survey of 143 programs around the world, UNESCO-UIS (2006) finds that more than two-thirds of the countries only offered institution-based TVET programs from the upper secondary level onward. TVET enrollments are also generally higher in the more developed countries, as suggested by about 50 percent participation in OECD countries as compared to about 20 percent in Sub-Saharan Africa, East Asia, and the Middle East and North Africa in 2009.[17] Where overall coverage of secondary education is high, as is the case of wealthier countries, education systems are more comprehensive and diverse. These countries also tend to demand higher-level skills acquired through advanced formal technical and vocational training, resulting in higher TVET shares.

As with participation trends, the lack of data and the diversity of TVET programs suggest caution in drawing firm conclusions about the impact of TVET on labor market outcomes. The returns to investment in TVET vary widely across systems and over time, suggesting that the performance of pre-employment TVET is context-specific. Among OECD countries there is some evidence that, on average, the employability of students graduating from TVET and from general tracks are similar but students graduating from general tracks tend to earn higher wages.[18] However, isolating the effect of TVET is difficult as student characteristics, some of them unobservable, influence both the likelihood of selection into TVET and the level of labor earnings. Students following the TVET track typically have lower test scores and come from less favorable parental and family backgrounds than their peers in the general track. Findings from survey data on labor market outcomes associated with TVET for developing countries are also mixed and inconclusive. They illustrate that while returns to pre-employment TVET can indeed be positive, they are not consistently greater or worse than those associated with general education.

TVET nevertheless remains a significant route taken by many students and is thus responsible for the provision of a comprehensive set of job-relevant skills. Reflecting the rapidly advancing global economy, employers are increasingly demanding both technical and educational qualifications as well as behavioral qualities in their employees. The multifaceted dimensions of these job-relevant skills are acquired in various settings throughout different stages of an individual's life. Situated within this broader context of skills accumulation, TVET programs, by definition, build on an individual's foundational skills by imparting specialized technical knowledge and practical know-how. Contextual differences and various factors, however, lend diverse views on the role of pre-employment TVET. Survey results from England and Poland reveal how employers in different countries possess contrasting views on the skills sought in new recruits. While employers in both countries value strong work attitudes, communication skills, and the ability to work in teams, they diverge on the expectations for job-specific vocational skills. Polish employers desire already-trained candidates possessing the relevant technical skills, whereas English employers prefer workers with solid literacy and numeracy that can be trained on-the-job.[19]

Fostering economic relevance
Given the government failures discussed above, fostering the economic relevance of TVET programs is perhaps the most important policy challenge confronting pre-employment training systems. These mismatches between skills supply and demand often create a paradoxical situation in some countries: high rates of unemployment among the graduates of training programs alongside complaints of skills bottlenecks by employers. Low-income countries, in particular, face further challenges due to small, underdeveloped modern industries and a lack of funds for sustainable training programs.

The successful experiences of the Republic of Korea; Taiwan, China; and Singapore illustrate how economies can overcome these difficulties by having effective governance arrangements and explicitly incorporating demand-driven TVET into their national industrialization strategies.[20] These Asian tigers understood the type of coordination failures that can emerge in training markets in the early stages of development. They pursued strategic government-led coordination that encouraged a more effective alignment of skills demand and supply as well as sustainable investments in higher-level skills. Key institutional mechanisms for coordinating economic and training policy ensured that TVET programs were effectively linked to the overall strategy for industrialization. Singapore's Economic Development Board (EDB) is one such coordinating mechanism that is credited for leading successful skills development schemes during the agency's first three decades (1961–91). EDB's approach involved partnering with prominent international firms with proven training systems to learn effective training strategies that could be adapted to the local context. Through the establishment of company-affiliated training centers, EDB spurred the development of a skills pipeline that effectively fostered Singapore's industrialization. As Singapore's economic strategy evolved to place more focus on technology and innovation, EDB employed further foreign support to upgrade their training curricula and resources accordingly.

There is also the story of India, where the private sector took the lead. Indeed, in countries with a dynamic modern sector, the role of TVET is crucial in stimulating a virtuous cycle of job-relevant skills provision toward technology- and innovation-driven growth. This growth in turn increases the demand for higher-level skills and helps make an improved education and training system sustainable. In India, the strong demand for information technology (IT) and IT-enabled services (ITES) propelled firms to take the lead in improving the supply of industry-relevant skills. IT/ITES companies have stepped forward to create new training courses with more appropriate content, establish partnerships with academia and government, and apply explicit standards to assess and certify skills.[21]

Given the market failures discussed above, governments can also have a role in providing information to prospective students about career prospects, the relevance of different programs, and the quality of different providers.[22] This implies developing certification mechanisms for training institutions as well as the various diplomas they offer.

Responding to social and equity concerns

Pre-employment TVET may also be an important policy tool in addressing social and equity concerns, and responding to the needs of the disadvantaged and marginalized. With wealthier students earning places in the more competitive academic programs, TVET enrollments often experience a disproportionately high percentage of those from poor and disadvantaged backgrounds. These students face tighter liquidity and information constraints, may expect lower returns to investments in training, and have lower levels of cognitive and noncognitive skills than optimal to compete for and succeed in the best programs. They are thus caught in less desirable programs that often suffer from a lack of political support, funding, and relevant, quality instruction. For more popular TVET programs, such as in the ICT-related fields, other obstacles such as lack of information, high costs, and poor transportation may hinder access by the disadvantaged. Gender discrimination preventing women from obtaining training for better-paying jobs is another major concern in many countries.[23]

Efforts to better serve the poor and marginalized through pre-employment TVET can occur in various ways, including financial support and improvements in training content. As many in this population find jobs in the informal and, more increasingly, the nonagricultural sectors, this chapter highlights the importance of teaching entrepreneurship skills to supplement technical training for the disadvantaged.[24] Other nontraining measures, such as access to credit, business advice for graduates, and evaluations of income-generation prospects, also serve the disadvantaged. Against this array of measures, successful interventions tend to incorporate targeted, customized programs that link to employment opportunities. Larsen and Toubro's Construction Skills Training Institute (CSTI) is an example of an industry-led pre-employment training initiative targeting poor, low-skilled, rural youth in India. This nationally and internationally benchmarked training program enrolls 1,200 new entrants annually and deploys 100 trained workers monthly for the company's construction projects. Employing a modularized approach, CSTI ensures steady skills acquisition and continuous assessments through short-term courses that incorporate mostly work-based training supplemented by classroom learning.[25]

While systemic reforms are necessary to improve TVET programs to better serve the disadvantaged, they are not sufficient. In the longer term, especially for equity reasons, there is a case for building strong literacy and numeracy skills in primary and lower secondary education before students enter TVET streams.

Ensuring effectiveness and efficiency in pre-employment TVET

Chapter 3 discusses the final challenge of ensuring TVET's effectiveness and efficiency by addressing a common government failure pertaining to the design of education and training systems: how to integrate TVET with general education and improve governance and accountability. Stemming from the question of whether TVET should be integrated into general education, countries continue to grapple with key challenges of *when* and *how* to introduce vocational content into general academic curricula. "Vocationalization" of general curricula appears to produce mixed results, depending on factors such as content, cost of inputs, and ease of implementation.[26] Increasing demands for strong technical skills based on a solid general education are also driving more countries to delay vocational specialization until the upper secondary level.[27] A study of Poland's 1999 Education Reform highlights how the deferment of vocational specialization may indeed improve TVET's effectiveness: the result of postponing student tracking by one year raised test scores of likely vocational students who remained in the general track by an estimated 100 points.[28] Premature tracking and limited flexibility across the separate tracks also emerge as related challenges that may hinder the effectiveness and efficiency of TVET. The Career and Technical Education programs in the United States may serve as exemplary cases, where students in secondary schools are able to earn skills qualifications through elective courses and industry-approved tests.

The chapter concludes by discussing effectiveness and efficiency concerns in light of TVET's governance and accountability mechanisms. Fragmented organization, unclear or overlapping mandates, and poor coordination across several ministries is not uncommon in many, especially developing, countries. Neglected responsibilities and duplication of efforts often result in ineffective and inefficient service delivery of training, as discussed previously. Such concerns have led governments to establish apex training authorities to better organize and manage the oversight of training provision. Although structurally diverse, the more successful organizations all enjoy strong partnerships with employers and other stakeholders, decision-making power over funding and resource allocation, and authority to oversee (without direct involvement in) the operations of individual TVET institutions.[29] Singapore's Institute for Technical Education (ITE) exhibits these key features in the management of their education and training system: a statutory board exercises centralized oversight functions under the Ministry of Education, while training delivery is decentralized to its three colleges.[30] This separation of oversight functions from the execution of service delivery enables these institutions to more effectively manage training providers. They have the capacity to encourage participation of nonstate providers as well as improve the service delivery of public training providers. By fostering competition in the training market and linkages between training institutions and stakeholders, these apex institutions are able to ensure more optimal TVET provision.

On-the-Job Training (OJT)

A substantial amount of a person's lifetime human capital is accumulated after individuals leave formal schooling and while on the job. In the United States, for instance, more than half of the lifetime human capital is accumulated through post-schooling investments that take place on the job.[31] OJT is thus an important channel through which workers upgrade skills and remain competitive in the labor market, and firms are able to adopt new technologies and innovate. In fact, continuous training for new technologies (including new organization and business processes) can be best accomplished by workplace training rather than by more general-purpose education if workers have a sufficient general foundation to be able to learn new skills. Chapter 4 discusses the main patterns of investment in OJT throughout the developing world, the potential market failures affecting firms that do not train, and the types of interventions that governments can consider. The evidence reviewed shows that there is a strong and positive correlation between the incidence of job training at the worker or firm level and higher productivity. At the worker level, several country studies for the developing world suggest wage returns to workers may be as high as 20 percent per training episode.[32] At the firm level, the incidence of job training is linked to higher firm productivity, a more schooled workforce, and more frequent technology adoption.[33] The usual criticism of most studies is that they do not usually take into account individuals' and firms' characteristics that likely also affect earnings and productivity and are strongly correlated with training (for example, the ability of workers). But in the few studies that attempt to correct for this "selection bias," the returns to training remain positive, even though they are substantially smaller and may even be close to zero for labor earnings.[34]

Nevertheless, the incidence of OJT in the developing world is still quite low, with only a small share of formal firms engaging in training. Moreover, there is substantial heterogeneity within countries. For instance, while the incidence of training is higher in high technology sectors, even within narrowly defined sectors, some firms invest much more than others. Even though it is hard with the existing data to address the potential simultaneity and self-selection of firms, there are four patterns that are quite robust across most regions of the world.[35] First, the incidence of job training increases with the schooling of the workforce and the skill composition of jobs. Second, there is a strong complementarity between job training and innovation, including the recent adoption of a new technology and investments in R&D. Third, exporting firms or those with more foreign capital are much more likely to invest in OJT. Finally, training incidence is higher among larger firms.[36]

The important policy question then is why some firms do not train.[37] Chapter 4 classifies firms into two groups. A first group of firms does not invest in training simply because their expected rate of return is smaller than the return on other investments. This happens either because firms have low expected benefits from training or because training costs are high. Low expected benefits usually relate to the lack of complementary inputs, including the use of production technologies operating mostly with unskilled labor. There is also some evidence for developed countries that the fixed costs of investments in OJT are high, making it a less attractive investment for smaller firms.[38]

A second group of firms may have profitable expected returns to investments in OJT but cannot realize these due to market failures. In particular, firms may face liquidity constraints and be unable to access credit. Other firms may not train because of high worker turnover, in part due to poaching by other firms. Evidence for Central America shows that almost 40 percent and 20 percent of firms not investing in OJT report, respectively, lack of financing and high turnover as the binding constraints. Moreover, around 30 percent of the firms specifically report poaching as a core obstacle for not investing. The patterns are similar for larger countries like Brazil. Although more difficult to assess, there could also be some firms that do not invest due to the lack of adequate information about the benefits of training. Indeed, these firms would have lower expected rates of return on investments and would train less.

Based on the analysis, Chapter 4 presents different recommendations to foster investments in OJT among each group of firms. For the firms in the first group, the strategy to increase skills and productivity would involve increasing the expected rates of return on training by getting the fundamentals right. These would include policies to promote good governance, foster product level competition, support innovation, and support the integration of firms in global markets.[39] For the second group of firms, however, other policies need to be considered, which are along the lines discussed earlier in the section "Linking Market and Government Failures to the Design of Training Related Interventions." Note that this framework does not clarify into which group small and medium enterprises (SMEs) will fall. Most likely some are under the first group and do not invest in training simply because their expected rate of return is smaller than the return on other investments. Others, however, may have profitable expected returns to investments in OJT but cannot realize these due to market failures, like information or liquidity constraints and difficulties in having access to credit.

Recommendations to foster investments in OJT are summarized below.

Contracts to deal with poaching externalities

There can be enforceable institutional arrangements that create adequate incentives for employers and individuals to invest in skill development. Payback clauses and apprenticeship contracts are the most popular arrangements, with the former being most common in middle-high-income countries and OECD countries as they are more difficult to enforce. Chapter 4 discusses in detail the apprenticeship program in Germany, which coordinates both school-based and on-the-job training and follows a standardized curriculum. It has well-monitored and high-quality standards for engaging effectively with the private sector. In some cases, these contracts even specify the precise type of cost sharing arrangement by the two parties. It is important, however, not to confuse these arrangements with other policies that may promote job security and that could have unintended consequences, such as reducing hiring rates, labor mobility, and productivity growth.[40] Apprenticeship contracts reach thousands of the most vulnerable in Africa and are also discussed in detail. An important feature in their design is to have them coupled with other types of training and certification systems, which helps address the often weak educational base of informal sector workers and the lack of quality standards for training.

Credit to deal with liquidity constraints

Because firms and workers may face liquidity constraints that prevent them from investing in OJT, there is room for policies to provide and improve the financial support to some firms and individuals. For individuals, solutions are relatively straightforward and focus on improving their access to training loans or the provision of training vouchers. In the case of firms, however, one of the main problems is the information that is needed to target the right firms without producing large deadweight losses and substitution effects.[41]

The most popular instrument in developing countries to provide subsidies is *training funds*. Although most of these funds are based on payroll levies, in practice, they may take various forms.[42] Under, a *levy-grant* mechanism all firms pay taxes and those that train receive grants. The Mauritius's Enterprise Training Fund, for instance, has some features of this mechanism. In *cost-reimbursement* schemes all firms pay taxes and finance their training but then can be reimbursed for incurred expenses (this can impose a high administrative burden on the training fund). In practice, however, the reimbursement is often set below the levy paid to cover administration costs. For example, in the Nigerian Industrial Training Fund, firms qualify for not more than 60 percent of the levy paid, and in practice less than 15 percent of firms apply for reimbursement for training costs.[43] Finally, in *levy-exemption* schemes, only those firms that do not train pay taxes. One good example is Côte d'Ivoire's *Fonds de Developpement de la Formation Professionnelle*.[44] The overall effects of the three types of levy are nonetheless similar: the tax provides incentives for firms to train since firms that train pay lower net training taxes (the training tax net of the transfer to cover the cost of the training). Interestingly, and in spite of evidence that smaller firms are more affected by credit constraints, this is rarely incorporated into the design of the training funds. However, nothing in this system ensures that the resulting training is efficient. For instance, firms might simply organize training to reduce the tax burden and larger firms might be better at playing the system and getting their money back than small firms. At the end, the distribution of taxes and subsidies across firms (some firms will pay more than they receive and others will pay less) can be highly nontransparent and be delinked from firm- or sector-specific market failures that need to be addressed.

General principles for designing the programs

A review of the available evidence strongly suggests that almost everywhere there is room to improve current arrangements to promote OJT. Training funds could pay closer attention to issues related to governance, targeting, financing mechanisms, and M&E systems:

- **Governance.** First, training funds should avoid excessive centralization and minimize the size of administrative bodies, focusing on their financing function and not on training provision. Therefore, training arrangements that allow firms the freedom to select their own training providers (possibly among a group of accredited providers) and manage their programs will minimize bureaucracies and make the program more cost-effective. For example, Dar et al. (2003) show that in Hungary employers felt that government exerted excessive control over funds and that this limited their effectiveness. Second, given that in most countries these training funds are financed through taxes, the public sector should seek a stronger buy-in from the private sector. A good example is Chile's National Training and Employment Service (*Servicio Nacional de Capacitación y Empleo*—SENCE), where training agencies and funds avoid a direct training role. In Brazil, however, the National Service for Industrial Training (*Serviço Nacional de Aprendizagem Industrial*—SENAI) operates its own network of training institutions.

- **Allocating subsidies.** The discussion earlier in the section "Linking Market and Government Failures to the Design of Training Related Interventions" argues that training subsidies may be effective in cases where workers and firms fail to coordinate investments in training. This may result from either innovation externalities or low-productivity traps, which will more likely affect small firms and low-income workers facing liquidity constraints. There is little rationale, however, for developing training funds that subsidize (or tax less) large firms that might have trained in any case. One possible approach to allocate subsidies is to identify priority areas based on broad consultations with the private sector, including SMEs. One example could be high-value-added sectors where investments are not taking place because of the lack of workers with the right skills and because the private sector is unwilling to risk training such workers.[45] The government could subsidize part of the training (the rest would be financed by either firms and/or workers) in exchange for the investment. Another example relates to low-productivity traps due to coordination problems discussed previously in the section "Linking Market and Government Failures to the Design of Training Related Interventions." In the tourism sector, for instance, the quality of services could be improved by training a large number of unskilled workers. Governments could coordinate and subsidize the cost of part of this training where there is potential demand. If subsidies are going to be allocated based on idiosyncratic demands by firms, then the focus should probably be on small enterprises that have less means to train on their own. Subsidies could be allocated in the form of matching contributions to a training project through competitive bidding.

- **Financing.** If the purpose of the training levy is to finance subsidies to promote training—as opposed to taxing firms that may or may not train—it would be preferable to rely on general budget financing. Even if earmarked taxes are desired to secure part of the government budget, it would be more prudent to rely on taxes on profits or sales rather than on payroll taxes that can reduce formal employment. In general, it is very important to separate the financing of the training fund from the allocation of funds.

Training Programs for Unemployed, Low-Income, and Low-Skilled Workers

Not all workers have access to TVET or OJT, and thus many countries have developed parallel training programs for unemployed, low-income, and low-skilled workers. Chapter 5 recommends that these programs be tailored to the needs of specific groups. Three groups are discussed: (i) unskilled workers unemployed or working in the informal sector or small enterprises; (ii) skilled workers transiting from school to work; and (iii) skilled workers in transition between jobs, be it as a result of idiosyncratic unemployment or because of major reallocations of labor/capital across economic sectors. These workers differ in terms of basic socioeconomic characteristics (such as age and gender) and income levels. Most cannot access OJT because they are not employed in firms that train, or TVET, because there are administrative and academic requirements that they usually do not fulfill.

There are several reasons why these workers may not invest in training that may ultimately improve their employability and increase their earnings. The main problems are related to liquidity and credit constraints; lack of information about how and where to get training; biased expectations about returns to investments in training; and weak incentives to invest when there is a limited supply of higher productivity jobs that demand skilled labor because of information and coordination problems.

The chapter starts by discussing the case of *unskilled and low-skilled workers*. These are workers who dropped out of the education system, usually before having completed secondary school. Across regions, these workers represent sizable shares of the labor force. For example in South and in West Asia only 50 percent of girls and 57 percent of boys are enrolled in secondary education. In Africa these numbers are even more discouraging, with only 30 percent of girls and 38 percent of boys enrolled. Whether young or adults, they lack sufficient skills, are engaged in low-productivity activities, and have low earnings. The problem tends to be more severe among youth who, in addition to the lack of skills, do not have work experience. The goal of training programs in all cases is to provide some technical skills, as well as cognitive and behavioral skills.

Given the characteristics of the beneficiaries and the market failures they face, the most successful program would likely include the following elements: (i) subsidies to finance all or parts of the cost of the training, (ii) counseling, and (iii) job-search assistance or support to self-employment. Subsidies, and not only access to credit, are needed to provide incentives to acquire skills, given potentially high discount rates and/or expected low private rates of return to training. However, subsidies probably would be insufficient without counseling and job-search assistance or support to self-employment, in part because of the information problems discussed previously. These two interventions are important to increase the expected private rate of return to training. The first (counseling) would provide information about the potential gains from training and the types of training that can be considered, given individual aptitudes. The second (job-search assistance or support to self-employment) would link individuals to jobs that will use the skills acquired. Indeed, left to their own devices, trained workers using their social networks might not find jobs that value the new skills. This would depress the value of the training and reduce the demand for the program.

Training, employment services, and wage subsidies

These programs offer a package of services including counseling, training, job-search assistance, and workplace internships. Qualified private firms, nongovernmental organizations (NGOs), or public institutions provide training and other services on a competitive basis. To be eligible for funds, training providers are required to line up internships and identify the types of skills that are needed. The training then focuses on the provision of these skills, including cognitive skills (such as problem solving) and behavioral skills (such as correct workplace behavior, conflict management, job-search techniques, and building self-esteem). Countries pioneering this type of program among youth include Argentina (*Proyecto Joven*), Chile (*Chile Joven*), Colombia (*Jóvenes en Acción*), the Dominican Republic (*Juventud y Empleo*), Panama (*ProCaJoven*), and Peru (*ProJoven*). There is evidence that for some of these programs, like *Jovenes en Accion*, beneficiaries (especially women) are more likely to find a job. These results, however, depend heavily on how programs are designed and implemented.[46] The downside of these programs is that per capita costs can be high, on the order of US$600–$2,000, and governments facing tight budgetary constraints might not be able to afford them.

Training and support to self-employment

This is training tailored toward self-employment and can be linked to the provision of business services and access to credit. Some of these programs, particularly in low-income countries, are targeted to craftsmen and their apprentices. The focus is on the use of production techniques that are better adapted to market demands. Some advantages of the programs are that they provide trainees with flexible and demand-driven skills; cost little; and do not require much skills or experience from the beneficiary. One example is the Benin Support Project, which provides hands-on job training in the informal sector and combines several innovative features. One feature is the institutional development of a marketplace for training proposals, which leads to a competitive selection process. A second feature is the analysis of specific training needs and skills mismatches in selected areas, which leads to a more targeted training curricula. In principle, variants of the two types of programs described above could also be used for unskilled adult workers—including those benefiting from welfare programs. One such program is the California GAIN program, which combines training with counseling and job-search assistance. Evaluations have shown positive long-term impacts of the training component of the program on employment rates.

In middle- and low-income countries, there are also examples of training programs for unskilled adults linked to public works. The additional requirements attached to workers may include saving some of their wages, learning technical skills, and eventually finding a job. One example of this type of program is Argentina's *Jefes y Jefas*, which required participants to work or participate in training or educational activities for 4–6 hours a day (no less than 20 hours a week) in exchange for the payment. Evaluations showed that the program had positive long-term effects on labor market outcomes. Other programs include the Rural Maintenance Program (RMP) in Bangladesh, the Temporary Income Support Program (TISP) in El Salvador, and the Expanded Public Work Program (EPWP) in South Africa. Evaluations of these programs, however, are still pending.

For *youth transiting from school to work*, interventions should focus on assessing competencies, providing information and counseling, supporting self-employment, and, when necessary, training and retraining. The bulk of the interventions could be handled by employment service offices (public or private), which could be in charge of assessing skills and aptitudes, identifying work opportunities, and advising on training needs—including for the preparation of business plans.[47] As in the case of the programs for low-skilled workers, training could be provided through private or public agents that arrange internships with employers or prepare workers for self-employment. One potential difference in this case, however, is that because beneficiaries would have in principle higher earnings capacity, part of the financing of the program could come from the young graduates (who internalize parts of the benefits from training). One modality could be that the government opens a credit line to finance the cost of training, the internship (wage subsidy), and/or start-up credit. Reimbursements for the credit would commence once individuals start to receive salaries or earn profits.

Regarding **skilled workers in transition between jobs,** the main goal is to prevent the depreciation of skills or to develop new skills that match changing demands in the labor market. Designing interventions for these groups is not fundamentally different from dealing with first-time job seekers and similar programs can be considered. The main reference for this group of programs is still the activation programs in OECD countries and especially the German system. There, access to training is not automatic but depends on the decision of a caseworker or advisor. Based on an assessment of individual skills, aptitudes for certain jobs, and the likelihood of success in a training program, the caseworker specifies the type of training needed and refers the client to a designated training provider (contracted on a competitive basis). Recent evaluations of the German system suggest that training programs may have positive impacts on employment probabilities.[48]

There are also successful interventions to enact more structural changes in the economy. In Romania, for example, the government successfully implemented training and retraining programs, along with self-employment assistance, public employment programs, and job-search assistance. Program design and implementation was handled by public employment agencies, while the actual service provision was contracted out to public and private service providers.

General principles to design the programs

The task of designing training-related ALMPs that can be easily adapted to different local conditions and institutional realities is not simple. However, a review of the evidence suggests a few general principles. Countries could consider systems that operate through "one-stop shops." These may be public or private "employment offices"—including NGOs—that would be the interface between the applicants and the training providers. The offices do not need to be passive agents, however, and in some cases (for example, unskilled, low-income youth) would be expected to develop outreach activities to bring individuals into the programs. Regardless of the mechanism used to register individuals, however, the process would start by assigning a counselor to each applicant. The counselor would assess competencies and aptitudes; discuss job prospects and training needs with the applicant; and, when needed, refer the applicant to training providers. These would be ideally selected on a competitive basis and offer *training packages* that respond to different needs. Short-term packages could focus on basic technical and life-skills needed by unskilled workers (including vulnerable youth); medium-term packages (1–2 years) could focus on vocational training to help skilled workers change careers. In many cases the training programs would include workplace internships and/or would connect participants with credit institutions.

In general, a successful system of ALMPs should be able to address issues related to possible government failures:

- **Governance**. Policy makers should avoid excessive centralization in program administration by giving local labor offices the flexibility to manage their programs, and by outsourcing implementation to public and private companies through contracts that reward performance. The latter should meet clearly defined standards regarding the qualifications of staff, particularly for counselors, and follow protocols for methods to assess competencies and aptitudes, provide career advice, and identify training needs. This model is essentially what some European countries are doing, including Germany and the United Kingdom.
- **Financing.** Usually stakeholders assume that training-related ALMPs will be financed exclusively through government subsidies. As discussed above, this can be the desired arrangement in the case of low-skill/low-income workers with no or limited savings, and for whom capital market restrictions or information constraints are particularly severe. However, it does not have to be the norm for all workers. On the contrary, to be able to expand these programs and improve their impact, individuals with savings capacity would need to finance part of the costs. There are two modalities: (i) *social security contributions* (not mandatory for employers), and (ii) *credit lines*. The first would apply to workers in the formal sector who already contribute for different social security benefits. These workers would have training accounts where contributions accumulate to finance training and employment services. Depending on the level of subsidy (that is, the level of the matching contributions by the government) a given dollar amount in the account would be equivalent to a certain number of hours of training and counseling. Given the discussion of the importance of labor market conditions in determining externalities related to training as discussed previously, it is reasonable to expect that different types of training will have different tariffs. These tariffs will be negotiated by the government with the training providers. The other system would be geared to informal sector workers and first-time job seekers and would involve credit to be reimbursed once individuals are productively employed.[49]
- **Administration**. The administrative complexity of well-designed training-related ALMPs should not be underestimated. Key processes include registering applicants, contracting employment offices and training providers, setting up tariffs, managing individual contributions and/or credit lines, and reimbursing providers. It is thus indispensable to build institutional capacity within the public agencies in charge of the management of the system at the central and local levels. Strengthening institutional coordination and the ability to manage multiservice programs can be important for reducing operational costs.

Open Methodological and Policy Questions: Building a Research and Operational Agenda

The discussion in the various chapters of this report identifies areas for future research and policy analysis. One area for research is the development of tools for measuring skills and assessing market failures. Other areas include the design and implementation of particular policies and programs.

Measuring Skills

An important question is how to define and measure the set of skills that determine individuals' employability and labor market outcomes in developing countries. Indeed, indicators such as school attainment are very weak proxies for the distribution of skills and are largely insufficient to inform policy. One of the main avenues for further research is thus the development of sound, country-level, regularly administered surveys of workers and firms that measure the supply and demand of technical, cognitive, and noncognitive skills. Surveys of this type have been pioneered by the World Bank in developing countries, including Lebanon and Peru (see box 1.2). Cognitive skills capture the individual's "ability to understand complex ideas, to adapt effectively to the environment, to learn from experience, to engage in various forms of reasoning, and to overcome obstacles by taking thought."[50] The most common examples relate to literacy, numeracy, and the ability to solve abstract problems. Noncognitive skills relate to multiple characteristics across various domains (including social, emotional, personality, behaviors, and attitudes) that are not included under cognitive skills. Examples of these skills translate into the individual's work habits (including the level of effort, discipline, or determination); his/her behavioral traits (including self-confidence, sociability, or emotional stability); and the individual's physical characteristics (including strength, dexterity, and endurance). In addition, the surveys also try to measure the set of technical skills that are simply the combinations of cognitive and noncognitive skills frequently used to accomplish specific tasks at work.[51]

The importance of exploring standardized instruments across countries and combining them with regular data on labor markets cannot be overemphasized.[52] Such standardization will not only increase the possibility of making comparisons among countries, but also will enrich the value of the information collected for each country. By linking the information from these various data sets, for example, it will be possible to assess problems of skill mismatches. It is important that all these data are in the public domain so that various analysts can assess their policy implications. It is also important that clear summaries of the main statistics are made readily accessible to workers and employers.

BOX 1.2

Recent Developments in International Skills Assessments

The importance of international skills assessments is increasingly apparent in today's rapidly advancing global economy. In an effort to more accurately understand the existing knowledge gaps, organizations such as the Organisation for Economic Co-operation and Development (OECD) and the World Bank are developing comprehensive, innovative assessments that measure beyond traditional literacy and numeracy skills. These initiatives are highlighted below.

Programme for the International Assessment of Adult Competencies (PIAAC)

PIAAC is a large-scale household-based survey that measures the level and distribution of key cognitive and workplace skills across 26 participating countries. Commissioned by the OECD, PIAAC measures core adult cognitive skills required in the information age, including problem-solving in technology-rich environments. This comprehensive assessment also measures the utilization of these competencies at the workplace through a "Job Requirements Approach" for those employed. A background questionnaire further collects information about every participant in the PIAAC survey to contextualize and analyze the determinants, development, and use of competencies. It was administered for the first time in 2011 to approximately 5,000 individuals between the ages of 16 and 65.

Source: http://www.piaac.sk/; http://nces.ed.gov/surveys/piaac; OECD 2010.

Skills toward Employment and Productivity (STEP) Measurement Study

Led by the World Bank, the Skills toward Employment and Productivity (STEP) Measurement Study is a multicountry research program that aims to identify those skill sets highly valued in the labor market and generate policy options to design effective training programs. Complementing the work of PIAAC, the program consists of developing harmonized survey instruments that assess the distribution of cognitive, noncognitive, and technical skills in the labor force of middle- and low-income countries, and the demand for these skills by employers. Subsequent phases of the program include adapting and administering the surveys in selected countries, identifying relevant policy interventions, and extracting the lessons learned from this multicountry perspective.

Source: World Bank (2011b).

Assessing market failures and the impact of alternative policies

There is urgent need for a much better assessment and benchmarking of the main market and government failures affecting the provision of training, and the impact of alternative corrective policy interventions. From the discussion above, one issue is how to assess the level of competitiveness of a given "labor market." This implies being able to define the relevant market(s) for the analysis (for example, is the market defined with respect to an economic sector or particular skills) and then having indicators of the degree of market power that employers have. Another issue is how to define a more systematic approach to identify constraints facing individuals or firms in different settings. For instance, how severe are information problems and myopia for different groups of workers? Can more information make a difference or are subsidies required as well? Similarly, in the case of SMEs, is the problem access to credit or are subsidies also needed and, in that case, should they go to employees or the firm? Pilot projects would need to be conducted to assess these issues, probably in the context of a coordinated effort involving governments, international organizations, and academic institutions.

A first step would be to conduct more systematic assessments of skills development policies and systems around the world. In this arena the World Bank has recently launched the Systems Approach for Better Education Results (SABER) initiative, of which workforce development (WfD) is one of several policy domains.[53] The SABER-WfD diagnostic tool focuses on assessing countries' policies and institutions for workforce development in light of global good practice. The initiative aims to inform policy dialogue on achieving better results in workforce development in low- and middle-income countries.

A second step would be, at the program level, to improve current data collection and ongoing M&E systems. Programs need to be adjusted and re-optimized continuously, and this can only be done if real-time data are collected and made available quickly to managers about program costs, operations, and performance. Furthermore, M&E is the only mechanism allowing the rigorous quantification of deadweight losses and substitution effects commonly associated with many government interventions. Although impact evaluations are becoming more common, they remain relatively rare and most reports provide only descriptive analysis with few counterfactual scenarios (see box 1.3 for an example).[54]

As a consequence, it is impossible to determine whether most interventions, ranging from direct provision of TVET to job training subsidies and to training for the unemployed, have sufficiently large gains to compensate for their costs. In addition, many programs try to address several market and/or government failures simultaneously and it is not possible in most cases to assess which are the most important. Related to this, we know little about which features of a given program increase its likelihood of success.

> **BOX 1.3**
>
> ## Identifying Market Failures through Impact Evaluations: Spotlight on Turkey
>
> Thorough evaluations are essential in identifying the potential market failures associated with training programs. The World Bank is currently engaged in the evaluation of vocational and technical training programs provided by the Turkish Public Employment Agency (ISKUR). The ISKUR impact evaluation is the first rigorous evaluation of a nationwide, public training program in Europe and Central Asia. The sample consists of more than five thousand beneficiaries across 95 training courses in more than 20 ISKUR provincial offices.
>
> The main objective of this evaluation is to shed light on the average effect of participation in an ISKUR training program on job placement, labor earnings, and employment quality. The evaluation also examines how the effects of the program differ for beneficiaries with different profiles, including their (i) human capital, (ii) work history (including unemployment and inactivity episodes and length), (iii) gender, (iv) age, (v) behavioral preferences including psychological traits, and (vi) household decision-making power. In addition, the evaluation will identify the main *channels* through which ISKUR trainings may influence the beneficiary's labor market outcomes. For example, ISKUR trainings may increase individual productivity (or wages) through the acquisition of relevant job skills, either cognitive or noncognitive. Alternatively, trainings may increase employment by reducing the costs of a job search or making a job seeker's searching or networking more effective. Understanding these intermediate outcomes will help clarify how public trainings can make a difference in Turkey. This knowledge will also help regional offices improve the effectiveness of ISKUR's vocational programs by linking them with other services (like counseling and job intermediation).
>
> Finally, if these trainings are effective, their success should inform discussion of the economic rationale for public intervention and the main bottlenecks preventing private investment. Among other things, the World Bank's evaluation is measuring individual assets and credit constraints; the degree of risk aversion (to human capital and other investments); and individual expectations and perceptions of the importance and quality of the training. The results will show which factors are important and who benefits the most.
>
> *Source:* World Bank (2011b).

Another question is how to make more effective use of regularly collected monitoring data in rigorous evaluation work. Indeed, most evaluation exercises are expensive and finding a way to collect and analyze data more effectively would be of much help.

Identifying key policy issues

Regarding **pre-employment TVET** in developing countries, there are many questions that will require more research. Among the most important concerns are the changes in employment opportunities and their implications for skills formation in a fast-changing global economy. Both opportunities and challenges are being created by the widening web of global production networks (in manufacturing and increasingly in services); the spread of digital information systems; and the emergence of China, India, Brazil, and other economic latecomers. Much work will therefore be required to inform countries' assessment of how they might adapt their TVET strategies to this emerging global landscape in order to ensure a close match between skills supply and demand. In addition, consistent feedback from employers underscores the importance of "soft" skills (teamwork, thinking skills, problem-solving capacity, and so forth) and the importance of teaching them in TVET programs. Other issues relate to options for expanding TVET in a financially sustainable manner; for diversifying the pathways for youth to gain market-relevant skills; for dealing with market and government failures concerning information and coordination problems; and for motivating service providers, whether in the public or private sector, to be accountable for the quality and market relevance of their services. In the years ahead, there is need for more evaluations to shed light on creating better linkages between disbursement of funds and performance. Evaluations can also help make voucher systems, which allow individuals to choose and directly pay training providers, become more effective.

Regarding the investment in **OJT**, the knowledge gaps are even more pervasive. This is likely related to the fact that investments in OJT, although partly subsidized, are largely supported by the private sector and consequently are less scrutinized than other public investments, including in TVET and ALMPs. More analysis of the scope, scale, and quality of the investment in OJT is needed to inform policy. This implies collecting better data to quantify the extent of underinvestment in training across the developing world. While for some skills and in some markets the extent of underinvestment may be clearly the case, for others the situation is more subtle. Unfortunately, most data sets do not collect information about the content and quality of OJT provided and complementary activities that also affect worker and firm productivity. Thus, most analyses of the effects of OJT could be biased by serious estimation issues. In general, better data and more systematic analyses are needed to document externalities, assess training costs, and generate more robust estimates of the private and social costs and returns to training.

At a more operational level, there are two important issues. First, it is important to better understand the factors that influence firms' decisions to invest in training and/or develop cost-sharing arrangements with employees. Indeed, as discussed above, much of what governments can do to promote training is likely to be related to the economic and institutional environment in which firms develop and operate, and not inside firms. Second, it is necessary to improve the targeting of programs in general, and more specifically the targeting of subsidies. Most programs are focused on SMEs because it is perceived that market failures are likely to be more pressing there than among larger firms. However, it is unclear that all SMEs require some sort of intervention on efficiency grounds. In some sectors, technology is old and the workforce does not necessarily need to constantly adapt and innovate.

Finally, regarding **_training for the most vulnerable_**, there is a strong need to better understand the effectiveness of various programs under different circumstances. Most of the very scarce impact evaluations in this field focus on the effectiveness of programs in influencing final employability and earnings outcomes. However, in addition to understanding whether programs work, it is important to know how they work, and why they work. This is particularly important when comparing alternative channels for delivery or when scaling up (given that initial conditions are usually different than the ones in pilots). Given that counseling and job-search assistance programs are likely to be important complements to training programs, it is also important to know how to optimize them. So far, there has been consensus about the need to minimize public infrastructure and increase reliance on private employment offices. However, there is still little consensus on best practices to create the right institutional arrangements to improve incentives. A review of these processes at the international level is needed along with the evaluation work.

Notes

1. See Cho et al. (2011).
2. "Skills toward Employability and Productivity" (StEP) framework in Banerji et al. (2010).
3. See Rigolini et al. (2010). For example, 52 percent of employers identify work attitude as the top skill lacking among unskilled workers. This is followed by the lack of a foreign language and then by technical skills. Soft skills appear to be a severe constraint in particular for out-of-school youth: 89 percent of employers state that they have difficulties working with out-of-school youth because of behavioral issues.
4. http://enterprisesurveys.org/.
5. See Banerji et al. (2010). For instance, in Turkey, employers in SMEs—even in the more labor-intensive sectors such as furniture, food processing, textiles, and clothing—cite the inadequacy of skills at all levels as a key constraint on their capacity to acquire and use new and more advanced technology.
6. There are too many analyses to cite here, but core references include Middleton et al. (1993) and Gill et al. (1998).

7. Skills include, for example, the knowledge, expertise, and behaviors that the job holder needs in order to execute his or her responsibilities competently. They also include mastery of a body of knowledge relevant to the job; familiarity with the tools and technologies used to perform the tasks associated with the job; understanding of the materials that are worked with; and the fostering and use of interpersonal relationships and interactions to accomplish the tasks required in the job.

8. Heckman et al. (2006) show that cognitive skills and noncognitive skills are important in explaining a diverse array of labor market outcomes. Although there are important gender differences in the effects of these skills, for most behaviors, both factors play an important role for both men and women. Carneiro and Heckman (2003), Heckman and Masterov (2004), Cunha et al. (2006), and numerous other papers establish that parents play an important role in producing both the cognitive and noncognitive skills of their children.

9. The distinction between pre-employment TVET and ALMPs is not always clear. Pre-employment TVET tends to be offered while students are in the formal schooling system and usually has a duration that overlaps with the school year. TVET also tends to be managed by the ministry of education. On the contrary, ALMP-style training is typically managed by the ministry of labor or the ministry of social protection. It tends to last three to six months and usually targets individuals who have already left the formal schooling system. Because TVET often is part of the formal schooling system, it usually has an International Standard Classification of Education (ISCED) categorization, which can go from level 2 to level 5 and beyond. On the contrary, ALMP-style training does not always lead to a skills certification.

10. These externalities, however, would not affect firms enjoying full-market power for a given set of skills (a monopsony), for which employers would be able to internalize the returns on their investments.

11. http://enterprisesurveys.org/.

12. See Thaler and Sunstein (2009) and Ariely (2010).

13. See Wolf (1979).

14. See Stein et al. (2008) and Schmidt-Hebbel (2009).

15. In particular, employers in these sectors are increasingly demanding advanced technological skills as well as the so-called "soft skills" such as leadership and teamwork.

16. UNESCO-UIS (2006).

17. UNESCO-UIS. As discussed above, caution is needed in interpreting these numbers. The 50 percent or more students in OECD countries who are enrolled in TVET likely receive very different instruction than the smaller proportion of students enrolled in secondary TVET in developing countries. Furthermore, even when comparing countries with similar levels of development (for example, OECD countries), there are likely important variations in the skills provided. This is due to selection of students, and differences in the structures and instructional content of programs.

18. OECD 2009.

19. Martin et al. (2008); Rutkowski (2011).

20. See Ashton et al. (2002) and Kuruvilla et al. (2002).

21. With the backing and participation of IT/ITES companies, the National Association of Software and Service Companies (NASSCOM) introduced the NASSCOM Assessment of Competence (NAC) in 2006 to assess entry-level employment in the ITES industry. NASSCOM has now added a NAC-Tech certificate to test candidates' engineering skills for the IT industry (NASSCOM-Everest 2008).

22. See Sondergaard and Murthi (2012) for examples from Hungary, Romania, and the Netherlands.

23. King and Palmer (2010).

24. However, reorienting formal school-based pre-employment TVET programs to provide suitable training in entrepreneurship skills for disadvantaged groups has proved to be difficult (see, for example, Johanson and Adams 2004). The challenges include weak incentives and inadequate knowledge among staff to redesign the training programs. Most of these interventions tend to be offered to individuals outside the formal schooling system. Some of these programs are discussed in chapter 5. Although the evidence is increasing for interventions targeting microfinance clients (see, for example, McKenzie 2009), it is still thin for publicly provided programs targeting the most disadvantaged groups. One exception is Almeida and Galasso (2010), who show that self-employment can be fostered among special needs beneficiaries, especially women with previous and related experience in the labor market.

25. CSTI explicitly bars software professionals and diploma or degree holders from admission. Training courses range from one to three months; 80 percent of the coursework is site-based practical training and 20 percent is classroom-based learning. See http://www.lntecc.com/homepage/CSTI/pdfs/English-Brochure.pdf; http://www.lntecc.com/homepage/CSTI/ for more information.

26. See ADB (2008); Johanson and Adams (2004).

27. See UNESCO-UIS (2006) and Adams (2007).

28. See Jacubowskl et al. (2010) for more information

29. ADB (2008).

30. Law (2008).

31. Heckman, Lochner, and Taber (1998).

32. Middleton et al. (1993).

33. Acemoglu (1998); Almeida and Carneiro (2009); Barron et al. (1997); Black and Lynch (1996, 2001); Frazis and Loewenstein (2005); Lynch (1992).

34. Few papers have accounted for this in a developing-country setting. Dearden, Reed, and Van Reenen (2006) explore panel data for the United Kingdom and find that on-the-job training in British industries was associated with significantly higher productivity between 1983 and 1996. Raising the proportion of workers trained in an industry by one percentage point is associated with an increase in value added per worker of about 0.6 percent and an increase in wages of about 0.3 percent. Almeida and Carneiro (2009) use a similar econometric approach on panel data and show that an increase in the amount of training per employee of 10 hours per year leads to an increase in current productivity of 0.6 percent. Leuven and Oosterbeek (2004) explore the 1998 law in the Netherlands that introduced a tax deduction for a firm's expenditures on work-related training. Leuven and Oosterbeek use the tax deduction as an

instrumental variable to investigate training participation and the effect of training participation on wages.

35. Almeida and Aterido (2010, 2011a, 2011b) document these patterns all over the world. Some of these patterns are also described by Tan and Batra (1995) and López-Acevedo and Tan (2005), who also analyze job training for a set of Latin American countries. These patterns have been found by others for developed countries (Bassanini et al. 2005).

36. For example, Almeida and Aterido (2010) estimate that the probability of investing in OJT is approximately 40 percentage points higher in Latin America or in Eastern Europe for large firms (more than 250 employees) than for micro firms (less than 10 employees). Differences of approximately 10 percentage points exist in the incidence of job training across firms that are present in foreign markets or with foreign participation.

37. This discussion follows Almeida and Aterido (2010).

38. Almeida and Carneiro (2009).

39. The effects of some institutions like product market competition, unionization, or minimum wages are theoretically ambiguous. Take, for example, a market with increased deregulation and higher product market competition. This could reduce rents through lower wages and profits after training and thus reduce the benefits of training. But training could improve as deregulation fostered productivity (and hence wages and profitability after training) by forcing firms to improve efficiency and to innovate. Moreover, because firm entry increases, product competition may also promote agglomeration economies and thus more training. Although the link between OJT and product completion is theoretically ambiguous, there is evidence supporting a negative correlation between product market concentration and OJT (see, for example, Autor 2004).

40. Theoretically there is ambiguity on the link between unionization and OJT. On the one hand, unions flatten wage profiles, which reduces wage dispersion and distorts workers' incentives to invest in training. On the other hand, the effect could be positive as unions may directly negotiate better training opportunities for unionized workers, especially in noncompetitive product markets. Unionization may also reduce turnover, producing an indirect positive effect on returns to firms due to longer tenures.

41. Deadweight losses result from the fact that subsidies might induce investments that would otherwise have also taken place. Substitution effects relate to the fact that firms might substitute away from the nonsubsidized training into the subsidizing training.

42. *Cost-reimbursement* training funds force firms of a certain size to pay a levy into a training fund, based on their payroll. The approved training expenditures are reimbursed in part, within the limits of the levy paid by the firm. *Levy-grant* (or cost-redistribution) seeks to redistribute training expenditures among several firms to minimize the "poaching" of workers within sectors. Funds typically administer a levy to finance national or sector funds. These funds then decide on the distribution of training grants among all enterprises. Finally, *levy-exemption* (train or pay) training funds exempt firms from paying the levy if they

spend resources on training workers. The employers are free to manage their mandated training allocation within agreed regulations.

43. See Ziderman (2003).

44. The *Fonds de Developpement de la Formation Professionnelle* (FDFP) manages an apprenticeship tax (0.4 percent of the total wage bill) and an additional tax for continuous vocational training (1.2 percent), levied through compulsory contributions. Firms qualify for a tax exemption of half the continuing vocational tax obligation (0.6 percent) on approval by the fund of a company training plan, including internal and external training of employees. In addition, firms have an additional incentive of retaining up to an additional half of the tax (0.9 versus 0.6 percent) by implementing approved training plans for three years and justifying training expenditures beyond 1.6 percent of payroll (see Johanson 2009).

45. See Robalino and Marouani (2008) for a discussion in the case of Morocco.

46. For a detailed discussion on activation and ALMPs policies, see Almeida et al. (2011).

47. See Robalino and Sanchez Puerta (2010).

48. See Kluve et al. (2010) and Lechner, Miquel, and Wunsch (2011).

49. The idea underneath this scheme is similar to the extension of the unemployment insurance to workers in the informal sectors, through the development of the Unemployment Insurance Savings Accounts (UISA). Under a UISA system, each worker saves part of his/her earnings in an individual account that defines eligibility (in this case for expenses in ALMPs). In case of exiting employment, benefits may be withdrawn from this account. In Chile, to introduce redistribution, the individual account is complemented by a solidarity fund that is only accessible if the individual account expires before the end of the maximum duration. This self contributory component will be easier to apply and enforce in the formal sector but may in principle also apply to the informal sector. For example, within the context of UISA, Jordan is pushing the model by allowing the participation of beneficiaries who have not saved enough before becoming unemployed but have already accumulated some pension wealth.

50. See the American Psychological Association (1996).

51. Examples of these skills include whether the individual in his or her job uses a computer to do data entry or how much of the workday is spent doing physical tasks such as standing, handling objects, operating machinery or vehicles, or making or fixing things with one's hands.

52. World Bank (2011a).

53. For more information on SABER, see http://go.worldbank.org/NK2EK7MKV0.

54. Other exceptions include the recent randomized evaluations of youth training programs in Latin America. See Attanasio, Kugler, and Meghir (2008) and Card et al. (2011). The World Bank, as well as many other international organizations, is supporting the evaluation of several other training interventions (see Muzi 2010).

References

Acemoglu, Daron. 1998. "Why Do New Technologies Complement Skills? Direct Technical Change and Wage Inequality." *Quarterly Journal of Economics* 113(4): 1055–89.

Adams, Avril V. 2007. "The Role of Youth Skills Development in the Transition to Work: A Global Review." Human Development Network Children and Youth Working Paper Series. World Bank, Washington, DC.

Almeida, Rita, Juliana Arbelaez, Maddalena Honorati, Arvo Kuddo, Tanja Lohmann, Mirey Ovadiya, Lucian Pop, Maria Laura Sanchez Puerta, and Michael Weber. 2011. "Improving Access to Jobs and Earnings Opportunities: The Role of Activation and Graduation Policies." Background Paper to the New SP&L Strategy. Human Development Social Protection Discussion Paper 1204. World Bank, Washington, DC.

Almeida, Rita K., and Reyes Aterido. 2010. "Investment in Job Training: Why Are SMEs Lagging So Much Behind?" Policy Discussion Paper 5358. World Bank, Washington, DC.

———. 2011a. "On-the-Job Training and Rigidity of Employment Protection in the Developing World: Evidence from Differential Enforcement." *Labour Economics* 18: S71–S82.

———. 2011b. "The Incentives to Invest in Job Training: Do Strict Labor Codes Influence This Investment?" Social Protection Discussion Paper 46189. World Bank, Washington, DC.

Almeida, Rita K., and Pedro Carneiro. 2009. "The Return to Firm Investments in Human Capital." *Labour Economics* 16 (1): 97–106.

Almeida, Rita K., and Emanuela Galasso. 2010. "Jump-Starting Self Employment? Evidence Among Welfare Participants in Argentina." *World Development* 38(5).

American Psychological Association. 1996. "Intelligence: Knowns and Unknowns." *American Psychologist* 51(2).

Ariely, Dan. 2010. *The Upside of Irrationality: The Unexpected Benefits of Defying Logic at Work and at Home.* New York: HarperCollins Publishers.

Ashton, David, Francis Green, Johnny Sung, and Donna James. 2002. "The Evolution of Education and Training Strategies in Singapore, Taiwan and South Korea: A Development Model of Skill Formation." *Journal of Education and Work* 15(1): 5–30.

Asian Development Bank (ADB). 2008. *Education and Skills: Strategies for Accelerated Development in Asia and the Pacific.* Manila: ADB.

Attanasio, Orazio, Adriana Kugler, and Costas Meghir. 2008. "Training Disadvantaged Youth in Latin America: Evidence from a Randomized Trial." NBER working paper 13931. National Bureau of Economic Research, Cambridge, MA.

Autor, David H. 2004. "Why Do Temporary Help Firms Provide Free General Skills?" *Quarterly Journal of Economics* 116(4): 1409–48.

Banerji, Arup, Wendy Cunningham, Ariel Fiszbein, Elizabeth King, Harry Patrinos, David Robalino, and Jee-Peng Tan. 2010. "Stepping Up Skills for More Jobs and Higher Productivity." World Bank, Washington, DC.

Barron, John M., Mark C. Berger, and Dan A. Black. 1997. *On the Job Training*. Kalamazoo, MI: W. E. Upjohn Institute for Employment Research.

Bassanini, Andrea, Alison Booth, Giorgio Brunello, Maria de Paola, and Edwin Leuven. 2005. "Workplace Training in Europe." IZA Discussion Paper 1640. Institute for the Study of Labor, Bonn, Germany.

Becker, Gary S. 1964. *Human Capital*. Chicago: University of Chicago Press.

Black, Sandra E., and Lisa M. Lynch. 1996. "Human Capital Strategy and Productivity Outcomes." *American Economic Review Papers and Proceedings* 86(2): 263–67.

———. 2001. "How to Compete: The Impact of Workplace Practices and Information Technology on Productivity." *Review of Economics and Statistics* 83 (3): 434–45.

Card, David, Pablo Ibarraran, Ferdinando Regalia, David Rosas-Shady, and Yuri Soares. 2011. "The Labor Market Impacts of Youth Training in the Dominican Republic." *Journal of Labor Economics* 29(2).

Carneiro, Pedro, and James J. Heckman. 2003. "Human Capital Policy." In James J. Heckman, Alan B. Krueger, and Benjamin M. Friedman, eds., *Inequality in America: What Role for Human Capital Policies?* Cambridge, MA: MIT Press.

Cho, Yoon, David Margolis, David Newhouse, and David Robalino. 2011. "Labor Markets in Middle and Low Income Countries: Challenges and Implications for the Social Protection Strategy." Background paper to the New Social Protection and Labor Strategy. Human Development Social Protection Discussion Paper Series. World Bank, Washington, DC.

Cunha, Flavio, James J. Heckman, Lance J. Lochner, and Dimitriy V. Masterov. 2006. "Interpreting the Evidence on Life Cycle Skill Formation." In Eric A. Hanushek and Finis Welch, eds., *Handbook of the Economics of Education*. Amsterdam: North Holland.

Cunningham, Wendy 2009. "Active Labor Market Programs for Youth in Africa: A Framework for Engagement." World Bank, Washington, DC.

Dar, Amit, Sudharshan Canagarajah, and Paud Murphy. 2003. "Training Levies: Rationale and Evidence from Evaluations." World Bank, Washington, DC.

Dearden, Lorraine, Howard Reed, and John Van Reenen. 2006. "The Impact of Training on Productivity and Wages: Evidence from British Panel Data." *Oxford Bulletin of Economics and Statistics* 68(4): 397–421.

De Ferranti, David, Guillermo E. Perry, Indermit S. Gill, William F. Maloney, Carolina Sanchez-Paramo, Jose Luis Guasch, and Norbert Schady. 2003. *Closing the Gap in Education and Technology*. Washington, DC: World Bank.

Diamond, Peter, and Hannu Vartiainen. 2007. *Introduction to Behavioral Economics and Its Applications*. Princeton, NJ: Princeton University Press.

Frazis, Harley, and Mark A. Loewenstein. 2005. "Reexamining the Returns to Training: Functional Form, Magnitude, and Interpretation." *Journal of Human Resources* 40(2): 453–76.

Gill, Indermit S., Amit Dar, and Fred Fluitman. 1998. *Skills and Change: Constraints and Innovation in the Reform of Vocational Education and Training*. Washington, DC and Geneva: World Bank and the International Labour Office.

Gill, Indermit S., Fred Fluitman, and Amit Dar, eds. 2000. *Vocational Education and Training Reform: Matching Skills to Markets and Budgets*. New York: Oxford University Press for the World Bank.

Greenhalgh, Christine, and George Mavrotas. 1994. "The Role of Career Aspirations and Financial Constraints in Individual Access to Vocational Training." *Oxford Economic Papers* 46(4): 579–604.

Heckman, James J., Lance Lochner, and Christopher Taber. 1998. "Explaining Rising Wage Inequality: Explanations with a Dynamic General Equilibrium Model of Earnings with Heterogeneous Agents." *Review of Economic Dynamics* 1(1): 1–58.

Heckman, James J., and Dimitriy V. Masterov. 2004. "The Productivity Argument for Investing in Young Children." Technical Report Working Paper No. 5. Committee for Economic Development, Washington, DC.

Heckman, James J., Jora Stixrud, and Sergio Urzua. 2006. "The Effects of Cognitive and Noncognitive Abilities on Labor Market Outcomes and Social Behavior." *Journal of Labor Economics* 24: 411–82.

Helpman, Elhanan. 2004. *The Mystery of Economic Growth.* Cambridge, MA: Harvard University Press.

Jakubowski, Maciej, Harry Patrinos, Emilio Porta, and Jerzy Wisniewski. 2010. "The Impact of the 1999 Education Reform in Poland." Policy Research Working Paper No. 5263. World Bank, Washington, DC.

Johanson, Richard. 2009. "A Review of National Training Funds." Social Protection Discussion Paper 0922. World Bank, Washington, DC.

Johanson, Richard, and Arvil Van Adams. 2004. *Skills Development in Sub-Saharan Africa.* World Bank Regional and Sectoral Studies. Washington, DC: World Bank.

King, Kenneth, and Robert Palmer. 2010. "Planning for Technical and Vocational Skills Development." Fundamentals of Educational Planning No. 94. UNESCO: International Institute for Educational Planning.

Kluve, Jochen, Hilmar Schneider, Arne Uhlendorff, and Zhong Zhao. 2010. "Evaluating Continuous Training Programs Using the Generalized Propensity Score." Revised version of IZA Discussion Paper 3255. Institute for the Study of Labor, Bonn, Germany.

Kuruvilla, Sarosh, Christopher L. Erickson, and Alvin Hwang. 2002. "An Assessment of the Singapore Skills Development System: Does It Constitute a Viable Model for Other Developing Countries?" *World Development* 30(8): 1461–76.

Law, Song Seng. 2008. "Vocational Technical Education and Economic Development: The Singapore Experience." In Sing Kong Lee, Chor Boon Goh, Birger Fredriksen and Jee-Pen Tang, eds., *Toward a Better Future: Education and Training for Economic Development in Singapore since 1965.* Washington, DC: World Bank and National Institute of Education, Singapore.

Lechner, Michael, Ruth Miquel, and Conny Wunsch. 2011. "Long-Run Effects of Public Sector Sponsored Training in West Germany." *Journal of the European Economic Association.*

Levy, Frank, and Richard J. Murnane. 2005. *The New Division of Labor: How Computers Are Creating the Next Job Market.* Princeton, NJ: Princeton University Press.

Levy, Santiago. 2006. *Progress Against Poverty: Sustaining Mexico's PROGRESA-Oportunidades Program.* Washington, DC: Brookings Institution.

Leuven, Edwin, and Hessel Oosterbeek. 2004. "Evaluating the Effect of Tax Deductions on Training." *Journal of Labor Economics* 22(2): 461–88.

Lillard, Lee A., and Hong W. Tan. 1986. "Private Sector Training: Who Gets It and What Are Its Effects?" R-3331-DOL/RC. The RAND Corporation, Santa Monica, CA.

López-Acevedo, Gladys, and Hong Tan. 2005. "Evaluating Training Programs for Small and Medium Enterprises: Lessons from Mexico." Policy Research Working Paper 3760. World Bank, Washington, DC.

Lynch, Lisa M. 1992. "Private-Sector Training and the Earnings of Young Workers." *American Economic Review* 82(1): 299–312.

Martin, Rob, Frank Villeneuve-Smith, Liz Marshall, and Ewan McKenzie. 2008. "Employability Skills Explored." Learning and Skills Network (LSN), London.

McKenzie, David. 2009. "Impact Assessments in Finance and Private Sector Development: What Have We Learned and What Should We Learn?" *World Bank Research Observer* 25(2): 209–33.

Middleton, John, Adrian Ziderman, and Arvil Van Adams. 1993. *Skills for Productivity: Vocational Education and Training in Developing Countries.* New York: Oxford University Press.

Muzi, Silvia. 2010. "Summary Notes on Impact Evaluations in the Active Labor Market/Youth Employment Programs Cluster Supported by SIEF." Unpublished paper. World Bank, Washington, DC.

NASSCOM-Everest. 2008. "NASSCOM-Everest India BPO Study: Roadmap 2012—Capitalizing on the Expanding BPO Landscape." New Delhi. http://www.britishcouncil.org/learning-nasscom-report.pdf.

Organisation for Economic Co-operation and Development. 2009. *Education at a Glance 2009. OECD Indicators.* Paris: OECD.

———. 2010. "How Technology Changes Demands for Human Skills." OECD Education Working Papers Series, EDU/WKP(2010)8.

Rigolini, Jamele, Laura Pabon, Mariana Infante, Andrew Jones, and María Laura Sánchez-Puerta. 2010. "Providing Skills for Equity and Growth: Preparing Cambodia's Youth for the Labor Market." Working Paper, Human Development Department, East Asia and Pacific Region. World Bank, Washington, DC.

Rutkowski, Jan. 2011. "Skills for Productivity and Competitiveness: The Employers' Perspective." In *Europe 2020 Poland: Fueling Growth and Competitiveness in Poland through Employment, Skills, and Innovation.* Washington, DC: World Bank.

Robalino, David A., and María Laura Sánchez Puerta. 2010. "Managing Labor Market Risks." In Andrew Mason and Helena Ribe, eds., *Building an Effective and Inclusive Social Protection System in Latin America: Diagnosis and Policy Directions.* Washington, DC: World Bank.

Robalino, David A., and Mohamed Marouani. 2008. "Assessing Interactions among Education, Social Insurance, and Labor Market Policies in a General Equilibrium Framework: An Application to Morocco." World Bank Policy Research Working Paper 4681. World Bank, Washington, DC.

Schmidt-Hebbel, Klaus. 2009. "Chile's Growth and Development: Leadership, Policy-Making Process, Policies, and Results." Working Paper No. 52, Commission on Growth and Development. World Bank, Washington, DC.

Sondergaard, Lars, and Mamta Murthi. 2012. *Skills, Not Just Diplomas: Managing Education for Results in Eastern Europe and Central Asia.* Directions in Development Series. Washington, DC: World Bank.

Stein, Ernesto, Mariano Tommassi, Pablo T. Spiller, and Carlos Scartascini, eds. 2008. *Policymaking in Latin America: How Politics Shapes Policies.* Cambridge, MA: David Rockefeller Center for Latin American Studies, Harvard University.

Tan, Hong, and Geeta Batra. 1995. *Enterprise Training in Developing Countries.* Washington, DC: World Bank.

Thaler, Richard H., and Cass R. Sunstein. 2009. *Nudge: Improving Decisions about Health, Wealth, and Happiness.* New York: Penguin Group.

United Nations Educational, Scientific and Cultural Organization (UNESCO), Institute for Statistics (UIS). 2006. *Participation in Formal Technical and Vocational Education and Training Programmes Worldwide: An Initial Statistical Study.* Bonn: UNESCO-UNEVOC International Centre for Technical and Vocational Education and Training.

Wolf, Charles J. 1979. "A Theory of Non-Market Failure." *Journal of Law and Economics* 22(1): 107–39.

World Bank. 2011a. "PERU Labor Skills Programmatic AAA—Strengthening Skills and Employability in Peru." Report No. 61699-PE. Human Development Sector Management Unit, Andean Country Management Unit, Latin America and the Caribbean Region. World Bank, Washington, DC.

———. 2011b. "Policy Note on the ISKUR Vocational Trainees Profile, Job-Search Behavior, and Expectations." Unpublished paper. World Bank, Washington, DC.

Ziderman, Adrian. 2003. *Financing Vocational Training in Sub-Saharan Africa.* African Region Human Development Series. Washington, DC: World Bank.

2

Policy Framework: The Economic Rationale for Skills Development Policies

David Robalino, Rita Almeida, and Jere Behrman

More often than is desirable, skill development policies are designed and implemented by policy makers who lack a full understanding about why markets alone do not generate an efficient distribution of skills in the labor force. For example, most countries have technical and vocational education and training (TVET) systems that promote short-term training for technical careers and offer a safety net to those dropping out of primary or secondary schools. Often governments also build and manage training centers, decide on the content of the training programs, and subsidize tuition. Probably in the past this was the only mechanism to rapidly expand coverage. Today, however, many countries have a private sector that could play a more prominent role. What should then be the role of the government? Similarly, countries have setup schemes to promote on-the-job training (OJT), which often use payroll taxes to subsidize training provided by firms. What is the rationale for this type of scheme? More generally, if investments in skills produce high returns that justify the use of subsidies, why are individuals and firms not investing on their own?

This chapter attempts to improve our conceptual understanding of skills development policies. It discusses the most common market and government failures that affect the supply of skills and proposes specific policy interventions to address them. It shows that the most common interventions are not necessarily the best ways to address the underlying problems.

Why Do Markets Fail in the Provision of Training and How Can Policies Help?

This section discusses reasons why private mechanisms can lead to suboptimal levels of investments in training and/or a misallocation between the supply and demand for skills. Market failures can be generally grouped into four categories: (i) imperfections in labor markets, (ii) imperfections in capital markets, (iii) coordination failures, and (iv) decision-making failures that affect an individual's decision making (see table 2.1).

Table 2.1 The Training Market: Market Failures and Suggested Policy Interventions

Market failure	Suggested policy intervention
Imperfections in labor markets	
• Imperfect competition for skills (poaching externalities)	• Payback or apprenticeship contracts
• Pecuniary externalities of training	• Training subsidies (for workers or firms)
• Imperfect job-search information and asymmetric bargaining power (matching externalities)	• Unemployment insurance for workers
	• Job intermediation services
	• Trial employment arrangements
Imperfections in capital markets	
• Credit constraints	• Direct provision of credit (credit lines to firms or government loans to workers)
	• Loan guarantees to finance training
	• Training vouchers
Coordination failures	
• Innovation externalities	• Training subsidies (for firms or workers) in sectors with high value added (through public-private partnerships)
• Vacancy externalities	• Research and development subsidies (for firms)
	• Relocation subsidies for skilled workers
	• Training subsidies conditional on employment creation or wage subsidies for internships (for firms)
Decision-making failures	
• Inaccurate information about returns to investment in training or the quality of providers	• Counseling (for workers) and other support services fostering the dissemination of information
• Inconsistent time preferences	• Accreditation and ranking systems
• Cognitive and psychological limitations	• Subsidies supporting the public disclosure of providers' quality
	• Training subsidies to increase expected rate of return on investments

Imperfections in Labor Markets

Two main sources of failures in the labor market are particularly relevant for training policies: (i) imperfect competition among employers for different types of skills that can lead to "poaching externalities," and (ii) imperfect information in the job-matching process that can create pecuniary externalities for training or "matching externalities."

Imperfect competition and "poaching externalities"

When many employers demand a particular skill, and none of them is large enough to affect its "price," the skill is considered *fully transferable*. It is valued by many—perhaps all—firms. When this happens *employees* can appropriate the returns from the investments in training because many or all employers will be competing for them. At the other extreme is the case of *firm-specific* skills, which are valued by a single employer (a monopsony for that skill). The returns from investments in this type of skill can then be fully appropriated by the employer, since workers cannot sell the skill elsewhere. In these two cases, government interventions would not be necessary; either employees or employers would invest in training to generate the right set of skills.

In the real world, however, not all skills fall into one of these two categories. Many skills, such as plumbing, the use of particular software, or medical skills, are valued by some but not all employers.[1] Most skills are therefore *partially transferable*. In this situation neither employers nor firms can fully appropriate the returns from their investments in training. Employers invest less because they now face the threat that other employers will poach their skilled workers. Employees will also invest less because limited competition for their skills gives market power to employers that can depress wages—and therefore the rate of return on investments in training. It is in this middle ground, when the labor market is not fully competitive but there is not a single employer, that there can be a role for government intervention. The state can, for instance, enforce payback clauses or apprenticeship contracts, or provide training subsidies to workers or firms.

Figure 2.1 illustrates this point. The horizontal axis measures the degree of competition in the labor market for a particular skill, from zero for a monopsony to one with perfect competition. For a given skill, the gap between the marginal product of labor relative to the wage reaches a maximum in the case of a monopsony (normalized to be one). The curve for this gap slopes downward as firms' power in the labor market for this skill declines, reaching zero in the case of perfect competition. On the contrary, the probability of workers with that skill separating from their employers increases from zero under a monopsony until it reaches a maximum under perfect competition (normalized to be one). The value of the externality

Figure 2.1 Degree of Competition in a Skills Market and the Poaching Externality

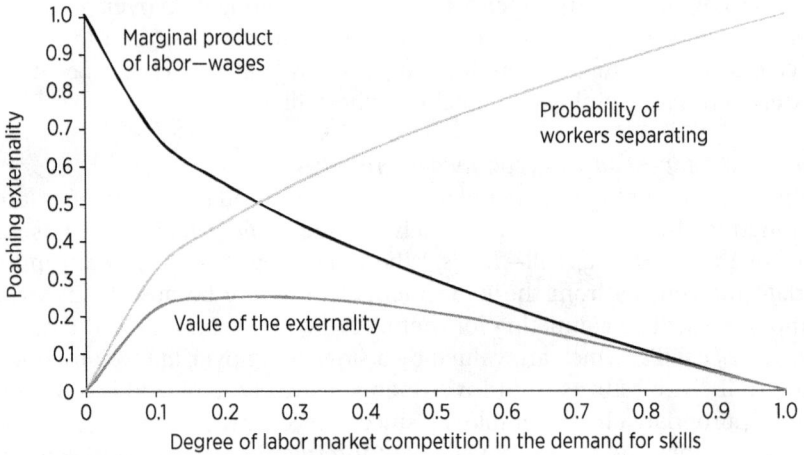

Source: Based on Stevens (1996).

depends on the combined effect (that is, the product) of the excess of the marginal product of labor relative to the wage rate and the probability of workers with that skill separating. This is indicated by the concave curve in figure 2.1. The social returns from addressing this externality thus are the greatest in oligopsonistic markets.

Imperfect information for job searching and pecuniary and matching externalities

Another factor that may lead to underinvestment in training is imperfect or limited information in the labor market for a particular skill. Workers and firms often have only partial information about the demand and supply of different skills. One consequence is that most employers and workers do not take wages as a given, but rather bargain for them. The relative bargaining power of employers and workers is determined by both the share of job vacancies relative to the stock of job seekers and by the fallback position of employees and employers when they cannot reach an agreement.[2] If employers have more bargaining power than employees, then wages will be lower than in a perfectly competitive labor market and workers will have fewer incentives to invest in training.[3] This is referred to as a "matching" externality. A consequence is that an increase in the supply of skilled workers, by making it easier to fill a vacancy, increases the market power of employers. Subsidizing training in this case can have unintended consequences.[4] Subsidies can increase the market power of employers and thus further reduce wages and incentives to invest in training. Workers who once invested in training on their own may stop.

Remedial policies include reducing the asymmetries of information or improving the bargaining power of workers. Employment, intermediation, skill certification services, and the promotion of internships could be effective tools to this end. Income protection programs for workers could also lead to more investment in training, because they improve the worker's bargaining power.

Imperfections in Capital Markets

Often individuals or employers might not have the necessary liquidity to finance investments in training. In principle, they could borrow, as long as the rate of return on the investment is higher than the interest rate. In practice, however, financial institutions usually have little information about the effect of training on earnings and the creditworthiness of the individual or employer. As a consequence, they may choose not to lend. In fact, there is empirical evidence that training decisions among low-income workers are negatively affected by the lack of financing.[5]

One way to mitigate this problem is for governments to facilitate individual and firm access to credit. They can do so through direct provision of credit or guarantees to financial institutions that finance specific types of training. For low-income workers, straight subsidies to finance training (for example, through training vouchers) may also be considered. These interventions, however, are not consensual among economists. Many would argue that such programs simply shift the risks from the financial institutions to the government. In doing so they may provide too much encouragement for risky investments. Therefore, developing mechanisms for assessing and monitoring such investments is likely to be critical. It is also not clear why governments would necessarily have advantages over financial institutions in developing such mechanisms—although they might be able to pool more risks over larger geographic areas and more markets.

Coordination Failures

Even assuming perfect labor and capital markets, firms and workers may underinvest in job training if they fail to coordinate to realize mutual benefits. The discussion in this section shows that underinvestment can happened both in high- and in low-productivity sectors.

Innovation externalities
Innovation externalities typically arise at the high end of the skills spectrum. When workers invest in the acquisition of high-end technical skills,

they are better able to invent or develop new technologies or adopt and adapt current technologies. More skilled workers make innovations possible within firms. This, in turn, determines how successfully firms compete in domestic and international markets and how labor productivity and wages evolve over time.[6] However, there can be situations where workers do not invest enough in high-end skills because there are not enough companies that introduce innovations and demand them, and firms do not innovate and create high-productivity jobs because there are not enough skilled workers.[7,8]

Policy interventions in this case could involve subsidizing training for individuals and firms in high value-added sectors (probably in the context of public-private partnerships), subsidizing research and development, facilitating the diffusion of technologies, and lessening migration costs for highly skilled workers. A big challenge, however, is identifying the strategic sectors. When these are not well defined, there is a large risk that subsidies end up in infant industries that never grow or do so very slowly. Furthermore, the vested interests of those who benefit from the subsidies can make it difficult to phase them out. In this context, explicit and well-defined sunset provisions for subsidies would be required.

Vacancy externalities

Vacancy externalities affect all skill levels but are likely to be more common at the low end of the skill spectrum. The problem is that employers may be reluctant to open vacancies for skilled workers because they are few in number and the associated costs are high. Instead, they settle for an unskilled labor force and lower levels of productivity (and profits). At the same time, workers do not invest in training because there are not enough vacancies for skilled workers. For example, in the construction or hospitality sectors, firms often operate with low-skilled labor and choose not to open more skilled job vacancies because of the higher labor costs (see box 2.1). The result is, again, a low-skills/low-productivity trap. To address this type of failure, governments could design policies to stimulate job training among low-skilled workers, conditional on firms posting vacancies for these same skills. One example could be subsidized internships for unskilled workers who acquire specific skills.

Decision-Making Failures

Investment decisions in training are often complex and individuals might not be able to collect and process all the relevant information.[9] This section discusses briefly three common problems that affect the decision-making process and can lead to low levels of investment in training or the wrong type of investment: (i) inaccurate information on the returns to training, (ii) limited information on the quality of training providers, and (iii) limited cognitive abilities and irrational behaviors.

BOX 2.1

Looking at the Hospitality and Construction Sectors in Cambodia: Skills Gaps and Mismatches for University Graduates

The hospitality, garments, and construction sectors are growing in the Cambodian economy. Anecdotal evidence shows significant skills gaps even among new graduates across these sectors. For example, Rigolini et al. (2010) show that only 20 percent of firms affirm that vocational training graduates are equipped with the necessary skills to perform their jobs, and 80 percent claim that workers have skill deficiencies (figure B2.1.1)

Figure B2.1.1 Vocational Training Skills Gap

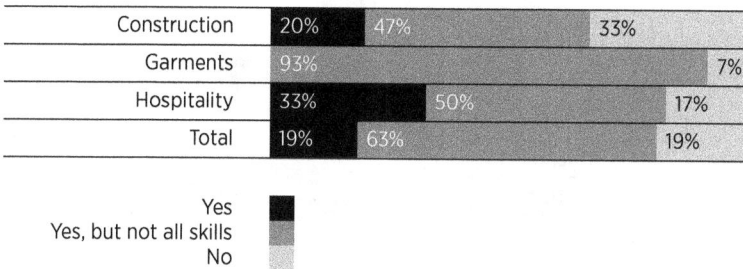

Construction	20%	47%	33%
Garments	93%		7%
Hospitality	33%	50%	17%
Total	19%	63%	19%

Yes
Yes, but not all skills
No

Source: Rigolini et al. (2010).

There are, however, important variations by sector in how severe firms deem the skills gaps to be. In the garment sector, for instance, firms do not appear to deem gaps as excessively severe; in contrast, in the construction sector, one out of three firms considers the gaps severe. These differences are likely to stem from differences in technologies and tasks that workers are expected to perform. In the garment sector, for instance, it remains relatively easy to train a worker to use a specific machine. Skills required in the hospitality sector are much broader in scope.

Figure B2.1.2 shows that, in the hospitality sector, employers identify foreign language proficiency as the most difficult skill to find. In this sector this is a strong demand for knowledge of foreign languages, even among the unskilled workers. Foreign languages are important to serve tourists, offer quality customer service, and remain competitive in an increasingly active sector. Nevertheless, only 12 percent of the hospitality labor force is able to speak a language other than Khmer (NIS 2008),

(Box continues on next page)

BOX 1.1 *(continued)*

Figure B2.1.2 Foreign Language Proficiency and Behavioral Skills Gaps

Skills gap in higher education

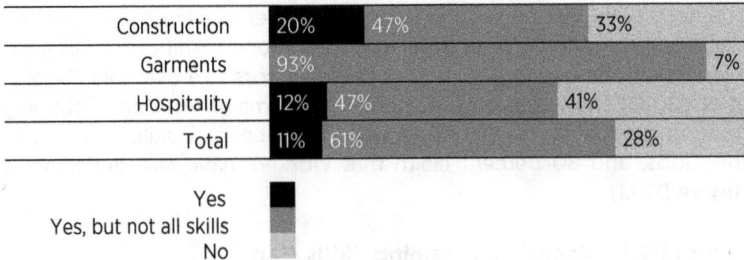

Construction	20%	47%	33%
Garments	93%		7%
Hospitality	12%	47%	41%
Total	11%	61%	28%

■ Yes
Yes, but not all skills
No

Skills mismatch in higher education

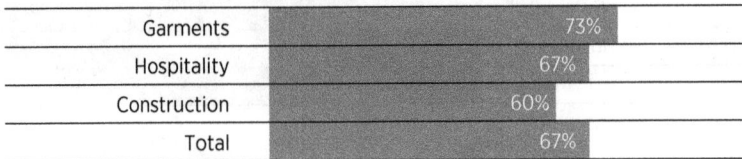

Garments	73%
Hospitality	67%
Construction	60%
Total	67%

Source: Rigolini et al. (2010).

and the proportion is even lower for unskilled workers. Accordingly, 61 percent of employers complain about the difficulty in finding unskilled workers with knowledge of foreign languages. Employers also complain about the lack of technical and soft skills among unskilled workers. It appears to be particularly difficult to find workers with technical skills related to service, housekeeping, and room grooming. The lack of behavioral skills such as team spirit, self-motivation, and commitment is also mentioned as a constraint (28 percent)

Source: Rigolini et al. (2010).

Inaccurate information on the returns to training

Individuals make their own assessments about the costs and benefits of investments to upgrade their skills. Their expectations are based on partial observations of labor market outcomes in the local economy as well as the experience and advice of peers, friends, and family that can be unrepresentative of the average experience. Expectations, therefore, are not necessarily accurate, particularly among individuals with low levels of cognitive skills, and can lead to investments in training that are too low or too high or allocated to the wrong skills.

Governments can have a role to play here by disseminating information on the costs of different types of training and their impacts on labor market outcomes. This can be done, for instance, through employment offices, publications, websites, and the general media. Clearly, given rapid changes in technologies and markets, there are high levels of uncertainty about the evolution of the demand for different skills. This emphasizes the importance of promoting investments in broader and more flexible skills that ease individuals' adaptation to changing working conditions.

Limited information on the quality of training providers

Even with good access to information about the benefits and costs of training, individuals may have difficulty identifying the right training providers. In the absence of information to systematically compare the content and quality of the courses offered, individuals may end up with low-quality providers or with providers who are not good matches for their needs. Even though in the long run the market should separate good providers from bad providers, the process can be long and costly. Moreover, there may not be perfect competition and free entry in the training market, perhaps because of inadequate regulations. In this case, the best policy intervention is probably to develop accreditation mechanisms for training providers or to facilitate the emergence of rating agencies. In all cases, governments should ensure that information about the quality of each training center is publicly available. Given the nature of such information as a public good, there is an efficiency argument for public subsidies. Moreover, subject to the provision of such information, governments should encourage entry into the training market—or at least not restrict entry—by subsidizing only certain types of providers (such as those operated by the public sector).

Limited cognitive abilities and irrational behaviors

Psychologists and behavioral economists have identified various reasons why individuals might fail to do the "right thing," be it saving more or investing more in human capital—both health and education.[10] First, individuals have limited cognitive abilities to analyze and solve complex problems, even if they have the knowledge and access to the right information. For instance, individuals may lack self-control and overconsume (and underinvest) when young—and then regret it when older.[11] Even if they opt to invest in education and training, they may lack the discipline to complete a given diploma. There is evidence by now that noncognitive skills developed during the first years of life (such as self-control and discipline) influence these decisions and behaviors.[12] Thus, failure to develop the right set of noncognitive skills at early ages can lead to suboptimal investment in training later in life.[13] Government interventions in these cases would need to focus on providing counseling and life skills training, and possibly provide financial incentives such as matching contributions to investments in training.

Why Do Governments Also Fail in the Provision of Training?

The market failures just discussed may be partially offset or fully corrected through government interventions. Often, unfortunately, the treatment can be worse than the disease. This does not mean that all government interventions should be avoided (see box 2.2). But it does mean that careful consideration should be given to the gains and costs of particular policies and programs. This section discusses some of the most common types of government failures and analyzes the main reasons behind them.

BOX 2.2

Challenges in National Training Funds to Promote Job-Relevant Skills

National training funds have long been a popular instrument for encouraging firm-based training and promoting skill development of the workforce. They buy training services for firms and target groups and offer a practical way to consolidate and administer government and donor spending on training in a cohesive and strategic manner. Training funds usually support short-term training for firm employees to meet rapidly changing skill needs of a particular sector.

However, they usually impose high administrative costs and often promote routine training programs instead of new programs. Moreover, program coordination is quite cumbersome and costly. This is in part the result of high administration costs and the often diverse and fragmented communities of training providers. Ministries of education, ministries of labor, other technical ministries, national and regional training authorities, nongovernmental organizations, and private training providers all must work together with employers under the administrative umbrella of training funds to deliver the training that firms demand. So that these various actors can be accommodated, training funds are usually administered under the aegis of federal governments and managed by a governing board that includes employer representatives. This method helps ensure that feedback from the labor market is incorporated into the training content.

Training funds can be financed out of general or payroll taxation or supported by donor agencies. In many countries, training funds use competitive procedures or levy-grant arrangements to disburse funds to firms to carry out board-sanctioned training programs and courses, but this is not always the case. Only in recent years have some Latin

(Box continues on next page)

BOX 2.2 *(continued)*

American countries begun to introduce innovative financing mechanisms, such as performance-based budgeting or competitive funding
schemes. Among the best-known training funds are Brazil's National
Industrial Apprenticeship Service (SENAI) and Malaysia's Human
Resource Development Fund (HRDF).

Source: Di Gropello et al. (2011); Dar et al. (2003); Johanson 2009; World Bank 2010.

Table 2.2 summarizes the main types of government failures that preclude the emergence of effective skill development programs. Policies to
address these failures are also suggested.

**Table 2.2   The Training Market: Government Failures and Policy
Recommendations**

Government failures	Suggested policy designs
Weak policy-making process	• Establish a national and well-articulated strategy for skills development policies. • Ensure transparency in the objectives of policy and on the role of the different stakeholders.
Inappropriate governance and institutional arrangements that reduce accountability	• Develop a strong regulatory framework for skill development policies, establishing clear responsibilities for the different players. • Develop sound institutional arrangements for implementation agencies, awarding them sufficient autonomy. These arrange-ments may include (among others) the following features: – autonomy of training centers to hire teachers, charge tuition, and select students – vouchers for individuals for increased choice over training providers – well-structured human resource policies for teachers and training staff members to improve their performance – budget allocations based on performance and not on historical disbursements.
Imperfect Information	• Support strong monitoring and evaluation systems with regular data collection and continuous evaluation that feed into program designs and managerial decision making. • Promote the disclosure of information (for example, on quality of training providers) to private parties.

Weak Policy-Making Process

Policy makers often lack the incentives and means to design policies that maximize social welfare. Governments are composed of individuals or groups that have their own interests (see figure 2.2). These groups can have incentives to favor politically powerful groups or to focus on short-term returns, possibly realized before the end of a political cycle. In addition, government policies also usually create their own interest groups. The most common example is probably teachers.

Addressing this problem is not easy. The emerging consensus is that much depends on the quality of the policy-making process (PMP), which is understood as the process of discussing, approving, and implementing public policies.[14] The quality of the PMP depends on the set of political actors and the incentives they face. These factors are, in turn, determined, at least in part, by political institutions (such as legislative bodies, the party system, and the judiciary) and institutional rules (for example, electoral rules). What the countries that have been able to introduce successful reforms have in common is a PMP in which political actors cooperate and are able to reach and enforce agreements. Cooperation is more likely to exist under the following conditions:

- leadership is strong and there is a vision
- there are good "aggregators" to reduce the number of actors with direct influence on policy making
- the key actors plan for the long term and interact repeatedly
- there are institutionalized arenas for political exchange

Figure 2.2 The Main Actors in the Provision of Skills

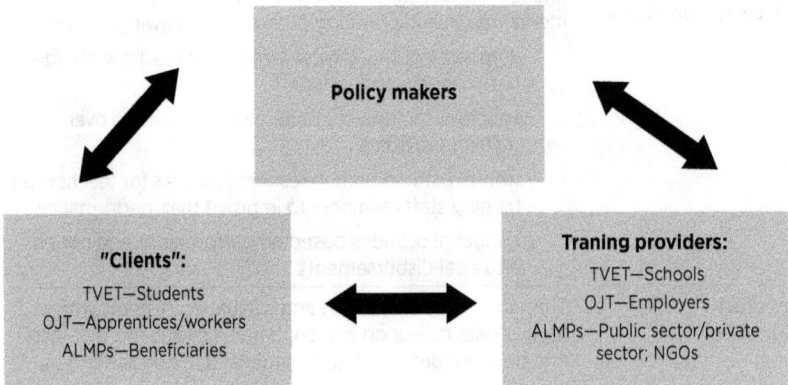

Policy makers

"Clients":
TVET—Students
OJT—Apprentices/workers
ALMPs—Beneficiaries

Traning providers:
TVET—Schools
OJT—Employers
ALMPs—Public sector/private sector; NGOs

- there are credible institutions to enforce agreements and prevent corruption, such as an independent judiciary
- there is a strong bureaucracy to which the analysis and implementation of policies can be delegated.

A start is to have a transparent process to discuss and design policies involving different stakeholders, set a clear strategic vision for skill development, and rely more on technical staff members within ministries who can ensure the continuity in the policy dialogue.

Inappropriate Governance and Institutional Arrangements

Even when the PMP is right, policies will fail if they do not provide the right set of incentives and margin of flexibility for those involved in the delivery of services. One issue is having appropriate governance arrangements. Indeed, training policy will only be relevant if policy makers can ensure that providers actually deliver appropriate content and quality to their target groups. Governments therefore might need to establish an effective institutional and regulatory framework with a clear delegation of roles and responsibilities between central and local governments and the different institutions (public and private) involved in the provision of training. The situation facing many countries today is one of excessive centralization and insufficient autonomy among training providers. These training institutions often lack the flexibility to define the curricula and adjust many of the inputs in the production of skills (for example, infrastructure, quality and quantity of teachers, and selection criteria for students).

Devising institutional arrangements that improve accountability to students and employers is also critical. Training providers usually do not have incentives to make decisions in the best interests of the training recipients. The main underlying reason is that government interventions are not intermediated by incentive structures such as those that might be provided by markets. Beneficiaries are able to influence the provision of training only in an indirect way: as citizens they can always affect politicians through the political cycle. At the root of the accountability problem is the fact that beneficiaries usually do not have any control over choice of training providers (and ultimately of teachers and managers). Similarly, teachers and managers are rarely held accountable for the skill development and acquisition of trainees.

One of the key reasons for this failure stems from current financing mechanisms. Budgets for training providers often come from the central or local government on the basis of historic allocations. Teachers or managers of public training centers are rarely evaluated on the basis of measured performance indicators, because they are often hired at the central level from the central budget. Moreover, their career progression and wage growth are also often disconnected from their performance in class and research achievements.[15] Basing the allocation of funds on performance measures can therefore go a long way in improving incentives. Another option is to rely on training vouchers that allow individuals to choose and directly pay providers.

Limited Information

Another obstacle to public provision of relevant training is imperfect information across all major players, from policy makers to training recipients. Often public policies on skills development assume that government officials have better information than do private parties. One example is the provision of information to guide the content of training programs to support future innovations and technological developments. In most cases, it is unclear that the government has a comparative advantage in knowing about future developments, particularly in rapidly changing economies.

Governments also often fail to evaluate the economic and social impacts of the policies that they implement. Lack of evaluation prevents the fine-tuning and adjustment of programs to improve their effectiveness. As a consequence, training may be of low quality, outdated, and misaligned with the needs of the markets. Governments would need to focus on developing strong monitoring and evaluation systems. These systems should provide accurate information about program performance that would inform program adjustments. For example, designing incentive schemes for training providers on the basis of placement rates and successful integration in the labor market requires rigorous program evaluation so that the policy maker knows what is working and what is not. Labor market indicators and tracking surveys are also critical in determining the effectiveness of skill development programs. Nowadays, new technologies and large capacities to collect and store data make this task easier.

Conclusion

This chapter argues that governments likely have important roles to play in promoting skill development policies. Indeed, there are several reasons why markets alone may not generate an efficient allocation of investments in skills. However, the optimal response is not necessarily to subsidize training or to directly supply training. The policy response could be, instead, to make labor and product markets work better, to provide more and better information about training and labor market outcomes, to offer counseling services on career development, to provide accreditation and rate training institutions, and to ensure that firms have access to credit and that individuals can borrow for training. More direct interventions that involve subsidizing training need to be carefully thought through both in terms of (i) the individuals or firms to which subsidies should be allocated and (ii) ways to finance such interventions. And because of all the uncertainties and information imperfections, sound monitoring and evaluation systems are needed.

The discussion also suggests that public interventions should depend on the type of skills covered and on the characteristics of the labor market where these skills are traded. For example, in very competitive labor markets, poaching of workers could be an unimportant issue and provision of training subsidies to firms would be the wrong policy.[16] Similar considerations apply when devising subsidies for individuals. Certain cognitive and noncognitive skills (such as leadership and communication skills) are likely to be valued by all employers and thus training costs could be absorbed by individuals. There would be little rationale to subsidize their provision for some individuals and not others—except possibly for distributional reasons in the case of low-income workers. Subsidies are likely to be more relevant for high-level technical skills (to address innovation externalities) or in the presence of low-productivity traps.

With these considerations in mind, one sees that better policies will first require better instruments to measure skills and assess their effects on labor market outcomes in developing countries. Indeed, indicators such as school attainment are very weak proxies and are largely insufficient to inform policy. One of the main avenues for further research is thus the development of sound country-level surveys of workers and firms that are regularly administered and measure the supply and demand of technical, cognitive, and noncognitive skills. Surveys of this type have been pioneered in Lebanon (employees and employers) and Peru (only employees) and are now being considered in other middle- and low-income countries. Only through these surveys can policy makers understand how different skills affect employment profiles and earnings and whether skill mismatch problems exist. In the absence of these surveys, policy makers are ultimately navigating blind.

Another important issue is how to define a more systematic approach for identifying constraints facing individuals or firms that reduce investments in training in different settings. For instance, how severe are information problems and myopia for different groups of workers? Can more information make a difference, or are subsidies required as well? Similarly, in the case of small and medium enterprises, is the problem access to credit, or are other problems with the business environment constraining their growth or reducing their incentive to innovate and invest in training? Pilot experiments need to be conducted to assess these issues, probably in the context of a coordinated effort involving governments, international organizations, and academic institutions. A first step would be to improve current data collection and ongoing monitoring and evaluation systems to better identify where alternative interventions are having the desired effects.

Notes

1. In other words, there is an oligopsony in the skills market.
2. See Lillard and Tan (1992).
3. This is different from failure discussed in the previous subsection. There the problem of a noncompetitive labor market was related to the number of firms. Here the argument holds regardless of the number of firms.
4. See Burdett and Smith (1996).
5. See Chapman (2002) and Greenhalgh and Mavrotas (1994).
6. This finding is in line with endogenous growth theory. See Helpman (2004) for a review.
7. See Ulph (1996).
8. See also Acemoglu (1998) for a similar discussion of the case of an imperfect labor market where capital and labor are complements.
9. In fact, a growing literature shows that individuals make systematic mistakes when choices are complex and outcomes cannot be observed repeatedly over fairly short time intervals. See Thaler and Sunstein (2009).
10. See Ariely (2008, 2010).
11. For example, the low propensity of most individuals to save has led many governments to develop mandatory saving programs. See Diamond and Vartiainen (2007).
12. For example, Carneiro, Crawford, and Goodman (2007) show that noncognitive skills measures at age 7 and earlier are important for a host of socioeconomic outcomes, including whether or not an individual stays in school, whether they have obtained a degree by age 42, employment status, and work experience, as well as likelihood of smoking, teenage pregnancy, and involvement with crime. Heckman, Stixrud, and Urzua (2006) show that cognitive and noncognitive skills at age 16 and above also explain a variety of labor market and behavioral outcomes. In particular, noncognitive skills strongly influence schooling decisions and also affect wages, given schooling decisions.
13. The available evidence suggests that for many skills and abilities, later remediation for early disadvantages to achieve a given level of adult performance may be possible, but is much more costly than early remediation. The economic returns to job training, high school graduation, and college attendance are lower for the less able. See Carneiro and Heckman (2003) and Cunha and Heckman (2007).
14. See Schmidt-Hebbel (2009) and Scartascini et al. (2010)
15. See Salmi (2009).
16. Even where the market for certain skills (such as operating machines to produce textiles) is imperfect, training subsidies may not make sense if the returns to training are low. Bassanini et al. (2005) find evidence that in several countries, including the United Kingdom, returns are smaller for low-educated workers.

References

Acemoglu, Daron. 1998. "Why Do New Technologies Complement Skills? Directed Technical Change and Wage Inequality." *Quarterly Journal of Economics* 113(4): 1055–89.

Ariely, Dan. 2008. *Predictably Irrational: The Hidden Forces That Shape Our Decisions.* New York: HarperCollins Publishers.

———. 2010. *The Upside of Irrationality: The Unexpected Benefits of Defying Logic at Work and at Home.* New York: HarperCollins Publishers.

Bassanini, Andrea, Alison Booth, Giorgio Brunella, Maria de Paola, and Edwin Leuven. 2005. "Workplace Training in Europe." IZA Discussion Paper 1640, Bonn, Germany: Institute for the Study of Labor.

Burdett, Kenneth, and Eric Smith. 1996. "Education and Matching Externalities." In Alison L. Booth and Dennis J. Snower, eds., *Acquiring Skills: Market Failures, Their Symptoms, and Policy Responses.* Cambridge, UK: Cambridge University Press.

Carneiro, Pedro, Claire Crawford, and Alissa Goodman. 2007. "The Impact of Early Cognitive and Non-Cognitive Skills on Later Outcomes." Centre for the Economics of Education, London School of Economics, London, UK.

Carneiro, Pedro, and James J. Heckman. 2003. "Human Capital Policy." In James J. Heckman, Alan B. Krueger, and Benjamin M. Friedman, eds., *Inequality in America: What Role for Human Capital Policies?.* Cambridge, MA: MIT Press.

Chapman, Bruce. 2002. "A Submission on Financing Issues to the Department of Education Science and Training Inquiry into Higher Education." Centre for Economic Policy Research, Research School of Economics, Australian National University.

Cunha, Flavio, and James J. Heckman. 2007. "The Technology of Skill Formation." IZA Discussion Paper No. 2550. Institute for the Study of Labor, Bonn, Germany.

Dar, Amit, Sudharshan Canagarajah, and Paud Murphy. 2003. "Training Levies: Rationale and Evidence from Evaluations." World Bank, Washington, DC.

Diamond, Peter A., and Hannu Vartiainen. 2007. "Introduction." In Peter A. Diamond and Hannu Vartiainen, eds., *Behavioral Economics and Its Applications.* Princeton, NJ: Princeton University Press.

Di Gropello, Emanuela, Aurelien Kruse, and Prateek Tandon. 2011. "Skills for the Labor Market in Indonesia: Trends in Demand, Gaps, and Supply." Green Cover Report. World Bank, Washington, DC.

Greenhalgh, Christine, and George Mavrotas. 1994. "The Role of Career Aspirations and Financial Constraints in Individual Access to Vocational Training." *Oxford Economic Papers* 46(4): 579–604.

Heckman, James J., Jora Stixrud, and Sergio Urzua. 2006. "The Effects of Cognitive and Noncognitive Abilities on Labor Market Outcomes and Social Behavior." *Journal of Labor Economics* 24: 411–82.

Helpman, Elhanan. 2004. *The Mystery of Economic Growth.* Cambridge, MA: Harvard University Press.

Johanson, Richard. 2009. "A Review of National Training Funds." Social Protection Discussion Paper 0922. World Bank, Washington, DC.

Lillard, Lee A., and Hong W. Tan. 1992. "Private Sector Training: Who Gets It and What Are Its Effects?" *Research in Labor Economics* 13: 1–62.

National Institute of Statistics (NIS), Cambodia. 2008. *Cambodia Socio-Economic Survey (CSES)*. Phnom Penh, Cambodia: NIS.

Rigolini, Jamele, Laura Pabon, Mariana Infante, Andrew Jones, and María Laura Sánchez Puerta. 2010. "Providing Skills for Equity and Growth: Preparing Cambodia's Youth for the Labor Market." Working paper, Human Development Department, East Asia and Pacific Region. World Bank, Washington, DC.

Salmi, Jamil. 2009. "The Challenge of Establishing World-Class Universities." World Bank, Washington, DC.

Scartascini, Carlos, Ernesto Stein, and Mariano Tommasi. 2010 *How Democracy Works: Political Institutions, Actors and Arenas in Latin American Policymaking.* Washington, DC: Inter-American Development Bank; Cambridge, MA: David Rockefeller Center for Latin American Studies, Harvard University.

Schmidt-Hebbel, Klaus. 2009. "Chile's Growth and Development: Leadership, Policy-Making Process, Policies, and Results." Working Paper No. 52. Commission on Growth and Development. World Bank, Washington, DC.

Stevens, M. 1996. "Transferable Training and Poaching Externalities." In Alison L. Booth and Dennis J. Snower, eds., *Acquiring Skills: Market Failures, Their Symptoms, and Policy Responses*. Cambridge, UK: Cambridge University Press.

Thaler, Richard H., and Cass R. Sunstein. 2009. *Nudge: Improving Decisions about Health, Wealth, and Happiness.* New York: Penguin Group.

Ulph, David. 1996. "Dynamic Competition for Market Share and the Failure of the Market for Skilled Labour." In Alison L. Booth and Dennis J. Snower, eds., *Acquiring Skills: Market Failures, Their Symptoms, and Policy Responses.* Cambridge, UK: Cambridge University Press.

World Bank. 2010. *Reducing Inequality for Shared Growth in China: Strategy and Policy Options for Guangdong Province.* Washington, DC: World Bank.

3

Pre-Employment Technical and Vocational Education and Training: Fostering Relevance, Effectiveness, and Efficiency

Jee-Peng Tan and Yoo-Jeung Joy Nam[1]

Introduction

Pre-employment technical and vocational education and training (TVET) is a term commonly associated with skills development programs that provide young people with a stepping stone into the labor market.[2] It encompasses programs offered in educational institutions that lead to formal qualifications, as well as nonformal courses provided in various settings—typically of shorter duration and often modular in design—that give young people other avenues to acquire useful skills. As a complement to the next two chapters on on-the-job (OJT) training and active labor market programs (ALMPs), this chapter focuses on pre-employment TVET.[3] While not confined to a specific age group, programs falling under this rubric primarily target young people nearing the end of their initial formal schooling and about to enter the world of work. The main objective of TVET programs is to equip those enrolled with job-relevant skills that can facilitate—though not guarantee—a smoother transition to gainful employment.

In recent years, TVET has attracted renewed interest among policy makers. Progress in expanding basic education throughout the world, including in the poorest countries, has meant rapid increases in the number of youth who are now completing basic education and seeking opportunities for further education and training.[4] This trend is straining secondary and tertiary systems and increasing the pressure on governments to offer multiple pathways for school-to-work transitions, including pre-employment TVET. In the former socialist countries, moreover, the transition from planned to market economies has called for a reorientation of pre-employment TVET systems that were primarily designed to supply workers for state-owned enterprises. Interest in pre-employment TVET has also been fueled by its perceived role in facilitating the industrialization of East Asian countries (see, for example, Fredriksen and Tan 2008). Even in developed countries, pre-employment TVET is receiving fresh attention as countries consider options to boost workforce skills in an increasingly competitive global economy (see, for example, OECD 2010).

Country experiences around the world suggest that imparting job-relevant skills through pre-employment TVET continues to be a challenge in developing countries. Because agriculture and the informal sector account for the bulk of employment in developing countries—about 78 percent in Sub-Saharan Africa, for example—skills development for these sectors is a concern.[5] Although agricultural education and training can complement other investments to raise agricultural productivity, a host of obstacles, including, in particular, a lack of qualified faculty (see, for example, World Bank 2007), has made the hoped-for results generally elusive. Training for jobs in the informal sector suffers from unfulfilled expectations as well. While some of the expectations are unrealistic, as Adams (2007) has pointed out (for example, seeing it as the solution to unemployment among youth), inadequate and ad hoc provision is also part of the problem (see, for example, Walther and Filipiak 2007; Fretwell 2009).

The performance of pre-employment TVET with regard to skills for the modern sector raises separate issues. A common complaint from employers pertains to mismatches between skills supply and demand. The system for supplying skills tends, by nature, to be ponderous, making it difficult to keep up with changing labor market conditions as new opportunities and technologies combine to shift workplace processes and practices and hence the demand for skills, including the so-called "soft" skills for work in modern settings that emphasize team work and effective communication. The desire to accelerate growth creates additional expectations. Many developing countries see pre-employment TVET as crucial to efforts to upgrade their technological capabilities and hence their ability to engage in economic activities with a potential for higher returns.[6]

This chapter discusses the design of policies and strategies in pre-employment TVET in light of the foregoing concerns in developing countries. To set the context, it provides a brief overview of global trends in pre-employment TVET and the available evidence on its economic impact; it also considers the nature of skills demand and skills acquisition through pre-employment TVET. The chapter then focuses on three policy challenges relating to such programs that are especially pertinent in developing countries: economic relevance, social and equity concerns, and effectiveness and efficiency. The conceptual framework laid out in chapter 2 on sources of market and government failures provides a useful backdrop for the discussion. Governmental subsidies or other policy interventions for pre-employment TVET might be warranted in the presence of *imperfections in capital markets, coordination failures and limited information, and uncertainty and myopia on the part of individuals.* However, as chapter 2 indicates, government action may also be flawed by *weak policy-making processes, inappropriate governance and institutional arrangements, and inadequate information to clarify policy choices.* Thus, in both pre-employment TVET and other types of training, challenges exist in achieving the right balance between governmental interventions and private market activities in the context of important market and government failures.

Participation in Pre-Employment TVET

Pre-employment TVET provides learning experiences in essentially two types of settings: an educational or training institution (such as a school, college, training center, or polytechnic) or the workplace. Institution-based training often consists of formal programs at various levels in the education system whose outcomes are accredited.[7] In a survey of programs around the world, UNESCO-UIS (2006) found that in more than two-thirds of the 143 countries for which data were available, institution-based TVET programs were offered only from the upper secondary level onward.[8] Because TVET programs are intended to impart skills for the world of work, they often put greater emphasis on practical subjects and hands-on training than on theoretical instruction. The degree of practical orientation varies by type of institution and often depends on logistical constraints, despite the intended design (for example, availability of facilities, equipment, and staff with the relevant expertise). In diversified secondary schools, practical subjects may claim 15–20 percent of instructional time, while the share may rise to 40–60 percent in more specialized technical and vocational schools and even to 80–90 percent in vocational or rural training centers (ADB 2009). Pre-employment TVET provided through apprenticeships is part of the landscape but is often much better organized and typically more formalized in developed countries (for example, the so-called dual system in Germany) than in developing ones.

The diversity in pre-employment TVET and uneven coverage of the available statistics make it difficult to document participation rates with a high degree of accuracy. Nonetheless, the data collected by UNESCO and mapped using the International Standard of Classification of Education (ISCED) permit an overall assessment. Figure 3.1 indicates that the share of enrollments in TVET at the upper secondary level (the most prevalent level at which it is provided) is diverse across regions and income levels. In general, it is higher in the more developed countries: about 50 percent, on average in OECD countries in 2009, compared with the corresponding

Figure 3.1 Share of TVET Enrollments at the Upper Secondary Level, by Region and in Relation to Per Capita GDP

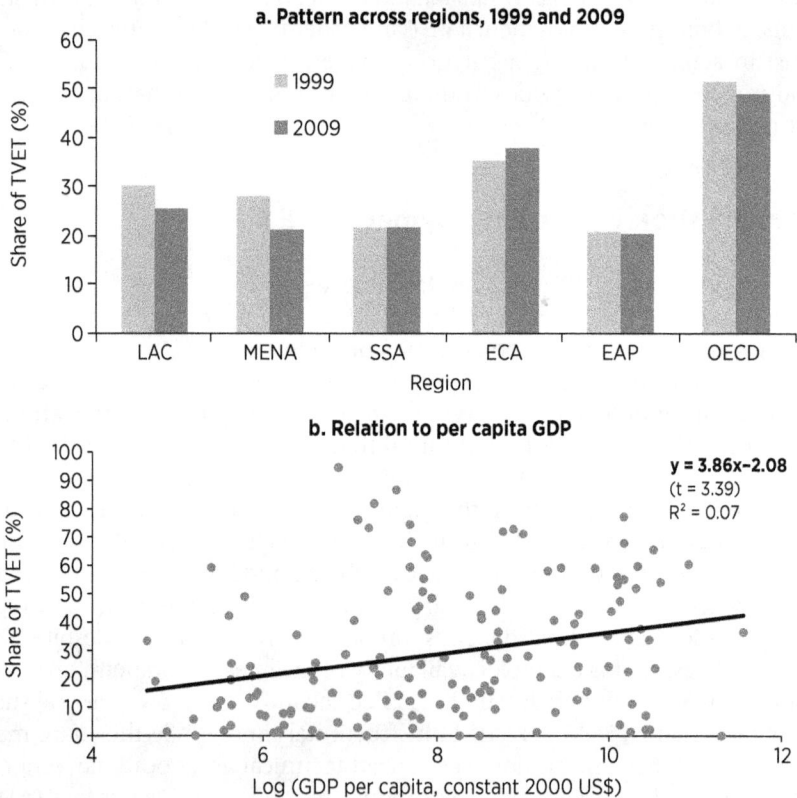

a. Pattern across regions, 1999 and 2009

b. Relation to per capita GDP

$y = 3.86x–2.08$
$(t = 3.39)$
$R^2 = 0.07$

Sources: UNESCO-UIS for data on TVET shares and World Bank WDI for data on per capita GDP.

Note: a. Sample contains 79 countries, South Asia excluded due to lack of data.
EAP = East Asia and Pacific; ECA = Europe and Central Asia; LAC = Latin America and the Caribbean; MENA = Middle East and North Africa; OECD = Organisation for Economic Co-operation and Development; SSA = Sub-Saharan Africa.

b. Sample contains 144 countries and data refer to the latest year between 2007 and 2010.

share of about 20 percent in Sub-Saharan Africa, East Asia, and the Middle East and North Africa. The share of TVET enrollments is generally higher in the Europe and Central Asia region than elsewhere among non-OECD countries, reflecting the legacy of the region's central planning past.

The share of TVET enrollments correlates positively with a country's level of income, as panel (b) in the figure shows. This pattern is consistent with the fact that as coverage rises and becomes universal (as they are in higher-income countries) education systems must offer more options to cater to and retain students with diverse interests and aptitudes for academic studies. At the same time, the economies of the higher-income countries are technologically more sophisticated and therefore exert a stronger demand for skills acquired through relatively advanced, institution-based, formal technical and vocational training. The relation between the share of enrollments in TVET and per capital GDP is nonetheless relatively weak (with an R-squared statistic of only 0.07), suggesting that pre-employment TVET can be organized in multiple ways even for countries at comparable levels of income.

Labor Market Outcomes of TVET Programs

Given the remit of pre-employment TVET, an important question is the pattern of employment and earnings among the graduates of such programs compared to their peers in the more academic tracks. Below we examine the evidence based on published aggregate data, mainly for the OECD countries and on the results from various statistical analyses of survey data for selected developing countries.

Employment and Earnings in OECD Countries

According to labor force survey data compiled by the OECD and Eurostat, the probability of being employed among the graduates of TVET is comparable to that among their peers from academic programs, at both the upper secondary and tertiary levels (panel (a) in figure 3.2). The pattern of earnings, on the other hand, suggests a more favorable outcome for the graduates of academic programs. The available data (panel (b) in figure 3.2), which pertain to tertiary level programs at the ISCED levels 5 and 6,[9] show a positive gap among both younger and older age cohorts. These comparisons are clearly only suggestive, given the possibility that the academic track may contain a higher concentration of the more capable students. Nonetheless, the gap in earnings (which appears to grow with age) provides one reason why pre-employment TVET programs are often perceived as a less desirable option. Analysis of life-cycle patterns, based on data for

Figure 3.2 Employment and Earnings among Graduates of TVET and Academic Programs, OECD Countries, 2007

a. Employment rate (%)

b. Earnings (below upper secondary = 100)

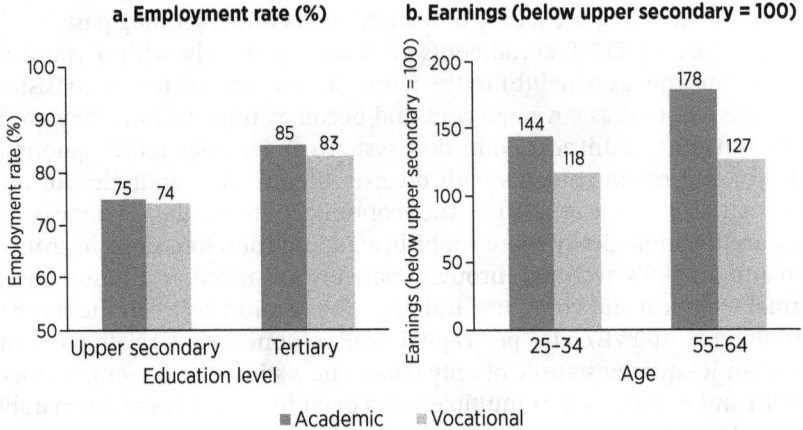

■ Academic ■ Vocational

Sources: Based on data in OECD 2009 (tables A6.1 and A7.1).

Note: At the upper secondary level, academic programs refer to those classified as 3A in the ISCED framework, while vocational programs include those classified as 3B or 3C. At the tertiary level, academic programs refer to those classified as 5A and 6, while vocational programs refer to those in the 5B category.

18 mostly OECD countries, suggests that programs with a heavy vocational orientation facilitate entry into the labor market but hurt employment at older ages, implying a tradeoff between benefits in the short run and costs in the longer term (Hanushek, Woessmann, and Zhang 2011).

Findings from Survey Data for Developing Countries

Survey data also exist for a number of developing countries that permit a closer look at differences between TVET and general education in terms of labor market outcomes. Researchers have evaluated the relationship using various regression techniques to control for factors other than individuals' training background that may affect labor market outcomes. A summary of the findings appears in table 3.1, for a total of 13 developing countries. An important caveat is that the available survey data typically do not distinguish between pre-employment TVET and other sources of training. They often capture accredited training rather than skills gained through other routes. And they tend not to control for the endogeneity of the schooling and training choices, making it difficult to isolate the effect of training net of the impact of other factors associated with an individual's intrinsic, unobservable, or unmeasured characteristics (for example, personal motivation,

Table 3.1 Returns to TVET and Other Labor Market Outcomes in Selected Developing Countries

Country and year	Impact on earnings	Methodology	Author(s)
Studies showing more favorable results for TVET than for general education			
Egypt, Arab Rep. (1998)	Returns to vocational secondary education are 35.4 percent, while returns to general secondary education are 6.1 percent for men.	Mincerian earnings regression (1st stage: ordered logit)	El-Hamidi (2006)
Singapore (1998)	Private returns to vocational/technical education are 10.3 percent at the secondary level and 12.7 percent at the post-secondary level, compared with the corresponding figures of 9.4 percent and 11.3 percent for general education.	Extrapolation of Mincer equation results from 1980s Singapore data	Sakellariou (2003)
Sri Lanka (2002)	Returns to formal vocational training are 17 percent compared with 7.9 percent for general education.	Mincerian earnings regression (not controlling for selectivity bias)	Riboud, Savchenko, and Tan (2007)
Thailand (1989–95)	Returns to vocational education at the upper secondary level exceed those to general education by 63.9 percent for men and 49.4 percent for women.	Mincerian earnings regression (1st stage: probit)	Moenjak and Worswick (2003)
Israel (1983)	Vocational school graduates employed in occupations related to their field of study earn between 8.1 percent (widely related) and 9.6 percent (directly related) more than peers who graduated from general education or who are working in fields unrelated to their studies.	Mincerian earnings regression (OLS, without first stage)[a]	Neuman and Ziderman (1991)

(Table continues on next page)

Table 3.1 (continued)

Country and year	Impact on earnings	Methodology	Author(s)
Studies showing no difference or mixed results			
India (2004)	Returns to formal vocational training are approximately 8 percent, comparable to returns to general education at 8.4 percent.	Mincerian earnings regression (not controlling for selectivity bias)	Riboud, Savchenko, and Tan (2007)
East Germany (1984–96)	No advantage exists in earnings or employment among graduates of public-sector-sponsored continuous vocational training and retraining in the first years following training.	Propensity matching score techniques	Lechner (2000)
Romania (1995–2000)	No significant differences exist in labor market participation or earnings between vocational and general education students.	Regression discontinuity	Malamud and Pop-Eleches (2008)
Tanzania (1997–2000)	Returns are higher for high levels of academic education than for vocational or lower levels of academic education; the returns to vocational or technical education are lower the higher the level at which it is entered.[b]	Mincerian earnings fixed effects regression	Kahyarara and Teal (2008)
Indonesia (1993, 1997, 2000, 2007)	For men, no significant differences exist in earnings between public general and vocational graduates, but public vocational graduates in the youngest cohort experience a large wage penalty. For women, public vocational graduates have greater wage returns than general graduates. Public vocational graduates are also more likely to obtain formal jobs than public general graduates.[c]	Mincerian earnings regression (OLS and LAD) (1st stage: multinomial logit regression)	Newhouse and Suryadarma (2011)

(Table continues on next page)

Table 3.1 (continued)

Country and year	Impact on earnings	Methodology	Author(s)
Studies showing less favorable results for TVET than for general education			
Pakistan (2004)	Returns to formal vocational training are 8.1 percent, while returns to general education are slightly higher at about 9 percent.	Mincerian earnings regression (not controlling for selectivity bias)	Riboud, Savchenko, Tan (2007)
Rwanda (1999–2001)	Returns to vocational education are 12.5 percent, while returns to general secondary education are 29.0 percent.	Mincerian earnings regression (1st stage: multinomial logit)	Lassibille and Tan (2005)
Suriname (1990, 1992, 1993)	Returns to both general language and mathematics tracks exceed returns to technical or vocational education for both males and females.[d]	Mincerian earnings regression (1st stage: probit regression)	Horowitz and Schenzler (1999)

Sources: See the chapter annex for detailed description of data sources.

Note:

a. No first stage because selectivity bias is controlled by comparing vocational education graduates employed in matched or study-related occupations versus their general education counterparts.

b. The returns for those who enter vocational schools after primary school are estimated at 9.6 percent compared with 8.8 percent for those who enter after completing lower secondary school, and only 3.2 percent for those who enter after completing upper secondary school. Similarly, the returns for those that enter technical colleges after completing lower secondary school are estimated at 10.5 percent compared with 7.3 percent for those that enter after completing upper secondary school.

c. Male public vocational graduates have a 6.2 percent greater chance of working in formal jobs than male public general graduates. The estimated wage penalty for male public vocational graduates in the youngest cohort was 20 percent in 2000, and 40 percent in 2007. Female public vocational graduates earn a wage premium (15.8 percent (OLS) and 14.3 percent (LAD)) and are 8.7 percent more likely to obtain formal jobs than public general graduates.

d. For males, the private returns to technical secondary education are 10.4 percent, compared with 11.6 percent for general education, 12.3 percent for the general language track, and 11.2 percent for the general mathematics track. For females, the returns to vocational secondary education are 2.5 percent, compared with 12.3 percent for the general language track, and 11.6 percent for the general mathematics track.

LAD = least absolute deviations; OLS = ordinary least squares.

social capital, and so forth). Two main points can nonetheless be distilled from the findings across the various studies: (i) TVET qualifications can yield favorable private returns, and (ii) the returns to TVET are not necessarily inferior to those associated with general education. The mixed picture from the aggregate and the survey data results may reflect limitations in the data (for example, no information on program content and quality) and also the possibility that context matters in determining the benefits of TVET relative to general education.

Skills Demand and Skills Acquisition through Pre-Employment TVET

The demand for skills and employers' expectations provide an important context for assessing the role and design of pre-employment TVET. In most developing countries, there is evidence of skills bottlenecks associated with mismatches between skills supply and demand (as documented in chapter 1 of this book) and with inadequacies in the quality and scope of skills. These problems undermine firm productivity and their competitiveness in global markets. Pre-employment TVET programs can help address some of these problems, but are effective only if they are closely linked to the demand for skills.

Skills Prioritized by Employers

Direct feedback from employers provides an interesting perspective on the types of skills valued in the workplace. A fairly typical finding in developing countries is that aside from formal educational or technical qualifications, employers also place a high value on attitudes and behaviors. In a 2009 survey of Indian firms that hire engineering graduates, the respondents prioritized such qualities as integrity, reliability, teamwork, willingness to learn, entrepreneurship, self-discipline, self-motivation, flexibility, ability to understand and take directions, and capacity to communicate in English (Blom and Saeki 2011). In a 2008 survey in the Philippines, employers placed a high value on their employees' ability to work independently, to communicate, and to solve problems. They also highlighted leadership and creativity skills for managers and directors; and teamwork and time management for employees engaged in production, administration, or sales (di Gropello et al. 2010). With regard to job-specific skills, employers in Indonesia, the Philippines, and Vietnam tend to prioritize practical, job-related knowledge over theoretical knowledge (di Gropello, Kruse, and Tandon 2011; di Gropello, Tandon, and Yusuf 2011).

Skills Acquisition through Pre-Employment TVET

The skills required by employers represent a mix of job-relevant competencies and personal qualities. To understand where pre-employment TVET might play a role in fostering these skills, it is useful to group them into broad categories that clarify the links to training programs. One useful conceptualization is the *Dictionary of Occupational Titles* used in the United States, which makes a distinction among skills according to the degree of involvement with *Data, People,* and *Things*.[10] These categories correspond to cognitive skills, interpersonal or interactive skills, and physical or manual skills.[11] In relation to a specific job, the skills encompass the knowledge, expertise, and behaviors that the job holder needs in order to execute his or her responsibilities competently. The skills include mastery of a body of knowledge relevant to the job; familiarity with the tools and technologies used to perform the tasks associated with the job; understanding of the materials that are worked with; and the fostering and use of interpersonal relationships and interactions to accomplish the tasks required in the job.

Acquiring multifaceted, job-relevant skills is a complex and cumulative process. General cognitive and noncognitive skills (such as literacy and numeracy for the former, self-control and discipline for the latter) accumulate from early childhood and are reinforced through general basic education, while job-relevant skills are acquired later on, either prior to entry into the labor market or on-the-job by building on the foundations laid (Banerji et al. 2010). It is also important to acknowledge that job-relevant skills can be acquired in multiple settings, including institution-based programs that may or may not lead to formal qualifications, formal apprenticeship arrangements, or informal learning in the process of working with others.

The two-dimensional framework in figure 3.3 offers one way to situate pre-employment TVET programs in the broader perspective discussed above. One dimension is the proximity of the skills being developed in relation to the requirements of specific jobs while the other is the focus of the learning goals. By definition, TVET programs build on the foundational skills identified in quadrants A and B, and are therefore designed to put more emphasis on the skills identified in quadrants C and D. Within these quadrants, a continuum of choices exists, making it necessary to reflect on such questions as these when deciding on the design of training programs: what skill sets are most effective in facilitating young people's transition to their first job and subsequent success in the labor market?[12] How are these skills produced? How important is a high level of literacy and numeracy to success in TVET programs and subsequently in the labor market? If such basic skills are important, do the students typically enrolled in pre-employment TVET have the necessary foundation to benefit from their programs? TVET? And if not, how can they be helped?[13]

Figure 3.3 Training Programs and the Building of Job-Relevant Skills

	Orientation of skills being developed	
	More general	*More specific to a job, task, or occupation*
More conceptual — Focus of learning — **More operational**	**A** **Meta-competence** (Knowledge to facilitate learning)	**C** **Cognitive competence** (Specialized technical knowledge)
	B **Social competence** (Attitude and behavior)	**D** **Functional competence** (Practical know-how)

Sources: Adapted from Winterton et al. (2005).

In reality, the specificity and orientation of the pre-employment training depend on many practical factors, including budget constraints, historical antecedents, and the political economy of balancing the interests and priorities of the different parties. With small budgets, the curricula options are likely to be limited to theoretically oriented, classroom-based courses that do not require the services of specialist teachers and that offer trainees only limited exposure to hands-on work experience. Stakeholders also exert an influence on the orientation of the programs. Large firms that have their own in-house training capability and firms with proprietary technology are less likely than other firms to value the acquisition of specialized technical knowledge as a learning goal in pre-employment TVET programs. Employers generally prefer training that imparts practical skills that are immediately useful in their business, whereas trainees might desire a greater focus on generic skills that are transferable to other jobs and that provide a basis for further learning. An example of striking contrasts in how employers in different countries view the role of pre-employment vocational training appears in box 3.1.

Policy Challenges in Pre-Employment TVET

Equipping youth with employable skills through pre-employment TVET has been the subject of policy debate in the international development community for many decades. A substantial literature also exists on many

BOX 3.1

Employers' Views on the Role of Pre-Employment Vocational Training in England and Poland

Surveys in England in 2008 and in Poland in 2009 asked employers to rank the skills they value in potential new recruits. In both countries employers expect workers to possess good work attitudes, to communicate well, and to be able to work in teams (figure B3.1.1 below). However, their views on the role of job-specific vocational skills are strikingly different. Polish employers expect young recruits to possess such skills already, while their English counterparts have no such expectations, preferring instead candidates with solid competency in literacy and numeracy. In other words, employers in England want trainable workers whereas those in Poland want trained workers. Rutkowski (2011) attributes this difference to the legacy of central planning in Poland, continuation of past attitudes, lags in the provision of on-the-job training by private sector firms, and the possibility that small firms in Poland cannot afford to train their recruits.

Figure B3.1.1 Employability Skills Prioritized by English and Polish Employers, 2008 and 2009, Respectively

a. English employers, skills priority, 2008
(scale of 1–14, 1 = highest)

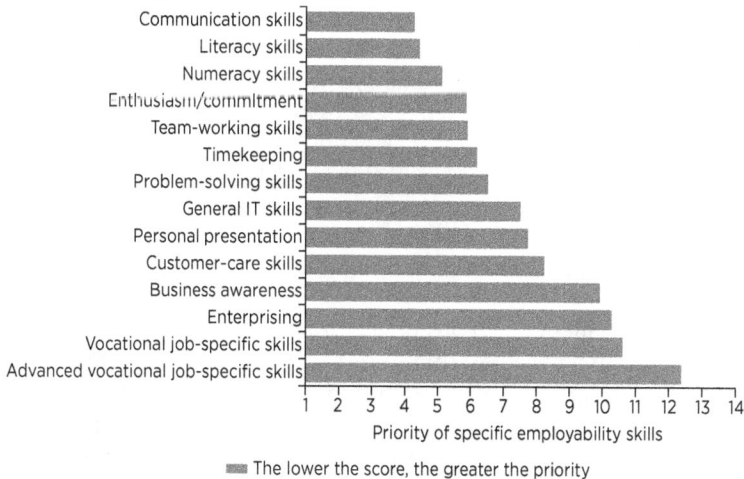

Priority of specific employability skills

▬ The lower the score, the greater the priority

Source: Martin et al. (2008).
IT = information technology.

(Box continues on next page)

BOX 3.1 *(continued)*

b. Polish employers, skills priority, 2009
(percentage of employers reporting a skill as "very important")

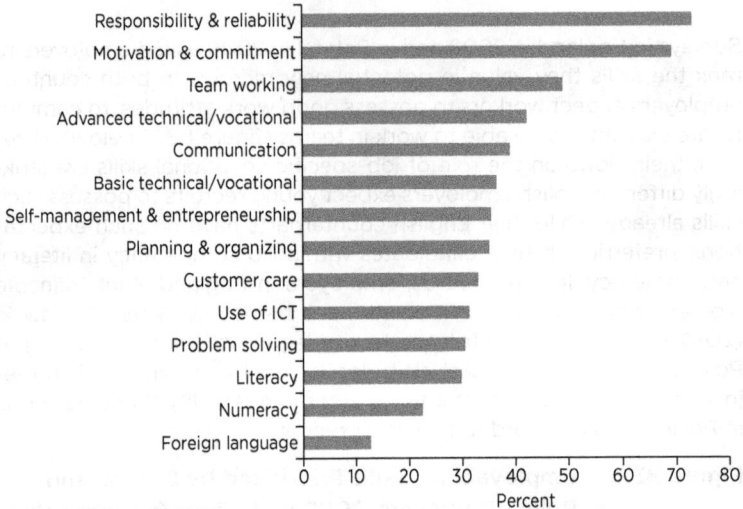

Source: Rutkowski (2011).
ICT = information and communications technology.

Although not confirmed by survey data reported in Martin et al. (2008), English employers' relative lack of interest in pre-employment vocational training is consistent with such factors as the availability of public funding for in-service training, a governance structure that gives employers more say in determining training provision, the need for customized training to suit local conditions, and protection of proprietary operational information and know-how through in-house training provision.

Source: Martin et al. (2008); Rutkowski (2011).

aspects of the challenges involved (see, for example, Maclean and Wilson 2009). The discussion below therefore highlights selected issues that may be of special relevance to the low- and middle-income countries served by the World Bank's development assistance. We focus on the following policy challenges: (i) fostering economic relevance, (ii) responding to social and equity concerns, and (iii) ensuring effectiveness and efficiency. By no means comprehensive, these themes are nonetheless highly pertinent to the World Bank's policy dialogue with its partner countries regarding pre-employment TVET.

Fostering Economic Relevance

The economic relevance of pre-employment TVET hinges on its potential role in fostering faster growth. Growth clearly requires certain preconditions: a stable macroeconomic environment, good governance and institutions, an environment supportive of the private sector, higher capital investment, and so forth. But without a skilled workforce, countries will lack the capabilities to grow new industries; diversify the range, quality, and sophistication of goods and services; and multiply linkages to the global economy. Although most developing countries, including the poorest ones, have made progress in basic education, the scarcity of job-relevant technical skills in the workforce can impede the development of viable, job-creating, and growth-accelerating modern industries and services.[14]

In low-income countries

In low-income countries, the role of pre-employment TVET for growth poses particularly difficult challenges. One major problem is that training programs are expensive—up to three times as costly as general secondary education (Mingat, Ledoux, and Rakotomalala 2010) as they often require specialized teachers and equipment. Thus, to afford them on a sustained basis, countries have to grow and generate the income and revenues to pay for the programs. A second difficulty is that modern industry is underdeveloped and small in poor countries. Most firms operate well within the production frontier in their relevant industries, rely on less sophisticated technology, and run on a relatively small scale with few workers. As a result, the demand for technical skills tends to be weak, fragmented across small firms, and poorly-coordinated; correspondingly, the supply of training programs is also limited. These difficulties create "a "chicken-and-egg" problem, at least in the short term. Countries need more skills to help modernize their economies and accelerate growth, but they also need a vibrant modern sector to create the demand for technical skills and sustain a training market, as well as faster growth to generate the revenues to finance skills development (Ansu and Tan 2011). In the framework of chapter 2, such coordination failures are likely to result in a suboptimal level of investment in skills and therefore to impede productivity gains.

Governments can help the country break out of this "chicken-and-egg" situation by making the formation of job-relevant skills through TVET an explicit part of their strategy for growth and development. We emphasize that pro-activity by the government to solve a coordination problem may not produce the desired results if it ignores the design of incentives for training provision. Indeed, among low- and middle-income countries, there is still limited experience with successful packaging of apex-level coordination with measures to foster market-responsive behavior by training providers. This rarity makes the successes of the Republic of Korea; Taiwan, China; and Singapore in the early years of their development experience worth distilling for possible lessons.

The experiences of these countries are documented in some detail in Ashton et al. (2002) and Kuruvilla, Erickson, and Hwang (2002). What appears to characterize these Asian tigers is that they understood the type of coordination failures that can emerge in training markets in the early stages of development. Consequently, they pursued a strategic, government-led coordination plan aimed at encouraging more effective alignment of skill demand and supply as well as sustainable investments in higher-level skills. In particular, they brought together three elements required to achieve results: (i) a clearly identified and well-focused source of demand for these higher-level skills; (ii) training curricula and pedagogy aligned with the skills to be developed; and (iii) arrangements for implementing the relevant training programs that include measuring success in terms of meeting explicit skill gaps. As with any innovation, making the pieces fit and work together entails a learning-by-doing process. The strategic value of governmental involvement in the process is to accumulate what might be described as "transactional" experience among those involved. Such hands-on experience is essential in building national capacity to design, implement, and manage locally adapted models of demand-led, pre-employment TVET for economic development and growth.

Intentional coordination of effort is especially relevant at the early stages of piloting a demand-led approach to pre-employment TVET. It is critical between those responsible for economic strategy and those responsible for training programs. In Korea, the powerful Economic Planning Board (EPB) fulfilled this function. Formed in 1961 and operating as a stand-alone entity until its absorption into the Ministry of Finance in 1994, it played a key role in aligning decisions about training funding and provision with the requirements of the new industry clusters targeted by the EPB (Lee 2009). During the 1970s, for example, a number of specialized high schools were created to supply the skilled workers for the heavy and chemical industries then targeted by the government. These schools were accordingly prioritized with generous funding to serve as models for replication elsewhere in the system. A similar coordinating function was fulfilled by Singapore's Economic Development Board, making it a key player in shaping the country's early experience with demand-led, pre-employment TVET for growth and development (see box 3.2 for details of the approach and its impact over time).

A more recent example of intentional coordination at the highest level of government is India's decision to create several new bodies for workforce development. These bodies are the National Council on Skill Development, chaired by the Prime Minister; the National Skill Development Coordination Board, chaired by the Deputy Chairman of the Planning Commission;

BOX 3.2

Demand-Led Pre-Employment TVET for Economic Growth in Singapore

Singapore's pre-employment TVET system is widely recognized as one of the best in the world. Its quality owes much to the skills development schemes sponsored by Singapore's Economic Development Board (EDB) during the agency's first three decades (1961–91) (see figure B3.2.1). Low et al. (1993) consider these schemes to be one of the agency's greatest innovations that supported Singapore's efforts to industrialize.

The start was inauspicious, however (Chiang 1998). EDB's training-cum-production workshops and worker retraining schemes in the late 1960s and early 1970s ended in failure. The regular technical education institutions were also inadequate: their programs offered only "remedial" options for weak students, and they took too long to produce graduates. EDB therefore decided to partner with leading international firms with proven training systems. The objective was to learn the training business from these partners, train to their requirements, and adapt the methods for local needs.

EDB's first foreign training partner was Tata Group, then India's largest engineering firm. The Tata-Government Training Center opened in 1972 to supply workers for Tata's precision engineering plant in Singapore. It trained Singapore workers the same way that Tata's workers in India were trained. The Singapore government provided the land and buildings, contributed 70 percent of the center's operating costs, and paid the stipends of the trainees (who signed a bond, valid for five years, committing them to work for the EDB or any company directed by the agency). The center trained twice as many people as Tata required. Tata had first pick of the graduates while EDB retained the rest as an asset to attract other engineering firms to Singapore. The agency's strategy thus created a skills pipeline to grow an industry cluster beyond the needs of a single company.

The arrangements with the Tata Group provided the template for other company-affiliated training centers. EDB later enlisted the help of foreign governments to upgrade the various training centers, and it convinced foreign investors to participate in the pooling of training resources. This development facilitated Singapore's access to advanced training resources for its emerging technology-intensive industries. Resource channels included the secondment of foreign experts to Singapore on request, the training of EDB lecturers and technical staff at the participating firms' overseas locations, assistance with curriculum

(Box continues on next page)

BOX 3.2 *(continued)*

and program development, donation or loan of equipment, commitment to upgrade equipment and software, and so forth. The evolution tracked the country's transition from being a skills-driven economy to one that is driven by technology, and ultimately, by innovation.

In 1993, EDB exited from direct involvement in training activities by consolidating its institutes to form Nanyang Polytechnic, which was brought under the purview of the Ministry of Education. In this way, EDB's innovative practices in industry-responsive skills development (such as the "teaching factory" model) were mainstreamed and institutionalized, thus benefiting the whole education and training system.

Figure B3.2.1 Evolution of EDB's Skills Development Schemes, 1972–93

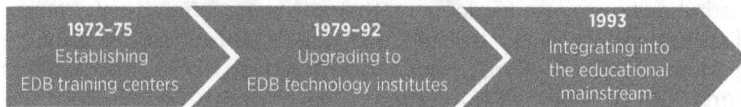

| 1972–75 Establishing EDB training centers | 1979–92 Upgrading to EDB technology institutes | 1993 Integrating into the educational mainstream |

Source: World Bank based on Chan (2008) and Chiang (1998).

and the National Skill Development Corporation, headed by an eminent private sector industrialist.[15]

Ireland and Costa Rica are other examples of countries with active government leadership that ensured close coordination between economic strategy and training provision. In Ireland, the government established new Regional Technology Colleges with an explicit orientation to train workers for the emerging industries targeted by the Ireland Development Authority (O'Hare 2008). In Costa Rica, new technical programs and enhanced curricula were introduced at three major educational institutions as part of the government's effort in the early 1990s to attract Intel, a leading technology company headquartered in the United States, to set up its US$300 million assembly and test plant in the country (Spar 1998; World Bank and MIGA 2006).

Countries with a more developed modern sector

In countries with a more developed modern sector, pre-employment TVET has the potential to be part of a virtuous cycle that supplies the skills to foster a technology- and knowledge-intensive pattern of growth. Globalization and rapid technological change have increased economic competition among countries and placed a premium on skills. Workers with higher-quality cognitive, technical, communication, and team skills are better able to assimilate and use technology, to push the knowledge frontier, to innovate, and to make efficient and informed decisions. Countries with these "capacity" skills can deepen their technological capability to compete in export markets, plug into global supply chains, and move more easily into new areas of economic activity where profit margins remain high.

Where the modern sector is more developed and where a critical mass of employers exists to drive the demand for higher-level skills, the "chicken-and-egg" problem cited earlier becomes less binding. Mobilizing the input of employers remains essential if pre-employment TVET is to minimize complaints about its failure to equip graduates with job-relevant skills. Employers know what skills are required for their operations; and firms that are innovating with new technologies are in the best position to articulate the implications of newly adopted technologies. The government can help enhance the economic relevance of pre-employment TVET by facilitating the transmission of clear signals about employers' skills requirements, by encouraging employers to codify and communicate their skills needs, and by incentivizing a responsive and flexible training supply to meet employer's demand for skills. Such demand can be signaled through timely and widely accessible information about the jobs and wages of recent graduates—information that can help guide current students in their choice of training options and enhance accountability for results in training provision.[16]

In the more-dynamic sectors of the economy, the demand for skills may be sufficiently strong to attract proactive participation by employers in shaping pre-employment TVET programs. The actions of Indian firms in the country's booming information technology (IT) and IT-enabled services (ITES) industries are an example. IT/ITES companies have powerful incentives to take the lead. The global market potential for their industries remains substantial and not yet fully tapped, and there is thus a large unmet demand for suitably qualified workers (the estimated shortfall is estimated at between 0.8 to 1.2 million workers in 2012).[17] Industry outreach to schools and colleges is a common practice to align courses to industry needs.[18] In a significant development for pre-employment training for the IT/ITES industries, Indian companies have joined forces through the National Association of Software and Service Companies (NASSCOM) on common skills assessment tests. Through this collaboration, the NASSCOM Assessment of Competence (NAC) was introduced in 2006 to assess entry-level skills for the ITES industry, followed subsequently by the NAC-Tech certificate to test engineering skills for the IT industry (NASSCOM-Everest 2008).

Responding to Social and Equity Concerns

By imparting job-relevant skills, pre-employment TVET can potentially boost the life chances of youth from marginalized populations. It is, however, not a panacea for the many economic and social problems faced by this population. For one thing, pre-employment TVET is no substitute for equipping disadvantaged youths with a strong foundation of basic literacy and numeracy skills. Much research has demonstrated the importance of such skills for success in the labor market. These skills are typically acquired beginning in primary and lower secondary education. The second point to recognize is that pre-employment TVET counteracts the effects of a general scarcity of jobs in weak economies. The solution requires broader strategies that go beyond TVET policies. Focusing more narrowly on social and equity concerns in pre-employment TVET, we highlight below two important aspects: its accessibility and responsiveness to the needs of the disadvantaged. The discussion complements the next two chapters in this volume in their exploration of the role of apprenticeships (as a form of OJT) and of the impact of ALMPs targeted toward vulnerable populations.[19]

Access to pre-employment TVET by disadvantaged groups
Access to pre-employment TVET by disadvantaged groups is a concern when these groups are shut out of programs that are effective in imparting job-relevant skills. In some countries, pre-employment TVET in fact enrolls a disproportionate share of the disadvantaged. These students tend to face tighter liquidity and information constraints, may expect lower returns to investments in training, and have lower levels of cognitive and noncognitive skills to compete for and succeed in the best programs. Because of the high correlation between educational achievement and socioeconomic status, most available studies show that students from higher-income families are more successful in gaining entry to the more-desirable academic streams. Their peers from poorer homes are then left to fill places in second- or last-choice options, (often) including TVET. The result is a vicious cycle of indifferent political support for TVET, inadequate funding, low quality of inputs, poor program image, and limited skills acquisition for employment. In many countries, the decline in pre-employment agricultural TVET, for example, is a manifestation of this dynamic (World Bank 2007). Reversing the situation is not easy: public interest in such programs is waning and school-based TVET programs tend to be more expensive than general education (see, for example, Mingat, Ledoux, and Rakotomalala 2010). Revitalizing pre-employment TVET that serves the poor is likely to require systemic reforms to modernize institutional governance, curricula design, and pedagogical methods. Ironically, one of the best approaches may be to enhance basic literacy and numeracy skills in marginalized populations, to establish a solid foundation for individuals to learn new skills throughout life.

Where pre-employment TVET programs are attractive (for example, in such fields as medical technology and ICT with good prospects for well-paid jobs), access by the poor can be constrained by such factors as geography, admission criteria, and costs. Lack of awareness about these programs and shortage of funds to cover fees, transport, and lodging expenses add to the barriers faced by the poor, particularly those in rural areas. Gender discrimination in pre-employment TVET has also been highlighted as a problem in many countries (see, for example, King and Palmer 2010). Stereotypes about the types of jobs suitable for men and women tend to channel boys and girls into different training programs and reinforce patterns of enrollment that limit women's ability to acquire skills for better-paying jobs. Interventions that can help enhance access to desirable programs of pre-employment TVET by marginalized groups include targeted scholarships or financial support, modification of selection criteria, and increased presence of female instructors in courses that prepare trainees for traditionally male-dominated occupations. Successful efforts are likely to be anchored by an explicit link with employment opportunities, for which a customized program of pre-employment training provides a stepping stone for the disadvantaged (see box 3.3 for a private sector–led example in India).[20]

BOX 3.3

Private Sector–Led Pre-Employment TVET for Construction Workers in India

Larsen and Toubro's Construction Skills Training Institute (CSTI) is an example of a structured, industry-led pre-employment training initiative that targets the disadvantaged. Established in 1995 by Larsen and Toubro (L&T), a US$9.8 billion technology, engineering, construction, and manufacturing company, CSTI reaches out to youth in rural India to equip them with skills required for the company's international and national construction business. Highlighted below are features of the CSTI program that make it an effective source of pre-employment TVET that benefits the disadvantaged.

Selection criteria: The admission criteria are geared to low-skilled workers capable of reaching high standards in the physically demanding construction industry. The qualifying educational attainment starts at Primary Grade 5 and it explicitly excludes those who possess a diploma, a degree, or qualification as software professionals. Selection into one of the several trade areas (such as formwork carpentry, bar

(Box continues on next page)

BOX 3.3 *(continued)*

bending and steel fixing, masonry, plumbing, electrical, and welding) offered by CSTI is made on the basis of written and practical entrance tests.

Curriculum and methodology: Courses in each trade have specific occupational standards of knowledge and skills grouped into three distinct levels: basic, intermediate, and high. All training courses are short term, ranging from 200 hours spread over one month to 600 hours over three months. About 80 percent of the courses is work-based practical training and the remaining 20 percent is classroom oriented. The emphasis is on "performing" rather than "knowing."

Assessment and certification: CSTI courses employ a modular approach, allowing for continuous assessments at each stage of training. Trainees at all levels take Trade Competency Tests at periodic intervals to ascertain progress in meeting the required standards in knowledge and skill. Individual progress is recorded and recognized through workmen referral cards. Highlighting personal data and skill levels of jobs performed, these cards are easily accessed, referenced, and updated.

International and national benchmarks: To comply with global standards of excellence, CSTI developed its training program in partnerships with Henry Boot Training Ltd and the Construction Industry Training Board of the United Kingdom. It is also registered as a vocational training provider under the Ministry of Labor and Employment's Skill Development Initiative Scheme, which makes its trainees eligible for public training subsidies and for a National Council for Vocational Training certificate upon passing the relevant tests.

Employment prospects: CSTI admits about 1,200 new entrants annually in its various campuses, and deploys 100 trained workers monthly to L&T's construction projects. Successful completers of CSTI training courses are employed initially on contract through subcontractors. At the CSTI in Mumbai, for example, less than a quarter of the trainees get hired directly by the company, while the others find employment elsewhere. The modularized training program allows for steady, incremental skills acquisition. At the end of six to seven years, good performers may progress to formal employment by L&T, including at the supervisory level.

Sources: World Bank based on http://www.lntecc.com/homepage/CSTI/pdfs/ English-Brochure.pdf; http://www.lntecc.com/homepage/CSTI/; http://www. bloomberg.com/news/2010-12-20/india-can-t-find-enough-laborers-to-build-roads-in-1-trillion-singh-plan.html.

Pre-employment TVET as a source of skills acquisition by the disadvantaged
Pre-employment TVET as a source of skills acquisition by the disadvantaged raises issues about the content of training in relation to the jobs and sources of income that most people in this population are likely to find. In urban areas, most of the jobs will be in the informal economy involving small-scale production and petty trade. In rural areas, nonfarm activities are gaining importance as a source of income.[21] In these circumstances entrepreneurship skills are a critical complement to the functional expertise that pre-employment TVET may impart. Such skills include the ability to identify and evaluate business opportunities, to estimate and keep account of input costs and the volume of sales, to manage production and personnel, interact with customers, market goods and services, and so on (see, for example, World Bank 2007). However, reorienting formal, school-based programs of pre-employment TVET to provide suitable training in entrepreneurship skills for disadvantaged groups has proved to be difficult (Johanson and Adams 2004), possibly because of weak incentives, inadequate knowledge among staff to redesign the training programs, and so forth. More fundamentally, it is also unclear that formal, school-based programs of pre-employment TVET are the right instrument. According to ADB (2009), such training in fact plays a minor role in helping the beneficiaries. Much more important are non-training measures, including evaluation of the prospects of income-generation, provision of business advice and access to credit for graduates, and regular tracer studies of graduates to ascertain the continued relevance of the training provided. Experience also suggests that provision of training through nonformal training centers and nongovernmental organizations is likely to be more cost effective than school-based formal arrangements (see, for example, ADB 2008).

Ensuring Effectiveness and Efficiency in Pre-Employment TVET

Although precise estimates are elusive, reflecting diversity in training provision across countries, pre-employment TVET programs often cost significantly more per student than general education programs at the same level.[22] Given their costliness, the revival of interest in such programs in recent years has highlighted questions about their effectiveness and efficiency and hence their affordability as an option for expanding secondary and post-secondary enrollments. Below we examine two issues that are relevant in this regard: (i) pre-employment TVET in relation to general education, focusing on the secondary level; and (ii) governance of and accountability in training provision.[23]

Pre-employment TVET in relation to general education
When to introduce vocational content into the curriculum and how much
emphasis to put on the vocational content are two recurring questions that
policy makers in many countries face. Poor choices by the government on
these matters can arise from weak policy-making processes, and they are
often perpetuated by inadequate attention to the monitoring and evaluation of alternative pathways for young people to make successful transitions from school to work. Introducing pre-employment TVET earlier
rather than later has an appealing logic in theory: it gives students a head
start in acquiring skills for employment and orientates them to the world of
work. The concept has been introduced in various formats in developing
countries, including vocationalization or diversification of the curriculum,
with mixed results (see, for example, ADB 2008; Johanson and Adams
2004). Success often depends on the type of vocational content being introduced. Where the content requires costly inputs of specialized teachers,
purpose-built facilities and equipment, and expensive materials, success is
usually elusive, particularly in low-income countries where tight budgets
make the arrangements financially unsustainable. The prospects improve
where training programs can be implemented easily; where the content
relates to both general learning and job applications (for example, training
in computer skills, business studies, and so forth); and where the programs
fit well into an academic setting (King and Palmer 2010). Some have argued
that a better approach than integrating TVET into general education is to
concentrate the resources in intensive training programs for those who are
about to take up a job or are already in one (ADB 2008).

Diversity in country conditions precludes a one-size-fits-all conclusion
about the most appropriate time to introduce vocational content. However,
against a backdrop of rising skills demands, more countries are deferring
vocational specialization until upper secondary education, to ensure that
students acquire a solid general education before training to acquire more
specific skills (see, for example, UNESCO-UIS 2006; Adams 2007).The benefit of delaying vocational tracking has been documented in several studies.
According to Jakubowski et al. (2010), the one-year delay in separating
students into general or vocational tracks in Poland's 1999 Education
Reform raised by an estimated 100 points (or a whole standard deviation)
the test scores of students who would have been channeled into the vocational stream. Pekkarinen, Uusitalo, and Pekkala (2006) examined the
impact of Finland's school reform of 1972–77, which raised the age at
which students are tracked from 12 to 16, and found that the reform had
reduced the intergenerational income correlation by seven percentage
points. Meghir and Palme (2005) examined the impact of Sweden's education reform in 1950, which extended compulsory schooling to nine years,

replaced ability-based placement of pupils after grade 6 into academic and nonacademic streams with one based on self-selected placement, and imposed a nationally unified curriculum. They found that the reform had raised the educational attainment and the earnings of children whose fathers were less well-educated. The adverse impact of early tracking on educational mobility and equality has been documented in Bauer and Riphahn (2006) in a comparison of Swiss cantons and by Hanushek and Wössmann (2006) in a cross-section of mostly developed countries. As shown by these studies as well as current trends, the deferment of vocationalization may be a key factor in improving the effectiveness of pre-employment TVET.

Another important concern with pre-employment TVET is that premature tracking may lock students into undesirable career paths with dead ends. Upper secondary education in Mexico, for instance, consists of three separate streams: (i) *general upper secondary* that prepares students for higher education, (ii) *technological upper secondary* that prepares students for both careers as professional technicians and for higher education, and (iii) *technical professional education* that includes various vocational and professional programs. The lack of mobility across these subsystems is seen as one factor contributing to the high dropout and low graduation rates at the upper secondary level (World Bank 2010). Addressing this problem has been the focus of the government's ongoing reforms of secondary education since 2007. By contrast, pre-employment TVET in secondary schools in the United States takes the form of elective courses through Career and Technical Education programs. Such programs enable students to earn skills qualifications while still in high school, through tests approved by various industry bodies. These qualifications enable students to build their careers through additional courses or use them to obtain employment.[24]

Governance of pre-employment TVET and accountability in training provision
Weak governance and lack of accountability are common problems of government failure that affect the effectiveness and efficiency of TVET programs. These challenges are themselves closely associated with poor policy-making processes and inadequate attention to monitoring and evaluation. In many developing countries, the responsibility for pre-employment TVET is often fragmented across several ministries, typically, education, labor, and social welfare, and across departments within ministries, often with unclear organizational structures and potential overlap in mandates. The resulting difficulties in coordination and collaboration raises the risk of duplication of effort and inadequate attention to public sector functions required for effective and efficient delivery of services in the system as a whole. Such functions include:

- developing policies and standards for quality assurance
- informing the public regarding the demand for skills and the quality, outcomes, and costs of training options, in both the public and private sectors
- supporting all training providers, public and private, to assure the quality of services through the development of common competency standards, instructional materials, and instructor-training programs
- incentivizing private providers to meet service delivery standards
- rationalizing training provision within the public sector
- targeting training resources and services to marginalized populations or underserved localities.

Concern about these issues has led governments to organize the oversight of training provision under apex entities such as national, subnational, or sector training authorities.[25] While such organizations differ across countries in their specific structures and powers, the more effective ones share at least three characteristics: (i) they are based on strong partnerships with and accountability to stakeholders, particularly employers; (ii) they have real authority to make decisions, backed up by control over budgets and resource allocation; and (iii) they oversee but are not directly involved in the administration of individual TVET institutions and the delivery of training programs (ADB 2008). Singapore's Institute for Technical Education (ITE), which enrolls some 25 percent of each cohort of 10th-grade graduates, is a good example of an organization that exhibits these attributes in the management of pre-employment TVET, following a 10-year process of sustained effort to transform the system.[26] Under its current "One ITE, Three Colleges" governance structure, oversight functions are centralized under a statutory board accountable to its parent ministry, the Ministry of Education, while the delivery of training programs is decentralized to each of the three colleges under the direction of a principal (Law 2008).

Separation of the oversight functions from those relating to service delivery puts the apex training authorities in a position to manage training providers more effectively. It can foster diversity and competition in the training market by enabling or attracting nonstate providers to participate more actively in training provision. In India, for example, the government's new policies allow private sector operators to manage governmental training institutions under contract (Goyal 2011). With regard to governmental training institutions, the apex authority has a variety of instruments with which to foster greater responsiveness and effectiveness in service delivery. These typically include devolving decision-making power to individual institutions, requiring industry representation on the boards of the institutions, and increasing their accountability for explicit results, especially in terms of the job destinations and earnings of their graduates and the satisfaction of employers. Fostering mutually beneficial linkages between training institutions and key stakeholders, among them potential future employers of their graduates, is another important avenue to enhance the effectiveness of pre-employment TVET providers in aligning their programs to the demand for skills.

Conclusion

Pre-employment TVET is, by definition, intended to equip young people with skills for work. It builds on the foundation established through early childhood education and general schooling and is often seen as a useful bridge between school and work. Pre-employment TVET encompasses a variety of programs, including those in formal settings such as secondary schools, typically in the upper grades, or post-secondary institutions (for example, polytechnics or community colleges), as well as the short-duration modular courses offered through various nonformal channels (such as training centers). This chapter has focused on the former type of programs; a later chapter addresses the issues related to nonformal programs.

Across countries, the share of enrollments in TVET tends to increase with the level of income, a pattern that is consistent with the greater demand for technical skills in more advanced economies. Evidence from studies on the returns to TVET shows no particular pattern, suggesting that the economic value of TVET is likely to be context-specific. For this reason, clear-cut conclusions about the operational design of pre-employment TVET are elusive. What is clear, however, is that most developing countries share concerns about the relevance, effectiveness, and efficiency of pre-employment TVET. The experience of such countries as Korea and Singapore underscores the potential relevance of TVET as a source of skills to support growth and economic development. However, the investment requires careful and sustained coordination of effort to overcome difficulties in aligning skills supply and demand. In general, ensuring coherence in skills supply and demand requires appropriate organizational and governance arrangements at both the systemic and institutional levels that give employers, among other stakeholders, a say in shaping pre-employment training. Filling our knowledge gaps regarding the best ways to design these arrangements is an important part of the research agenda to improve the relevance, effectiveness, and efficiency of pre-employment TVET in preparing today's youth for tomorrow's jobs.

Notes

1. We would like to thank, without implication for remaining errors, Arvil Van Adams, Cristian Aedo, Mohamed Ihsan Ajwad, Ariel Fiszbein, and Mamta Murthi for their thoughtful comments on an earlier version of this chapter.
2. According to UNESCO and ILO (2002) TVET refers to "aspects of the educational process involving, in addition to general education, the study of technologies and related sciences, and the acquisition of practical skills, attitudes, understanding and knowledge relating to occupations in various sectors of economic and social life."
3. Adams (2007) emphasizes the importance of separating the TVE from the second T (training) in discussing TVET policy issues. TVE is typically part of the formal education system, often under the purview of the ministry of education, while the second T tends to come under the other ministries, especially the ministry of labor, ministry of trade and industry, and other ministries with a sector focus. The second T is also more diverse in the clientele it serves, and in management, financing, and provision. In practice, however, the separation is not always clear-cut. In China, for example, both the Ministry of Education and the Ministry of Labor and Social Security operate education institutions offering TVE; whereas in Singapore, the TVE-offering Institute for Technical Education under the Ministry of Education also runs T-type courses on its premises. In the Organisation for Economic Co-operation and Development (OECD) countries, policy discussions refer to VET, thus dropping the first T instead of the second in the acronym (see, for example, OECD 2010).
4. Between 1999 and 2009, for example, the primary school completion rate among low-income countries in Sub-Saharan Africa rose from an average of about 43 percent to 63 percent (Majgaard and Mingat 2012).
5. Fretwell (2009) suggests that employment in the informal sector, including in nonformal agriculture, ranges from 34 percent in South Africa, to 62 percent in Mexico, to 93 percent in India, and reports that in North Africa, informal sector enterprises contribute about 27 percent to the nonagricultural GDP of the region. Adams (2008) cites research findings that put the informal sector's contribution to the GDP at an average of 42 percent for 23 African countries in 2000 and at 7–12 percent of GDP in South Africa, a middle-income country with a smaller informal sector than other African countries.
6. The finance minister of India, for example, in emphasizing the importance of skills for India, states that "our economy has to be technologically innovative if we are to realize this vision of inclusive development…. The most critical factor in realizing our vision is the human element be it at the level of leadership or at the level of a common worker on the floor of the factories, or in the fields and construction sites. We would need the right kind of expertise and skills at all levels. Personally, I attach the highest importance to skill development to ensure that the country benefits meaningfully from its imminent demographic dividend." (Press Information Bureau, Government of India. See http://www.pib.nic.in/newsite/erelease.aspx?relid=68693, accessed on April 4, 2011.)
7. The widely used International Standard Classification of Education (ISCED), developed in 1997 and updated in 2011 by the United Nations Educational,

Scientific and Cultural Organization (UNESCO), provides a systematic framework for categorizing educational programs. The data presented below rely on the 1997 classification, which distinguishes the following six levels of instruction: pre-primary education (level 0), primary education (level 1), lower secondary (level 2), upper secondary (level 3), post-secondary nontertiary (level 4), first stage tertiary (level 5), and advanced research or high-skills qualifications (level 6). The programs at levels 2–4 may be one of three types: general (A), pre-vocational (B), or vocational or technical (C). A distinction is made between vocational and other programs at level 5 while no distinction is made at level 6 where all programs are expected to terminate in exit from the system. See UNESCO-UIS (2006) and UNESCO 2011 for a mapping between the 1997 and 2001 classification categories.

8. UNESCO-UIS 2006 concludes that TVET provision is more common at the upper secondary (ISCED 3) level than at either the previous or subsequent levels (that is, postsecondary nontertiary (ISCED 4) or lower secondary (ISCED 2)).

9. See endnote 7 for the definitions.

10. http://www.oalj.dol.gov/PUBLIC/DOT/REFERENCES/DOTAPPB.HTM (accessed on October 10, 2011).

11. These categories correspond closely to the divisions in Bloom's (1976) taxonomy, which makes the following distinctions: (a) cognitive skills, as demonstrated by an intellectual grasp of the subject matter of various academic disciplines such as English, mathematics, various pure and applied sciences, history, and so forth; (b) affective skills relating to a person's perception of the meaning and value of work, concept of self and others, and attitudes toward timeliness, accuracy, and general commitment to quality and performance; and (c) psychomotor skills for the tasks to be performed in an occupation, job, or business (for example, operating a lathe, preparing architectural plans, and installing equipment) and the ability to apply the skills in practice.

12. Answering these questions requires data that are currently unavailable in most developing countries. To fill this data gap, the World Bank launched a multicountry study in 2010—the Skills toward Employment and Productivity (StEP) Skills Measurement Study. This study will measure the level and distribution of cognitive, noncognitive, and technical skills of the adult population, along the lines of the OECD's Programme for the International Assessment of Adult Competencies. It will also examine the relation between these skills and labor market outcomes, and the extent and nature of skills mismatches between skills supply and demand.

13. The importance of a strong foundation in literacy and numeracy has received renewed attention in developed countries in recent years. See for example, Wolf (2011) on vocational education and training in the United Kingdom and Arum and Roksa (2011) on college education in the United States.

14. The scarcity of managerial skills is often also an impediment but they are not the focus of our discussion here. For a discussion on the importance of such skills, see Ichniowski and Shaw (2009).

15. For more details of the arrangements in India, see Government of India (n.d.) at: http://labour.nic.in/policy/NationalSkillDevelopmentPolicyMar09.pdf (accessed July 19, 2011).

16. Tracer studies are a particularly relevant instrument in this regard and are routinely used in some countries to provide information both to guide student's choices and to shed light on the performance of training providers. Sondergaard and Murthi (2012) cite good practice examples from Hungary, Romania, and the Netherlands (where the practice has been in place since 1989 with regard to university education).

17. See NASSCOM-Everest (2008).

18. For example, through its "Campus Connect" program, Infosys, one of India's leading ICT firms, integrates a 130-hour, classroom-based, proprietary training program into the academic schedule of participating colleges. Students learn about the company's business and acquire some job-relevant skills while the company gives Infosys access to a pool of potential employees and reduces the training costs of new recruits selected from the pool (Wadhwa, de Vitton, and Gereffi 2008).

19. See Adams (2011) for a more detailed discussion on how skills development can play a role in overcoming social disadvantage.

20. In China's Guangdong province—one of the country's leading regions that has achieved sustained rapid growth over the past few decades—the demand for skilled workers is so strong that it has prompted efforts by training institutions to recruit students from rural areas to meet the demand. Qing Yuan Senior Technical Institute (QYSTI), a state school offering upper-secondary-level instruction in various engineering fields, is one such example. Over the past 15 years, the school has trained 30,000 skilled workers, of whom 18,000 come from poor families in the lagging regions of the province. More than 98 percent of its trainees land jobs upon graduation. The school hosted a World Bank–sponsored study visit in November 2010. (For the study, visit http://go.world-bank.org/TWWF6WKB80.)

21. World Bank (2007) cites a finding reported in DfID (2005) that up to 42 percent of total rural incomes in parts of Africa today come from nonfarm sources.

22. For example, according to Canning et al. (2007) public spending per student in secondary-level TVET exceeds the corresponding figure for general programs by 61 percent in Lithuania, 27 percent in Poland and 16 percent in the Czech Republic. Gill et al. (2000) report that in Chile, per student subsidies for secondary industrial and commercial schools are 25-100 percent more than those for general education; and in Egypt, secondary technical education costs 2.5 times as much as general education at the same level.

23. The effectiveness of pre-employment TVET also depends on the arrangements for service delivery. It is, however, beyond the scope of this paper to examine these arrangements in detail. Suffice it to say that teachers are a key factor, just as they are in the delivery of general education. To be effective, pre-employment TVET teachers require work experience in their subject area, but must also be skilled at handling students with academic and possibly also social deficits. See ILO (2010) for a useful discussion of a broad set of issues relating to TVET teachers.

24. Bishop (1989) notes that occupationally specific education in high schools lowers dropout rates of at-risk students and raises graduates' wages and employment if they obtain training-related jobs (less than 50 percent do). Measures to

raise training-related placement rates include ensuring that students' career choices before training are well-informed, that training is geared toward occupations in strong demand, that employers are involved in the delivery of training, and that vocational teachers take responsibility for the placement of their students.

25. A recent example of a regional apex entity is the Sindh Technical and Vocational Training Authority. It was set up by a provincial government in Pakistan in 2007 to consolidate 68 government pre-employment training institutions that previously had belonged to three different parent ministries (Government of Sindh 2009). Apex training authorities now exist in many countries, including in Sub-Saharan Africa. In a large country like India, the governance structure that was recently set up has three tiers: the National Council on Skill Development, chaired by the Prime Minister; the National Skill Development Coordination Board, chaired by the Deputy Chairman of the Planning Commission; and the National Skill Development Corporation (see http://dget.gov.in/).

26. In 2007, ITE won the inaugural IBM Innovations Award in Transforming Government, conferred by Harvard University's Ash Center for Democratic Governance and Innovation, based on the "innovation, effectiveness, significance, and transferability of its [transformation plan]." See http://www.innovations.harvard.edu/awards.html?id=93291 (accessed on March 14, 2011).

References

Adams, Arvil V. 2007. "The Role of Youth Skills Development in the Transition to Work: A Global Review." HDNCY Working Paper No. 5. Human Development Network, Children and Youth Department. World Bank, Washington, DC. http://siteresources.worldbank.org/INTCY/Resources/395766-1187899515414/RolcofYouthSkills.pdf.

———. 2008. "A Framework for the Study of Skills Development in the Informal Sector of Sub-Saharan Africa." Unpublished paper, Africa Region. World Bank, Washington, DC.

———. 2011. "The Role of Skills Development in Overcoming Social Disadvantage." Background paper prepared for the *Education for All Global Monitoring Report 2012*. Paris: United Nations Educational, Scientific, and Cultural Organization (UNESCO).

Almeida, Rita K. 2009."Does the Workforce in East Asia Have the Right Skills? Evidence from Firm Level Surveys." Human Development Network. World Bank, Washington, DC.

Ansu, Yaw, and Jee-Peng Tan. 2011."Skills Development for Economic Growth in Sub-Saharan Africa: A Pragmatic Perspective." In Noman Akbar, Kwesi Botchwey, Howard Stein, and Joseph E. Stiglitz, eds., *Good Growth and Governance in Africa: Rethinking Development Strategies*. Initiative for Policy Dialogue Series. Oxford: Oxford University Press.

Arum, Richard, and Josipa Roksa. 2011. *Academically Adrift. Limited Learning on College Campuses.* Chicago and London: University of Chicago Press.

Ashton, David, Francis Green, Johnny Sung, and Donna James. 2002. "The Evolution of Education and Training Strategies in Singapore, Taiwan and S. Korea: A Development Model of Skill Formation." *Journal of Education and Work* 15(1): 5–30.

Asian Development Bank (ADB). 2008. *Education and Skills: Strategies for Accelerated Development in Asia and the Pacific.* Mandaluyong City, the Philippines: ADB.

———. 2009. *Good Practice in Technical and Vocational Education and Training.* Mandaluyong City, the Philippines: ADB.

Banerji, Arup, Wendy Cunningham, Ariel Fiszbein, Elizabeth King, Harry Patrinos, David Robalino, and Jee-Peng Tan. 2010. "Stepping Up Skills for More Jobs and Higher Productivity." World Bank, Washington, DC.

Bauer, Philipp C., and Regina T. Riphahn. 2006. "Timing of School Tracking as a Determinant of Intergenerational Transmission of Education." *Economics Letters* 91(1): 90–97.

Bishop, John. 1989. "Occupational Training in High School: When Does It Pay Off?" *Economics of Education Review* 8(1): 1–15.

Blom, Andreas, and Hiroshi Saeki. 2011. "Employability and Skill Set of Newly Graduated Engineers in India." World Bank Policy Research Working Paper No. 5640. World Bank, Washington, DC.

Bloom, Benjamin S. 1976. *Human Characteristics and School Learning.* New York: McGraw-Hill.

Brown, Philip, Hugh Lauder, and David Ashton. 2011. *The Global Auction: The Broken Promises of Education, Jobs and Incomes.* New York: Oxford University Press.

Canning, Mary, Martin Godfrey, and Dorota Holzer-Zelazewska. 2007. "Vocational Education in the New EU Member States: Enhancing Labor Market Outcomes and Fiscal Efficiency." World Bank Working Paper No. 115. World Bank, Washington, DC.

Chan, Lee Mun. 2008. *Polytechnic Education.* In Sing Kong Lee, Chor Boon Goh, Birger Fredriksen, and Jee-Peng Tan, eds., *Toward a Better Future: Education and Training for Economic Development in Singapore since 1965.* Washington, DC: World Bank and National Institute of Education, Singapore.

Chiang, Mickey. 1998. *From Economic Debacle to Economic Miracle. The History and Development of Technical Education in Singapore.* Singapore: Times Edition.

Department for International Development (DFID), United Kingdom. 2005. "Growth and Poverty Reduction: The Role of Agriculture." A DFID policy paper. London: DFID.

di Gropello, Emanuela, with Aurelien Kruse and Prateek Tandon. 2011. *Skills for the Labor Market in Indonesia.* Directions in Development Series. Washington, DC: World Bank.

di Gropello, Emanuela, with Hong Tan and Prateek Tandon. 2010. *Skills for the Labor Market in the Philippines.* Directions in Development Series. Washington DC: World Bank.

di Gropello, Emanuela, Prateek Tandon, and Shahid Yusuf. 2011. *Putting Higher Education to Work: Skills and Research for Growth in East Asia.* World Bank East Asia and Pacific Regional Report. Washington, DC: World Bank.

El-Hamidi, Fatma. 2006. "General or Vocational Schooling? Evidence on School Choice, Returns, and 'Sheepskin' Effects from Egypt 1998." *Journal of Policy Reform* 9(2): 157–76.

Fredriksen, Birger, and Jee-Peng Tan. 2008. "East Asia Education Study Tour: An Overview of Key Insights." In Birger Fredriksen and Jee-Peng Tan, eds., *An Africa Exploration of the East Asian Education Experience*. Washington, DC: World Bank.

Fretwell, David. 2009. "Skills Development for the Informal Economy: Issues and Options in Vocational Education and Training in the Southern Partner Countries of the European Neighbourhood Policy." HTSPE Limited, European Commission.

Gill, Indermit, Fred Fluitman, and Amit Dar, eds. 2000. *Vocational Education and Training Reform. Matching Skills to Markets and Budgets*. A Joint Study of the World Bank and the International Labour Office. New York: Oxford University Press for the World Bank.

Government of Sindh. 2009. *Sindh Development Review 2008–09*. Planning & Development Department, Government of Sindh. www.sindhpnd.gov.pk (accessed on March 13, 2011).

Goyal, Sangeeta. 2011. "India: Vocational Training Improvement Project (VTIP)." Presentation. Government of India and World Bank.

Handel, Michael J. 2008. "Measuring Job Content: Skills, Technology, and Management Practices." Discussion Paper No. 1357-08. Institute for Research on Poverty. University of Wisconsin, Madison, WI.

Hanushek, Eric A., and Ludger Wössmann. 2006. "Does Educational Tracking Affect Performance and Inequality? Differences-in-Differences Evidence Across Countries." *Economic Journal* 116(510): C63–C76, 03.

Hanushek, Eric A., Ludger Woessmann, and Lei Zhang. 2011. "General Education, Vocational Education, and Labor-Market Outcomes over the Life-Cycle." National Bureau of Economic Research (NBER) Working Paper No. 17504. NBER, Cambridge, MA.

Horowitz, Andrew, and Christoph Schenzler. 1999. "Returns to General, Technical and Vocational Education in Developing Countries: Recent Evidence from Suriname." *Education Economics* 7(1): 5–20.

Ichniowski, Casey, and Kathryn L. Shaw. 2009. "Insider Econometrics: Empirical Studies of How Management Matters." National Bureau of Economic Research (NBER) Working Paper No. 15618. NBER, Cambridge, MA. Available at: http://www.nber.org/papers/w15618.

International Labour Organization (ILO). 2010. *Teachers and Trainers for the Future: Technical and Vocational Education and Training in a Changing World*. GDFVET/2010, Geneva: ILO.

Jakubowski, Maciej, Harry Patrinos, Emilio Porta, and Jerzy Wisniewski. 2010. "The Impact of the 1999 Education Reform in Poland." Policy Research Working Paper No. 5263. World Bank, Washington, DC.

Johanson, Richard, and Arvil Van Adams. 2004. *Skills Development in Sub-Saharan Africa*. World Bank Regional and Sectoral Studies. Washington, DC: World Bank.

Kahyarara, Godius, and Francis Teal. 2008. "The Returns to Vocational Training and Academic Education: Evidence from Tanzania." *World Development* 36(11): 2223–42.

King, Kenneth, and Robert Palmer. 2010. *Planning for Technical and Vocational Skills Development*. Fundamentals of Educational Planning No. 94. UNESCO: International Institute for Educational Planning.

Kuruvilla, Sarosh, Christopher L. Erickson, and Alvin Hwang. 2002. "An Assessment of the Singapore Skills Development System: Does It Constitute a Viable Model for Other Developing Countries?" *World Development* 30(8): 1461–76.

Lassibille, Gerard, and Jee-Peng Tan. 2005. "The Returns to Education in Rwanda." *Journal of African Economies* 14(1): 92–116.

Law, Song Seng. 2008. "Vocational Technical Education and Economic Development: The Singapore Experience." In Sing Kong Lee, Chor Boon Goh, Birger Fredriksen, and Jee-Peng Tan, eds., *Toward a Better Future: Education and Training for Economic Development in Singapore since 1965*. Washington, DC: World Bank and National Institute of Education, Singapore.

Lechner, Michael. 2000. "An Evaluation of Public-Sector-Sponsored Continuous Vocational Training Programs in East Germany." *The Journal of Human Resources* 35(2): 347–75.

Lee, Sing Kong, Chor Boon Goh, Birger Fredriksen, and Jee-Peng Tan, eds., *Toward a Better Future: Education and Training for Economic Development in Singapore since 1965*. Washington, DC: World Bank and National Institute of Education, Singapore.

Lee, Young-Hyun. 2009. *Vocational Education and Training in the Process of Industrialization. Understanding Korean Educational Policy, Volume 5*. Seoul: Korean Educational Development Institute.

Low, Linda, Toh Mun Heng, Soon Teck Wong, Tan Kong Yam, and Helen Hughes. 1993. *Challenge and Response: Thirty Years of the Economic Development Board*. Singapore: Times Academic Press.

Maclean, Rupert, and David N. Wilson, eds. 2009. *International Handbook of Education for the Changing World of Work: Bridging Academic and Vocational Learning*. Springer Science and Business Media.

Majgaard, Kirsten, and Alain Mingat. 2012. *Education in Sub-Saharan Africa: A Comparative Analysis*. Washington, DC: World Bank.

Malamud, Ofer, and Cristian Pop-Eleches. 2008. "General Education vs. Vocational Training: Evidence from an Economy in Transition." National Bureau of Economic Research (NBER) Working Paper No. 14155. NBER, Cambridge, MA. Available at: http://www.nber.org/papers/w14155.

Martin, Rob, Frank Villeneuve-Smith, Liz Marshall, and Ewan McKenzie. 2008. *Employability Skills Explored*. London: Learning and Skills Network (LSN).

Meghir, Costas, and Mårten Palme. 2005. "Educational Reform, Ability, and Family Background." *American Economic Review* 95(1): 414–24.

Mingat, Alain, Blandine Ledoux, and Ramahatra Rakotomalala. 2010. *Developing Post-Primary Education in Sub-Saharan Africa: Assessing the Financial Sustainability of Alternative Pathways*. Africa Human Development Series. Washington, DC: World Bank.

Moenjak, Thammarak, and Christopher Worswick. 2003. "Vocational Education in Thailand: A Study of Choice and Returns." *Economics of Education Review* 22(1): 99–107.

NASSCOM-Everest. 2008. "NASSCOM-Everest India BPO Study: Roadmap 2012—Capitalizing on the Expanding BPO Landscape." New Delhi. http://www.britishcouncil.org/learning-nasscom-report.pdf.

Neuman, Shoshana, and Adrian Ziderman. 1991. "Vocational Schooling, Occupational Matching, and Labor Market Earnings in Israel." Policy Research Working Paper Series 683. World Bank, Washington, DC.

Newhouse, David, and Daniel Suryadarma. 2011. "The Value of Vocational Education: High School Type and Labor Market Outcomes in Indonesia." *World Bank Economic Review* 25(2): 296–322. Oxford University Press for the World Bank.

O'Hare, Daniel. 2008. "Education in Ireland: Evolution of Economic and Education Policies Since the Early 1990s." In Birger Fredriksen and Jee-Peng Tan, eds., *An African Exploration of the East Asian Education Experience*. Washington, DC: World Bank.

Organisation for Economic Co-operation and Development (OECD). 2009. *Education at a Glance*. Paris: OECD.

———. 2010. *Learning for Jobs*. Paris: OECD.

Pekkarinen, Tuomas, Roope Uusitalo, and Sari Pekkala. 2006. "Education Policy and Intergenerational Income Mobility: Evidence from the Finnish Comprehensive School Reform." IZA Discussion Paper No. 2204. Institute for the Study of Labor, Bonn.

Riboud, Michelle, Yevgeniya Savchenko, and Hong Tan. 2007. *The Knowledge Economy and Education and Training in South Asia*. Human Development Unit, South Asia Region. Washington, DC: World Bank.

Rutkowski, Jan. 2010. "Demand for Skills in FYR Macedonia." Technical Note for a World Bank-Government of FYR Macedonia Workshop, Europe and Central Asia Department. World Bank, Washington, DC.

———. 2011. "Skills for Productivity and Competitiveness: The Employers' Perspective." In *Europe 2020 Poland: Fueling Growth and Competitiveness in Poland through Employment, Skills, and Innovation*. Washington, DC: World Bank.

Sakellariou, Chris. 2003. "Rates of Return to Investments in Formal and Technical/Vocational Education in Singapore." *Education Economics* 11(1): 73–87.

Sondergaard, Lars, and Mamta Murthi. 2012. *Skills, Not Just Diplomas: Managing Education for Results in Eastern Europe and Central Asia*. Directions in Development Series. Washington, DC: World Bank.

Spar, Debora. 1998. "Attracting High Technology Investment: Intel's Costa Rican Plant." Foreign Investment Advisory Service. Occasional Paper 11. International Finance Corporation and World Bank, Washington, DC.

United Nations Educational, Scientific and Cultural Organization (UNESCO). 2011. *Revision of the International Standard Classification of Education (ISCED)*. Paris: UNESCO. Available at http://www.uis.unesco.org/Education/Documents/UNESCO_GC_36C-19_ISCED_EN.pdf.

United Nations Educational Scientific and Cultural Organization (UNESCO) and International Labour Organization (ILO). 2002. *Technical and Vocational Education for the 21st Century: UNESCO and ILO Recommendations*. Paris: UNESCO and ILO.

United Nations Educational, Scientific, and Cultural Organization (UNESCO) Institute for Statistics (UIS). 2006. *Participation in Formal Technical and Vocational Education and Training Programmes Worldwide: An Initial Statistical Study*. Bonn: UNESCO-UNEVOC International Centre for Technical and Vocational Education and Training. Available at http://www.unevoc.unesco.org/2.0.html?&tx_drwiki_pi1[keyword]=UNEVOC-UIS%20Report.

Wadhwa, Vivek, Una Kim de Vitton, and Gary Gereffi. 2008. "How the Disciple Became the Guru: Workforce Development in India's R&D Labs." Report funded by the Ewing Marion Kauffman Foundation. Available at SSRN: http://ssrn.com/abstract=1170049.

Walther, Richard, and Ewa Filipiak. 2007. "Vocational Training in the Informal Sector." Research Department. Paris: Agence Française de Développement.

Winterton, Jonathan, Françoise Delamare-Le Deist, and Emma Stringfellow. 2005. *Typology of Knowledge, Skills and Competences: Clarification of the Concept and Prototype.* Centre for European Research on Employment and Human Resources Groupe ESC Toulouse. http://www.uk.ecorys.com/europeaninventory/publications/method/cedefop_typology.pdf.

Wolf, Alison. 2011. *Review of Vocational Education—The Wolf Report.* Department for Education, Government of the United Kingdom.

World Bank. 2007. *Cultivating Knowledge and Skills to Grow African Agriculture: A Synthesis of an Institutional, Regional and International Review.* Report No. 40997-AFR. Agriculture and Rural Development Department and Africa Region Human Development Department. Washington, DC: World Bank.

———. 2010. "Program Document for a Mexico Upper Secondary Education Development Policy Loan." World Bank, Washington, DC.

World Bank and Multilateral Investment Guarantee Agency (MIGA). 2006. *The Impact of Intel in Costa Rica. Nine Years After the Decision to Invest.* Investing in Development Series. Washington, DC: MIGA.

Annex: Detailed Data Sources for Table 3.1

Country and year of data	Data	Author(s)
Egypt, Arab Rep. (1998)	Egyptian Labor Market Survey, 1998; Sample: 4,843 urban private sector workers in 1998 (cross-sectional)	El-Hamidi (2006)
Singapore (1998)	Mid-1998 Labor Force Survey; Sample: 15,000 observations (cross-sectional)	Sakellariou (2003)
Sri Lanka (2002)	Labor Force Survey, 1992–93 (Sample: 24,535 observations); 1997–98 (Sample: 23,229 observations); 2001–02 (Sample: 20,838 observations) (cross-sectional)	Riboud, Savchenko, and Tan (2007)
Thailand (1989–95)	Thailand's Labor Force Survey, 1989 to 1995 inclusive; Sample: 4,885 individuals (2,633 males and 2,252 females) (cross-sectional)	Moenjak and Worswick (2003)
Israel (1983)	1983 Census of Population and Housing; Sample: 13,879 individuals (cross-sectional)	Neuman and Ziderman (1991)
India (2004)	National Sample Survey, 1983–84 (Sample: 81,521 observations); 1987–88 (Sample: 47,568 observations); NSS 1993–94 (Sample: 81,521 observations); 1999–2000 (Sample: 80,108 observations) 2004 (Sample: 39,190 observations) (cross-sectional)	Riboud, Savchenko, and Tan (2007)
East Germany (1984–96)	German Socio-Economic Panel, 1984–96; Sample: 1,411 observations	Lechner (2000)
Romania (1995–2000)	Six annual LSMS-type household surveys from 1995–2000 based on yearly cross-sectional representative samples, Sample: 13,133 individuals (LSMS)	Malamud and Pop-Eleches (2008)
Tanzania (1997–2000)	Fourth and fifth rounds of the Tanzanian Manufacturing Enterprise surveys (1997–2000); Sample: 2,527 individuals (panel)	Kahyarara and Teal (2008)
Indonesia (1993, 1997, 2000, 2007)	Indonesia Family Life Survey (IFLS), 1993, 1997, 2000, and 2007; Sample: 17,485 total labor market observations on 7,607 individuals (panel)	Newhouse and Suryadarma (2011)
Pakistan (2004)	Pakistan Integrated Household Survey 1993–94 (Sample: 10,553 observations); 1996–97 (Sample: 11,589 observations); 2000–01 (Sample: 16,200 observations) (cross-sectional)	Riboud, Savchenko, and Tan (2007)
Rwanda (1999–2001)	Rwanda Household Living Conditions Survey, 1999–2001; Sample: 2,013 observations (cross-sectional)	Lassibille and Tan (2005)
Suriname (1990, 1992, 1993)	Suriname Household Survey 1990 (4 waves), 1992 (2 waves), and 1993; Survey sample: 7,010 individuals (cross-sectional)	Horowitz and Schenzler (1999)

4

Employer-Provided Training: Patterns and Incentives for Building Skills for Higher Productivity

Rita Almeida and Yoonyoung Cho[1]

Programs for skills development while on the job are crucial for economic performance and growth. In fact, a significant part of human capital is accumulated through on-the-job training (OJT), and, over their lifetimes, workers acquire most of their new and improved skills on the job. Especially when tastes and technologies change rapidly, human capital investments are important in maintaining firms' competitiveness, innovation, and growth. Without a workforce that continually acquires new skills, appropriating all the returns from technological progress is difficult. As preemployment and technical training are increasingly criticized for producing skills that do not immediately align with the labor market, investment in job training by the private sector gains additional relevance for skills development policy. This chapter presents important patterns in OJT and discusses policy tools to promote that investment in the developing world. On-the-job skill development can be accomplished through both formal training, provided mainly by employers, and informal processes, including learning by doing. OJT can also take place at both formal and informal firms. Depending on the definition of formality in skill development at the firm level, the content and scope of OJT will vary. In this chapter, *on-the-job training* is defined as formal training provided by private sector firms to their workers. It will thus capture different forms of internships, apprenticeships, and training courses while individuals are working.[2]

The importance of OJT for an individual's lifetime human capital and a firm's productivity has been widely noted and researched to date, at least for the United States.[3] A substantial part of one's human capital is accumulated through post-school investments and OJT. Heckman, Lochner, and Taber (1998), for example, suggest that post-school human capital accumulation that takes place on the job explains more than half the lifetime human capital in the United States. OJT is an important channel through which workers upgrade skills and remain competitive in the labor market, and through which firms adopt technology and innovation. A large body of literature, mostly in developed countries, shows that OJT is positively associated with increases in individual workers' wage growth and firms' productivity and innovation.[4] Some studies on developing countries, though not as many as those of developed countries, also suggest that individuals' earnings can substantially increase with OJT and that the size of the returns may be larger in developing countries.

OJT can play an important role in equipping workers with relevant labor market skills in developing countries, where education systems and pre-employment technical training often suffer from severe limitations. In many developing countries, a large number of workers enter the labor market without basic abilities, let alone high-end technological skills. Even the lucky few who had a chance of receiving pre-employment technical and vocational education and training (TVET) may not have adequate skills either, due to the many existing issues discussed in chapter 3. In such cases, OJT can be an important alternative in producing skilled workers if well designed and implemented.

Despite the potential benefits and the important role of OJT, the incidence of OJT in developing countries is quite low, and the constraints to the provision of OJT are not fully understood. Early evidence suggests that firm characteristics, including size, sector of activity, and employees' human capital composition, partially explain firms' decisions on the provision of job training. Firms that provide training to their workers tend to be, on average, larger and more open to trade, and have higher foreign ownership and a workforce with more years of formal schooling. This suggests that small firms unable to take advantage of the economies of scale and faced with large initial costs of training, less-open firms with little information and incentives to innovate, and those with already low-skilled workers may experience particularly large barriers to OJT. Nevertheless, the large within-country differences in the incidence of training are not explained by observable firm or worker characteristics alone. In this chapter we will rely on combined information from micro surveys and empirical analysis together with theoretical arguments to identify the barriers that reduce skills development on the job.

The chapter highlights that, despite their pervasiveness, public-sector training funds throughout the developing world often fail to address the main market failures. Furthermore, the low level of investment in job training in most of Africa and South Asia does not necessarily imply the need for government intervention. In fact, for many firms, investment in training may pay off with little government intervention. Good examples of industry-led training initiatives include one of India's leading companies, Infosys. A software technology giant, Infosys, completed a new 300-faculty Global Education Center in 2009 with a training capacity of 14,000 seats, dedicated to enhancing the competencies of company staff. Another example is Malaysia's Penang Skills Development Center, a partnership of several enterprises coming together to benefit from industry-specific training services financed through membership subscriptions, fees, and a government subsidy. Its 17-year success inspired the Chittagong Skills Development Center in Bangladesh. The Ghana Industrial Skills Development Center, yet another industry-led training example, was formed through a partnership of private firms, government, and donors to support the country's budding manufacturing sector.

Underinvestment in OJT and poor implementation happen for a number of reasons. For example, many firms in developing countries may find OJT investment unnecessary given their technological base, the skill component of most of their jobs, or their reliance on informal training. Other firms may face severe constraints in identifying appropriate training programs (including relevant curricula), in recruiting training experts, or in financing the programs. For all these reasons, firms could fail to invest in OJT even if expected (or ex ante) returns are high. Finally, some firms may be willing to invest in training—and may actually have the required financial resources to invest—but do not allocate enough resources from a social perspective because they fear external poaching of trainees by other employers.[5] Implementing ad hoc OJT policies without addressing the core reasons of underinvestment and without having a firm-specific approach will also likely lead to government failures and efficiency loss. Therefore, policies should address the primary source of market failures to avoid unintended effects.

This chapter discusses potential failures in the area of OJT as well as policy interventions from selected countries that have addressed these failures, and highlights some principles to improve the efficiency of such interventions. Two broad areas of intervention are discussed: institutional and financial arrangements. The chapter argues that institutional arrangements, including payback clauses and apprenticeship contracts, are needed to address information asymmetries between workers and firms that prevent both parties from defining optimal training contracts. Training subsidies, widely used across many countries, may be useful for overcoming credit constraints and externalities if well designed and implemented. This chapter argues that promoting a private training market and allocating funds to a more targeted set of beneficiaries, together with ensuring governance and institutionalizing monitoring and evaluation (M&E), can enhance the efficiency and effectiveness of OJT-related policies.

The remainder of the chapter is organized as follows. The next section reviews the current status of OJT, including our understanding of the rationale for and returns to OJT, the incidence of OJT across the world, and some of the constraints faced by firms. The following section discusses policy tools that address constraints to OJT and promote OJT, focusing on best practices found from international examples. The last section summarizes the key findings and identifies knowledge gaps that future research can fill.

On-the-Job Training: What We Know and Where We Are

There is compelling empirical evidence that OJT can be beneficial both to individuals and firms, although the magnitude of the benefits compared to costs can be arguable due to the technical difficulties in measuring them. Nevertheless, the share of firms that provide training in low-income countries is low and lags far behind that of developed countries. Several factors, including the differences in the degree of development, skills level of the workforce, and firm characteristics, provide partial explanations for the gap and large heterogeneity across countries. However, there exists a knowledge gap on the constraints of OJT and policy measures to address them. This section discusses what benefits firms and individuals may receive from OJT, how widely OJT is practiced around the developing world, and why more investment does not take place.

Private Returns to OJT

The benefits of OJT ultimately translate into higher labor productivity of trainees over several periods, which may lead to higher earnings and profits. Participation or the provision of training though incurs some direct and indirect costs at the time of training. From firms' perspective, the current investment in human capital raises expected future productivity at a cost to the current period. In this sense, investment in human capital is very similar to investment in physical capital. However, unlike the latter, workers retain the ownership of their increased, embodied human capital. Thus, firms may discount their future benefits and transfer some of the costs of training to workers through lower wages to mitigate the risks of losing their invested human capital. This is particularly true when the skills are general and useful to other employers. From the perspective of workers, training while working is in general a good investment. OJT both helps workers accumulate human capital and signals their competence to the market—even if it involves some foregone earnings. As long as the benefits of OJT are larger than the costs, and the firms and workers can reach an agreement on sharing costs, one would expect the provision of and participation in OJT to be common in labor markets.

Efforts in both developed and developing countries to empirically estimate returns to OJT investment have encountered a few difficulties. First, measuring total training costs is not trivial. They comprise the opportunity costs of training, or the forgone earnings, as well as the direct costs of training. Direct costs of training include, for example, the one-off cost of identifying useful programs for the business, hiring training specialists, purchasing training materials, and delivering the actual programs. Because of this complexity, few surveys and empirical studies have accurately measured the cost of training.[6] Second, a lack of good measures of the training episodes is also a constraint to examining the returns. Surveys typically collect very different indicators of training, and information on the timing, duration, and type of training is difficult to obtain. Third, the outcomes of training over time—including productivity, profit, and earnings—are typically difficult to quantify and are often based on self-reported perceptions or data from one point of time. Finally, obtaining unbiased estimates that factor in selection issues is difficult, as training participants who choose to receive training are likely to differ from nonparticipants in both observed and unobserved ways.

With these issues in mind, we examine some returns to OJT in outcomes such as earnings and productivity. The empirical evidence consistently shows that OJT is positively correlated with higher labor earnings, although point estimates vary widely (see table 4.1).[7] This implies that workers engaged in formal training programs receive positive and statistically strong wage premiums. As emphasized above, almost everywhere the results should be interpreted with caution due to various issues, including the selection problem.[8] However, even studies that carefully address this selectivity problem in training or that measure the treatment effect on the treated still tend to find positive effects of training on labor earnings.[9] The magnitude of the measured premiums varies widely across different countries, worker and job characteristics, and types of training. In general, wage premiums are higher in developing countries than in developed countries.[10]

Table 4.1 Effects of OJT on Wages and Productivity: Evidence from Selected Countries

Country	Magnitude of effects	Data and methodology
Effects on wages		
United States (Lynch 1992)	• OJT: 0.20–0.36 percent wage increase per week of training • Apprenticeship: 0.10–0.26 percent wage increase per week of training	• Interviews with a panel of individuals 14–21 years of age in 1979, observed again in 1980 and 1983; data from the National Longitudinal Survey, youth cohort
United States (Bartel 1995)	• OJT: Increases in wage growth and a rate of return of about 13 percent	• 1986–90 personnel records of a large manufacturing company
United States (Frazis and Loewenstein 2005)	• Formal training: Median of 60 hours increases wages by 3–4 percent	• Panel analysis using data from the National Longitudinal Survey, youth cohort, 1979–2000.
Republic of Korea and Malaysia (Middleton, Ziderman, and Van Adams 1993)	• Republic of Korea: 28 percent rate of return • Malaysia: 21 percent rate of return	• Survey of previous studies (Cohen 1985; Lee 1985)
Kenya and Zambia (Rosholm, Nielsen, and Dabalen 2007)	• Formal training: 20 percent wage increase	• Matching estimation using cross-sectional data from the Regional Program on Enterprise Development
Malaysia and Thailand (Almeida and Faria, 2009)	• Malaysia: 5.5 percent wage increase • Thailand: 5.1 percent wage increase • Returns close to zero when using matching estimators	• Cross section of matched employer-employee enterprise surveys (World Bank, 2002 and 2004). Least squared and matching estimation

(Table continues on next page)

Table 4.1 (continued)

Country	Magnitude of effects	Data and methodology
Effects on productivity		
United States (Barron, Black, and Loewenstein 1989)	• 10 percent increase in training hours resulted in a 3 percent increase in productivity	• Cross-sectional survey collecting detailed information on training and wages in 1982
Ireland (Barrett and O'Connell 2001)	• Training resulted in 3–4 percent productivity growth	• Surveys of nationally representative enterprises in 1993 and 1995
Portugal (Almeida and Carneiro 2009)	• Rate of return from training of 6.7–8.6 percent	• Panel of large manufacturing firms, 1995–99
Chile, Colombia, Mexico, and Peru (Lopéz-Acevedo and Tan 2011)	• Effects of small and medium enterprise (SME) program participation on productivity (measured as sales, profits, or output): Chile, 7–9 percent; Colombia, 5 percent; Mexico, 5–6 percent; Peru, 21–26 percent	• Panel data of firms participating in SME programs
Ghana, Kenya, and Zimbabwe (Biggs, Shah, and Srivastava 1995)	• 49 percent increase in output after training	• Ordinary least squares estimation from cross-sectional data of the Regional Program on Enterprise Development

In addition to positive returns of OJT to individuals' earnings, studies also find a strong association between OJT and firms' productivity. In modern economies with constant technological changes and increased competition, firms worldwide struggle to find workers with the right set of skills.[11] Investment in job training allows workers to adopt and implement new technologies, eventually leading to increased firm productivity. Again, the main difficulty in identifying and measuring the effects of training on productivity comes from the fact that firms offering OJT tend to already have a set of better observable (and unobservable) characteristics. Even after controlling for these differences, however, studies show that increasing OJT can enhance productivity.[12]

The Incidence of OJT in the Developing World

Despite the benefits of job training around the world, the level of employer-provided training in developing countries is generally low and quite heterogeneous within and across countries. This section draws extensively on the Enterprises Surveys collected by the World Bank in more than 100 countries to document some of the main patterns.[13] The surveys contain harmonized information on training incidence and allow analysis on some core constraints for employers.

At the country level, the share of firms providing job training is strongly correlated with the level of development measured as GDP per capita, and the level of existing skills of the population measured as the average (expected) years of schooling (see figure 4.1). In addition to those factors, investment in research and development together with trade openness is also an important country-level correlate (Almeida and Aterido 2010; Tan et al. 2007). Labor policies and institutions such as hiring and firing regulations, the power of unions, and minimum wage laws are also expected to affect the incidence of training. For example, regulations increasing worker protection and decreasing employment flexibility may increase the incentives to train because firms are more likely to retain workers (Acemoglu and Pischke 2000; Bassanini et al. 2005). Meanwhile, minimum wage regulations for low-wage earners may reduce training to compensate for increased labor costs for the unskilled, inexperienced workers who would need training most. The empirical evidence regarding labor regulations is less robust in both developed and developing countries. Some studies of developing countries suggest that regulations that simultaneously accelerate the diffusion of temporary contracts and increase worker protection tend to generate negative effects on the investment in human capital by firms (Almeida and Aterido 2010; Bassanini et al. 2005).

Even among countries at a similar stage of economic development and education level, significant heterogeneity is observed in the incidence of

Figure 4.1 Training Incidence, Economic Development, and Human Capital

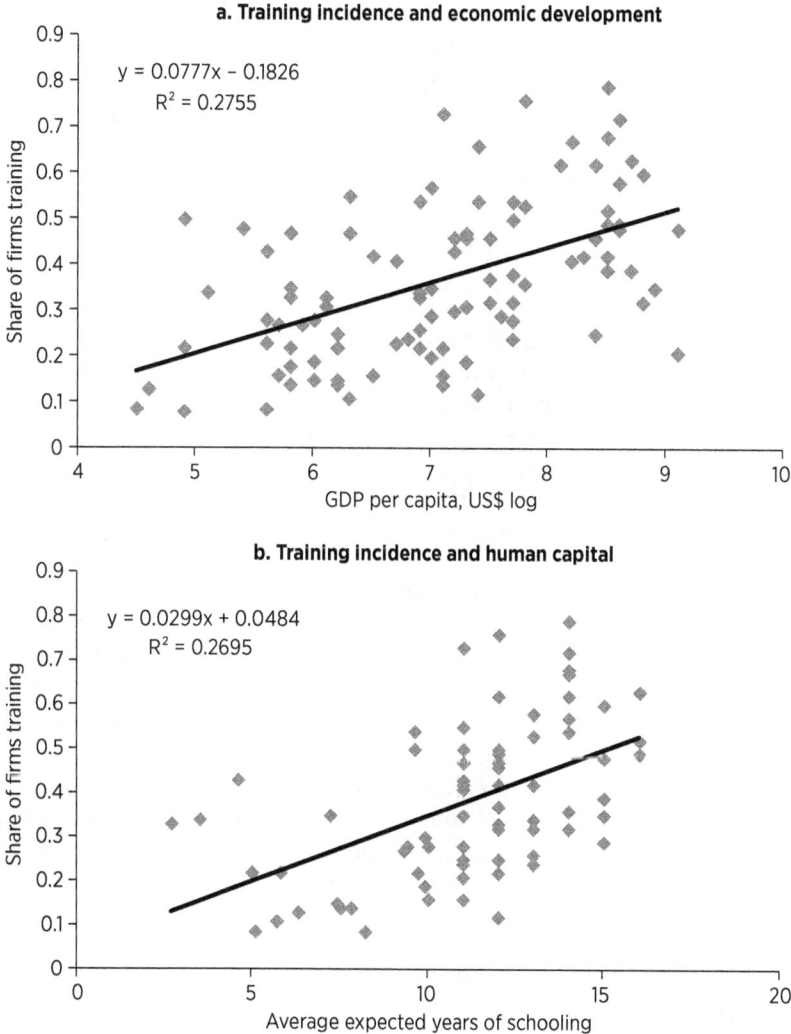

a. Training incidence and economic development

$y = 0.0777x - 0.1826$
$R^2 = 0.2755$

Share of firms training (y-axis, 0 to 0.9)
GDP per capita, US$ log (x-axis, 4 to 10)

b. Training incidence and human capital

$y = 0.0299x + 0.0484$
$R^2 = 0.2695$

Share of firms training (y-axis, 0 to 0.9)
Average expected years of schooling (x-axis, 0 to 20)

Source: Enterprise Surveys.

OJT. The differences in OJT investment, when controlling for country characteristics, are strongly related to the characteristics of firms and their workers. Training is more frequent among large and technologically intensive firms that are likely to be more integrated into global markets and exposed to competition. Training incidence also varies widely by worker character-istics, being less prevalent among less-educated and older workers, but increasing with the tenure for a same job (see, for example, Barron, Black, and Loewenstein 1987; Leuven and Oosterbeek 2004; Lillard and Tan 1992). Training incidence is also lower among women, arguably because of their higher turnover and less attachment in the labor market. Low levels of schooling and the widespread presence of small and micro enterprises are some of the most important reasons for the lack of formal employer-provided training across the developing world (Almeida and Aterido 2010; Bassanini et al. 2005; Middleton et al. 1993; Pierre and Scarpetta 2004).

Why Are Firms Not Training More?

An absolute low incidence of training in a given region or sector does not necessarily imply that firms are investing less than socially desired. If the rates of return are low, for example, because the skills required for certain professions do not improve with the available training, then the optimal level of training would also be low. In such cases, policies may aim at a broader goal of building training capacity and fostering a pool of skilled workers for effective transmission of skills and technology, rather than focusing on OJT-promoting policies. However, if failures in labor and capi-tal markets, coordination failures, and lack of information hinder a firm's investment despite high rates of return, then a low incidence of training implies underinvestment that should be addressed by public policies.

Several common reasons for not investing more in OJT emerge from the Enterprise Surveys for a few selected countries and regions (see figure 4.2).[14] This provides some suggestive evidence on the potential constraints to skills development on the job faced by many developing countries, though not informing definite sources of failures. A majority of firms con-sider informal training to be sufficient for their regular operation. It is pos-sible that the level of skills or technology is not advanced enough to require systematic training, implying that the coordination failures are widespread in the economy. A lack of OJT-promoting systems such as training funds, limited knowledge among firms about the benefits of training, or the lack of know-how for delivering training may also leave firms satisfied with informal training.[15] Firms' rejection of the need for OJT and skepticism about its effectiveness are probably due to the poor quality of training and low skills of the recipients. These conditions may encourage firms to stay with informal training without making efforts to provide formal training.

In the surveys, there are also some firm responses that particularly sug-gest market failures and call for public interventions. Examples include high worker turnover and poaching of workers, which suggests externali-ties, and financing difficulties and the lack of information and awareness,

Figure 4.2 Reasons for Not Investing in OJT in Central America

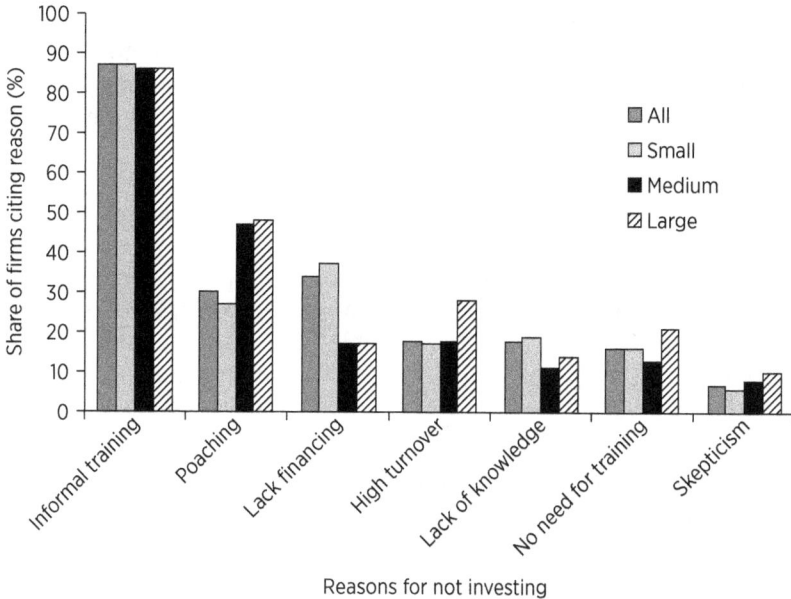

Reasons for not investing

Source: Enterprise Surveys.

Note: Small firms have 1–49 employees, medium firms have 50–99 employees, and large firms have more than 100 employees.

which also suggest market imperfections. As suggested in the next section, "Promoting On-the-Job Training," policy measures should be tailored to address the main constraints to investment.

Whether smaller firms are disproportionately affected by these constraints compared to their larger counterparts is not straightforward. It is often accepted without rigorous evidence that smaller firms are faced with greater constraints to skills development because OJT is substantially less common among these firms. However, it is also likely that smaller firms may simply find the returns to investment lower. In Central America, high worker turnover and the poaching of workers seem to be major deterrents for investment in job training, especially among medium and large firms, while financial difficulties and the lack of knowledge are more relevant for small firms. The importance of each of these factors across firm size is likely to differ across countries.[16] To create relevant public policy interventions, more study is needed of the constraints to OJT and of market failures in skills development across firm size, type, sector, and region.

Promoting On-the-Job Training

The previous section discussed why firms do not invest more in OJT despite the potentially high returns. Among other things, we presented evidence suggesting that market failures, including poaching externalities, credit constraints, and imperfect information, are prevalent around the developing world.

The following subsections discuss policy tools to promote OJT. For the interventions to work in fostering human capital accumulation in general, they need to be aligned with the constraints faced by many employers. We particularly focus on the two frequently discussed policy instruments: an institutional arrangement between employers and workers, and a financial arrangement that internalizes the possible poaching externality. In each case, we emphasize best practices in design and implementation of the program from the worldwide examples and discuss the lessons learned.

Shaping Institutional Arrangements and Getting Incentives Right

Governments can establish institutional arrangements that align incentives for firms and workers to invest in OJT. These arrangements are most effective when the key constraints to investment are high risk of worker turnover (the poaching externality) and firms' difficulty in appropriating the returns on the investment in training. These risks can be a major deterrent to investing in job training when knowledge is portable across firms (and thus is not firm specific). In that case, enforceable contracts that require workers to stay with the employer that provides the training for a certain period of time are a possible solution that enables the firm to recover the costs of training.

The two most common instruments designed to facilitate such arrangements are payback clauses and apprenticeship contracts. A payback clause is a type of labor clause specifying that the worker is required to stay with the firm providing the training for a minimum length of time. Otherwise, the worker will have to pay back the costs of job training. Because workers are required to stay with the training firm, employers can pay lower wages to recover the training costs and can benefit from improved productivity without the risk of losing workers to other firms. Because these instruments require good governance and effective legal enforcement mechanisms, they have been preferred by high- or middle-income countries.[17]

The apprenticeship contract is probably the most widely used instrument to promote OJT across the developing and developed world. An *apprenticeship* is defined as a period during which individuals and firms engage in a working relationship, firms benefit from low-wage workers (usually early in their careers), and individuals have the opportunity to receive firm-specific training. This arrangement is very popular and useful for promoting the transition from school to work because it gives youth the opportunity to develop skills that are directly relevant to the labor market after completing their formal studies. During the apprenticeship period, wages are usually set below the market rate with an expectation that they will rise afterward. Therefore, the apprenticeship usually promotes the sharing of training costs between firms and workers (by underpaying workers during training). Because the implementation is relatively easy, financing and regulations are flexible, and the curriculum can be customized, the apprenticeship is popular even among micro and informal sector firms. However, the weak educational base of informal sector workers (or the trainers), the lack of quality standards for training, and the limited potential for scaling up have been acknowledged as the main difficulties with apprenticeship.[18] Good implementation may require enforcing both an adequate length of training and certification systems, as well as improved access to new technology.

An example of a well-defined and established apprenticeship program with good regulation is found in Germany. As a part of a dual-education structure that distinguishes vocational and academic training, German apprenticeship plays a critical role in vocational training. It combines school-based and on-the-job training, follows a standardized curriculum and well-monitored quality standard, and incorporates private education (box 4.1). Adopting the long-standing traditions of German apprenticeship will not guarantee successful program implementation, but lessons from

---

BOX 4.1

Germany: An Institutional Arrangement for Contractibility

The apprenticeship is one of the best-known institutional arrangements for addressing the contractibility problem between employers and employees. This problem arises from the difficulty in defining a wage and training program prior to the start of the employment relationship. More recently, apprenticeships have also attracted the attention of policy makers in many countries as a way of promoting school-to-work transitions. The best examples come from countries with a long tradition of apprenticeships and where this tradition also works as an enforcement mechanism. This is the case in many African and some European countries.

(Box continues on next page)

BOX 4.1 (continued)

Traditionally, apprenticeships have two main components: (i) the contract and (ii) the certification. Government usually supports the apprenticeship through a subsidy to the individual or firm and through labor regulations. The contract is a private agreement between the apprentice and the firm. It covers a specific time period (typically three to four years) and a given type of training, and usually defines an hourly wage (typically below the market wage). The training curriculum is determined by the employer but is usually regulated by the government to ensure quality and relevance. Workers benefit from apprenticeship training by acquiring relevant labor market experience and skills. Upon completion of the apprenticeship, trainees are usually certified. They may or may not remain with the same firm but the certification signals the worker's competence to other employers. Employers benefit from the lower cost of labor during the training period and use apprenticeships as a screening procedure for prospective workers.

Germany provides a good example. It is a dual system based on (i) classroom training in vocational institutions and (ii) training in the workplace. Apprentices' wages tend to be lower than productivity, but after training they typically grow to be three to four times higher. For transparency and quality, the curriculum, content, and time structure of the training are carefully regulated by the Federal Institute for Training and other national committees. The evidence suggests that apprentices, especially in large firms, increase employability. However, the post-training benefit to firms is less obvious. The retention rates of apprentices are low, as the skills taught tend to be general and thus applicable at other firms. In addition, the total training costs are far from negligible.

Sources: Clark and Fahr (2001); Harhoff and Kane (1997); Soskice (1994); Winkelmann (1996).

the German program, including its structure and principle, would be useful in promoting private OJT.

Allocating Public Resources: The Principles of Subsidies

Because poaching externalities and credit constraints are often mentioned as key barriers to OJT, training subsidies may be an appropriate policy tool to increase the investment in skills. However, badly designed financial subsidies can crowd out nongovernmental provision of training that might have taken place even without subsidies, and reduce economic efficiency by creating labor market distortions. This section discusses the financing and operating principles of providing subsidies through national training funds by looking at some selected country examples. It argues that more attention needs to be paid to deadweight losses in financing training through payroll taxes because such taxes may discourage employers from investing in and hiring workers. It also emphasizes the importance of improving efficiency through better targeting of subsidies and improving governance and accountability within the funds through stronger M&E.

How to finance subsidies

In developing countries, the most popular way to provide subsidies is through training funds, particularly those based on payroll taxes.[19] At least in theory, training funds can be financed through either general revenue or payroll taxes. Training funds financed out of general taxation provide earmarked and secured funding for training and thus have been an appealing OJT financing source under tight government budgets. However, using general revenue for OJT poses some problems. First, OJT benefits only a fraction of the population, a selective group of firms and workers. Second, knowledge generated through training cannot widely be recognized as a public good. Third, investing in OJT is usually less of a priority than investing in general education.[20] For these reasons, many training funds are based on payroll taxes rather than on general revenue. For example, Brazil, Chile, Malaysia, Mexico, and Singapore collect payroll levies and use the funds to encourage firms to invest in OJT.

A common design challenge linked with subsidies financed through payroll taxes is the potential deadweight losses and substitution effects they may create. The deadweight losses from the training levy and increased tax rates could outweigh the benefits of incremental training induced by the financial incentive.[21] Efficiency losses also result from the fact that subsidies might be used for investments that would otherwise have occurred. In fact, most international experience shows that this type of incentive is focused on larger firms, for which the returns of training are arguably higher even without any public intervention. When training funds subsidize private OJT, they may crowd out privately financed training because firms likely use the subsidized training opportunity rather than the nonsubsidized one. Therefore, caution is needed in designing programs for subsidizing and financing training. Depending on how training funds are used, the efficiency of the program can improve.

Training funds based on payroll levies are usually employed to generate revenue or for incentive schemes. Revenue-generating levies were first developed in Latin American countries, where pooled revenues traditionally have been used to develop national training systems. National training systems emphasize public provision of training and cover a wide range of pre-employment training and OJT. Meanwhile, incentive schemes encourage private firms' training by compensating them for their costs. These types of levy-rebate schemes are generally categorized as cost reimbursement, levy grant, and levy exemption (train or pay). Cost reimbursement compensates actual expenses of training incurred; levy grant returns taxes for specified activities, including training; and levy exemption simply waives training levies contingent upon the training. Administration of these schemes varies from country to country, and many hybrids exist. A wide tax base in the formal sector and a reasonable administrative capacity would be needed to establish well-functioning training funds.

How to operate subsidies

In most countries, there is room to enhance the efficiency of training subsidies by improving targeting, ensuring good governance, and establishing a practice of M&E. Training funds are usually criticized on the grounds that they tend to benefit mainly large firms. They are also criticized because they subsidize through public training institutes that are often inflexible to demand-side needs or that they lack transparency in their operation. These drawbacks likely lower the efficiency of training funds. Large firms arguably have higher returns from training and thus would have invested in OJT regardless of the available subsidies. There are a number of overarching issues that need to be addressed to improve the effectiveness of operations. First, improving the targeting of training funds is important so as not to crowd out private training. Second, good governance arrangements giving flexibility and autonomy to the private sector for a more innovative and transparent use of funds is crucial to avoid the high administrative costs of centrally-managed funds. Finally, similar to other public programs, the M&E of training funds is necessary for a more results-based approach to skills development.

Improving targeting. Targeting based on firm size is not necessarily efficiency enhancing because little robust evidence exists that small and medium enterprises (SMEs) are disproportionally affected by market failures. However, addressing obvious constraints faced by SMEs compared to larger firms, such as lack of economies of scale, may improve efficiency when implementing training funds. A training consortium in the Republic of Korea, the Mexican Integral Quality and Modernization program (*Calidad Integral y Modernización,* or CIMO), Singapore's Skills Development Fund, and Malaysia's Human Resource Development Fund are good examples of programs that support SMEs, especially in their training, although the operational details vary.[22] Box 4.2 describes Korea's effort to support SMEs through an intervention that attempts to overcome large fixed costs and create economies of scale in training provision. In Korea, SMEs often did not take advantage of training funds for which they already paid levies,

BOX 4.2

The Republic of Korea: A Training Consortium for Small and Medium Enterprises

The Korean levy-rebate system, created in 1995, aimed at encouraging enterprises to invest in job training. The system set aside a portion of a payroll tax on employers for a training fund and provided reimbursement out of the fund if the employers offered training. The caveat is that the system was found to benefit mostly larger firms as SMEs had very low recovery rates (that is, reimbursement as a share of the training levy paid) due to a low incidence of training. In 2002, only approximately 17 percent of trained workers were from SMEs, while these represented almost 65 percent of the employed workforce. To encourage SMEs to provide more and better training, the Korean government introduced a pilot training consortium (TC) for SMEs in 2001.

The SME TC exemplifies a policy attempting to use training funds more efficiently. It works by targeting SMEs whose training programs arguably are more affected by market imperfections than large firms. The program encouraged SMEs operating in the same sector and geographic region to form a TC and jointly hire trainers. Some of the TCs' training expenses were subsidized, including facilities, equipment, and operational costs (such as textbooks, curriculum development, and financial managers). The consortium collectively mobilized resources and benefited from economies of scale. Working together through a consortium helped SMEs take advantage of the available training subsidies (obtained through the levy-rebate) and increase the incidence and quality of training.

When scaled up, the program introduced some modifications. Considering that a large number of SMEs rely heavily on a few dominant conglomerate firms, the government added a new way of operation linking SMEs and leading conglomerates: the BRIDGE model. This program combines the participation of large conglomerates, universities, and the SME consortium. Its first application was executed with a leading firm, Samsung Electronics, more than a hundred of its partner companies, and the Korea University of Technology and Education. Several other cases involving major conglomerates are currently being implemented. Through this collaborative model, the participating SMEs expect to receive cutting-edge skills development and upgrades while subsidized, and the conglomerates are able to obtain skilled partners. Anecdotal evidence suggests that both models helped promote training among SMEs and improve worker performance, although further rigorous evaluation should follow to examine their effectiveness.

Source: Lee (2009); Lee, Seol, and Kim (2009).

probably because of limited capacity to administer and finance training. In recognition of this, the Korean government encouraged SMEs in similar sectors and regions to form a consortium so that they could collaborate in providing training. Later the program vertically expanded; now the consortium includes large firms, and SMEs can achieve synergy with their large partners in acquiring and maintaining skills.

Although firm size is usually considered a good proxy for reflecting inefficiencies and externalities with respect to training, better proxies are needed to improve program targeting. A more rigorous examination would help improve the efficiency of training funds. For example, if the size of the poaching externality originates from the compressed wage structure (driven by market imperfections), sectors or workers facing larger discrepancies between wages and marginal productivity should be prioritized in the targeting. Therefore, better proxies should be developed to help improve program targeting beyond firm size. Some usually observable firm characteristics such as the firm's sector of activity, frequency of technology adoption, or the gaps between average wages and productivity in the sector, are promising proxies that can be used to improve targeting and thus the effectiveness of these interventions.

Ensuring good governance. As with most public interventions, a sound governance structure is a prerequisite for effective training funds. Governance, including administrative autonomy, transparent funds management, public and private partnership, and fair competition, is important for improving efficiency and better allocating funds. Several country procedures suggest the following best-practice principles for the operation of training funds. First, levy schemes should refrain from excessive centralization by avoiding large and heavy administrative bodies. Funds should give firms as much freedom as possible to pick their providers and manage their programs. Second, seeking a strong buy-in and collaborating with the private sector will improve employers' perception of the levy, showing them that it is not just another tax reducing their competitiveness. Moreover, to avoid conflicts of interest, training funds should not play a direct role in training provision. By directly providing training, they may also crowd out other (private or nongovernmental organization) training providers.[23]

A voucher program could be a good tool for developing the private sector training market. The Kenyan program in box 4.3 illustrates an innovative way to use a voucher program to improve governance and efficiency by developing the private sector. This program advances beyond conventional training subsidies in three ways: (i) it has a clear target group in a sector where the rate of churning is high and training can hardly take place, (ii) it uses vouchers to induce demand for training and to develop the private trainer market, and (iii) it tries to reduce information asymmetry by assisting firms in identifying areas for training. The evaluation shows that

BOX 4.3

Kenya: Training Vouchers for Small and Medium Enterprises

The Kenyan voucher program, Jua Kali, is a good example of a program that developed a private training market while supporting SMEs with workers' training.

Expected Effects of the Voucher Program

Training vouchers are expected to address a few problems faced by SMEs, including credit constraints and asymmetries of information. The voucher program mitigates credit constraints of individual firms by providing subsidies. It also facilitates access to the private training market and to information regarding service quality and program outcomes. Because vouchers promote competition in the market among private training providers, they should be useful in improving quality at a lower cost.

Stakeholders of the Kenya Voucher Program

The beneficiaries of Kenya's Jua Kali include very small, young firms (often with only one or two workers) that experience high rates of churning. The total employment, wages, and growth rates vary largely with firm size. Some firms operating at the subsistence level tend to be very small and heavily populated with women. In these firms, workers are mostly unpaid or earn minimum wage. They are likely to be in the retail sector and face highly competitive and saturated market conditions. Other types of firms, mostly in manufacturing, have higher employment, income, and growth. Thus, two different groups are identified as potential recipients of a voucher program: (i) micro enterprises (with 1–10 employees) and woman-owned start-ups and (ii) small enterprises (with 11–50 paid employees). Vouchers can be used for training providers, including master craftworkers; public training institutes adapted to Jua Kali; and technology institutions and consulting firms.

Depending on the service provider and the needs of the firm, training covers anything from basic skills and marketing to more sophisticated financial and technical advice. The Project Coordination Office assists firms in identifying their training needs and possible service providers and explains to them how the voucher works. The Project Coordination Office also contracts with service providers and maintains quality control and monitoring.

(Box continues on next page)

BOX 4.3 *(continued)*

Evaluation of the Kenya Voucher Program

Voucher beneficiaries and nonbeneficiary applicants were compared approximately 12 to 18 months after training. The results show that firms using vouchers experienced greater growth in business than those that did not (80 percent and 13 percent, respectively) and increased business assets (61 percent and 21 percent, respectively). Also, private training providers whose service was previously available only to larger enterprises actively participated in the voucher program and showed greater interest in training firms in Jua Kali. Quantifying the program's effects on the development of the private training market and its sustainability is difficult. One cannot fully examine the causal effects of the training program by simply comparing voucher recipients and nonrecipients without properly addressing selectivity. However, findings suggest that private sector involvement in training is a useful way of promoting training among SMEs.

Sources: Hallberg (2000); Phillips and Steel (2003); Riley and Steel (2000).

---

these vouchers and custom-made training programs have improved the business performance of the recipient firms, although it only partially addresses self-selection.

Building in strong M&E systems. Together with governance, M&E should be among the operating principles in managing training funds. Although several programs have been introduced and modified to promote OJT across many countries, few evaluations of those programs are available. The absence of evaluations makes it difficult to correctly assess the effectiveness of the intervention and to identify ways to improve and scale up the programs. Some training programs, such as the Korean consortium program and the Kenyan training voucher program, though they represent innovative efforts to promote training, could provide only limited evidence on their effectiveness because detailed data collection and rigorous evaluation was not incorporated.

One of the few programs that included an M&E component from the onset is Mexico's CIMO Program (see box 4.4). CIMO is a comprehensive strategy to support SMEs in Mexico by addressing not only specific training but also overall competency, including research and development, technology adoption, and managerial skills. CIMO was established in 1987 and has been particularly successful. By 2000 it was helping 80,000 enterprises each year with a package of training and industrial extension services and train-

BOX 4.4

Mexico: Building in Monitoring and Evaluation Systems

Mexico's Integrated Quality and Modernization program, or CIMO, is a good example of a comprehensive program targeted to foster productivity among SMEs. The program is particularly well known for its sound M&E system. From its inception in 1987 up to the early 1990s, CIMO focused primarily on training services. Later it became more comprehensive, including the provision of consulting and technical assistance in addition to training. In 2001, however, the program again shifted its focus more toward the training component, changing its name to Training Support Program (*Programa de Apoyo a la Capacitación,* or PAC). Among other things, the program provided subsidies for firms to hire independent instructors that design and deliver training programs for them. CIMO-PAC trained about 1.6 million workers between 2001 and 2006, and benefited more than 226,000 firms. It had an estimated total budget of about US$75 million during that period.

CIMO-PAC is one of several Mexican programs targeting SMEs. A noteworthy feature of the program, as well as of other Mexican SME programs, is its efforts in data collection for monitoring and evaluation (M&E). For example, an intersectoral commission (*Comisión Intersecretarial de Política Industrial,* or CIPI), apart from each ministry responsible for supervising its own SME programs, plays a coordinating role in M&E. Created in 1996, CIPI promotes a common approach to the design, implementation, and evaluation of SME programs. It maintains a unified database on all SME programs that puts together information reported by the different ministries. The database includes information on the supervising agency, the beneficiaries of each program by year, and the types of support services provided (capacity building, consulting, technical assistance, among others). In so doing, CIPI tries to monitor different types of services and any possible duplication across programs, and to assess the needs of SMEs.

The availability of this type of monitoring information over time allows for a more rigorous evaluation of these programs. Several studies have therefore examined the effectiveness of the CIMO program on firm productivity over time. For example, López-Acevedo and Tan (2005) examined the effects of CIMO during the early stage of the program (1991–95). They explored panel data to address pre-program differences between participating and nonparticipating SMEs, and found that the program was associated with an increase in productivity. A series of more recent studies focused on the later stages of the program and found little or no effects.

Sources: López-Acevedo and Tinajero-Bravo (2010); López-Acevedo and Tan (2005).

ing 200,000 employees. More than 300 business associations were participating in CIMO in 2000, up from 72 when it started. In addition, CIMO's M&E effort distinguishes it from other programs. CIMO administered data collection in such a way as to gather panel data over time. A great deal of effort to construct data over time has provided the policy makers with useful information on how the intervention has evolved and worked.

Conclusion

The importance of sound skill development systems while on the job is not controversial, given the amount of human capital generally accumulated in the labor market compared with in schools. Most evidence shows that OJT (with a mix of general and specific knowledge) is linked to better labor market outcomes for individuals and higher firm productivity, although the magnitude of effects varies. The lack of adequate data, difficulty in measurement of benefits and costs, and the econometric challenge of self-selection increase the difficulty of quantifying the causal effect of OJT on earnings and productivity and the returns to training. Nevertheless, it is generally agreed that skill development through OJT is an important source of fostering human capital.

However, there is no consensus on why low levels of training are observed and whether this implies suboptimality that calls for public intervention. International data clearly show that low-income countries tend to have less training, a consequence of their generally lower levels of education and skills development. Low levels of training do not necessarily imply a need for public intervention or market failure. Some firms simply find little need to invest because the skills they require are not technical enough to be improved through training.

This chapter argues that market failures hindering OJT, such as externalities, credit constraints, and lack of information, can be addressed by interventions. These targeted interventions can coincide with general efforts to promote an environment conducive to human capital accumulation. We paid particular attention to the theoretical background and empirical evidence to identify the source of market failures and corresponding interventions to address them. The chapter then discussed some best practices of institutional and financial arrangements across several countries and suggested guiding principles of public intervention in the area of OJT. Table 4.2 reviews the main failures and summarizes the interventions proposed. Institutional arrangements, including payback clauses and apprenticeship programs, are good examples of internalizing externalities without heavy public intervention or market distortion. Improving transparency and enforceability of contracts, standardizing and promoting quality train-

Table 4.2 Summary of Market Failures in OJT and the Corresponding Policies

Market failures or constraints to investment in OJT	Possible policies	Implementation challenges	Recommendations
Contractibility and poaching of workers	• Institutional arrangements against poaching and asymmetry of information, including payback clauses and apprenticeships	• Payback clauses: Sound governance and enforceability of contracts • Apprenticeships: Fostering and harmonizing quality, supervision, and transferability of skills	• Strong legal system needed to support these arrangements and strict enforcement of contracts and labor law • Standardized curriculum for apprenticeships and promotion of certification and accreditation systems
Imperfect and inadequate information and low complementarities with other factors of production	• Technical assistance such as business consulting to promote firm productivity, including strategies related to technology adoption, human resource management, and skill development • Direct provision of training through public or private institutes	• Technical assistance: Scope of consulting and of M&E • Training: Governance and effectiveness of public training provision	• An integrated approach to technical assistance to promote overall competency, information and knowledge sharing, and built-in M&E • Training based on industry, region, and similarity of technology to create economies of scale • Training for market-demanded skills through public-private partnerships
Externality	• Subsidies for training, including partial reimbursement of expenses or tax benefits for training	• Financing: Payroll taxes, general revenue, and earmarked budgets • Resource allocation: Priority setting • Governance: Administrative efficiency and transparency	• Financing done through general revenue and earmarked budgets for training purposes, which are less distortive than payroll taxes • Resource allocation to identify needy firms with growth potential rather than focusing only on firm size • Governance that reduces the involvement of administrative bodies and increases the involvement of employers

ing, and establishing a tradition of good public-private partnership in training could partially address the suboptimality of training. In conjunction with institutional arrangements, more efforts to improve the efficiency of financial support to promote OJT are needed. Financial support for OJT through training funds, which are often financed by payroll taxes, is likely to increase inefficiency and deadweight losses unless carefully designed and implemented. Better targeting, governance, and M&E systems need to be considered to further improve the effectiveness of interventions.

Notes

1. We would like to thank Mamta Murthi, Ariel Fiszbein, David Robalino, Zafiris Tzannatos, and Amit Dar for their excellent comments and suggestions at different stages of this chapter.
2. This chapter addresses skill development for the informal sector and for the most vulnerable workers.
3. Note that skills are developed through a series process throughout a worker's life. See World Bank (2010) for the STEP (Skills Toward Employability and Productivity) framework and a detailed discussion on each stage in lifetime human capital accumulation. This chapter focuses only on the formation of job-relevant skills as employees participate in formal OJT programs.
4. See Acemoglu (1998), Bartel and Sicherman (1998), Barron, Berger, and Black (1997), Black and Lynch (1996, 2001), Frazis and Loewenstein (2005), and Lynch (1992) for discussion of the role of OJT.
5. The poaching of workers creates an externality because when knowledge is partially transferable, some of the returns from OJT are captured by future employers and thus are not internalized by the firm undertaking the initial investment. For a detailed discussion, see chapter 2.
6. Exceptions include Almeida and Carneiro (2009).
7. Table 4.1 references several studies that estimate the effect of job training on labor earnings and productivity. Rather than being exhaustive, the table shows studies that present stronger estimates, either because they are based on panel data or because they present a more robust econometric approach. Most studies of developing countries, however, face more severe data limitations.
8. Thus, comparing the wages of trained workers with those of nontrained workers will yield a biased estimate.
9. A few studies have successfully done so. First, when longitudinal data are available, the selection based on time-invariant individual characteristics can be eliminated with a fixed effect. This approach will fully eliminate the bias when selection for training is based on time-invariant unobservable characteristics (see, for example, Lynch 1992). Second, an instrumental variable for training is available that directly affects wages only through job training. Leuven and Oosterbeek (2004) explore a discontinuity at age 40 on the tax deductions for training expenses as an instrument.

10. A priori, it is unclear whether returns should be larger or smaller in developing countries than they are in developed countries because developing countries have smaller stocks of human capital and smaller stocks of physical capital.

11. The concept of "right skills" will be further identified and discussed. Bloom's (1976) taxonomy still validly categorizes job-relevant skills into three groups: (i) psychomotor, (ii) cognitive, and (iii) affective (soft). Recent studies have also emphasized the importance of both noncognitive and cognitive skills in successful labor market achievement (for example, Heckman, Stixrud, and Urzua 2006).

12. It is difficult to compare estimates across countries because of different outcome measures and methodology. Almeida and Carneiro (2009) show that the point estimates obtained from estimating production functions cannot directly be interpreted as mean returns to training, because data on costs are unobserved and calculations on future benefits are rarely discussed.

13. http://www.enterprisesurveys.org/.

14. Evidence is also available for Brazil, China, Sri Lanka, and Central Asia, but is not reported because of the great similarity in the overall rankings.

15. In fact, few low-income countries have established training funds, whereas many middle- and high-income countries have them in practice. See Johanson (2009).

16. For example, in Central America smaller firms feel constrained by the lack of financing more frequently than do larger firms. However, this was not the case in Brazil or China.

17. Payback clauses as a part of employment law have been examined in middle income countries such as Poland and Romania benchmarking the cases of the United Kingdom, the Netherlands, and Germany.

18. See Middleton et al. (1993) and Ziderman (2003).

19. Training funds for pre-employment or enterprise training are found in more than 60 countries, most of which are large countries in Europe, Latin America, and Sub-Saharan Africa. See Dar, Canagarajah, and Murphy (2003) and Johanson (2009).

20. A few examples of financing training through general revenue include interventions in the 1970s in the Republic of Korea (see, for example, Ra and Shim 2009) and recent programs in the United States, where the government provided training directly to firms through public institutions. Ra and Shim (2009) review changes in skill development policies that accompanied economic development in Korea. Public policy for training evolved from the direct provision of training and subsidization to more sophisticated levy-rebate systems as the economy developed. Moore et al. (2003) summarize state-financed training programs for each U.S. state, with particular focus on California. State-financed training programs in the United States are part of local governments' efforts to help private firms gain competency and revive the local economy.

21. The deadweight loss rises approximately in proportion to the square of the tax rate.

22. Malaysia and Singapore have implemented different measures, including training vouchers to ease cash-flow constraints, training grants for firms with more pressing training needs, and simplification of administrative approvals. In Malaysia, for example, large enterprises with excess training capacities are

encouraged to offer training slots to employees of smaller firms, which are eligible for training grants from the Human Resource Development Fund (Tan 2001). Singapore's Skills Development Fund awarded grants to small firms to engage external consultants to help them meet their training needs and develop a worker training plan. Hence, smaller firms were able to access the specialized resources and design appropriate training programs.

23. A best-practice example is Chile's National Service of Training and Employment (*Servicio Nacional de Capacitación y Empleo*), whereas Brazil's National Industrial Training Service (*Serviço Nacional de Aprendizagem Industrial*) has been widely criticized for operating its own network of training institutions.

References

Acemoglu, Daron. 1998. "Why Do New Technologies Complement Skills? Direct Technical Change and Wage Inequality." *Quarterly Journal of Economics* 113(4): 1055–89.

Acemoglu, Daron, and Jörn-Staffen Pischke. 2000. "Certification of Training and Training Outcomes." *European Economic Review* 44(4–6): 917–27.

Almeida, Rita K., and Reyes Aterido. 2010. "Investment in Job Training: Why Are SMEs Lagging So Much Behind?" Policy Discussion Paper 5358. World Bank, Washington, DC.

———. 2011. "The Incentives to Invest in Job Training: Do Strict Labor Codes Influence This Investment?" *Labour Economics* 18.

Almeida, Rita K., and Pedro Carneiro. 2009. "The Return to Firm Investments in Human Capital." *Labour Economics* 16(1): 97–106.

Almeida, Rita K., and Marta Faria. 2009. "The Wage Returns to On-the-Job Training: Evidence from Matched Employer-Employee Data in East Asia." Unpublished paper. World Bank, Washington, DC.

Barrett, Alan, and Philip J. O'Connell. 2001. "Does Training Generally Work? The Returns to In-Company Training," *Industrial and Labor Relations Review* 54(3): 647–62.

Barron, John M., Mark C. Berger, and Dan A. Black. 1997. *On-the-Job Training*. Kalamazoo, MI: W. E. Upjohn Institute for Employment Research.

Barron, John M., Dan A. Black, and Mark A. Loewenstein. 1987. "Employer Size: The Implications for Search, Training, Capital Investment, Starting Wages, and Wage Growth." *Journal of Labor Economics* 5(1): 76–89.

———. 1989. "Job Matching and On-the-Job Training." *Journal of Labor Economics* 7(1): 1–19.

Bartel, Ann P. 1995. "Training, Wage Growth, and Job Performance: Evidence from a Company Database." *Journal of Labor Economics* 13(3): 401–25.

Bartel, Ann P., and Nachum Sicherman. 1998. "Technological Change and the Skill Acquisition of Young Workers." *Journal of Labor Economics* 16(4): 718–55.

Bassanini, Andrea, Alison Booth, Giorgio Brunello, Maria de Paola, and Edwin Leuven. 2005. "Workplace Training in Europe." IZA Discussion Paper 1640. Institute for the Study of Labor, Bonn, Germany.

Biggs, Tyler, Manju Shah, and Pradeep Srivastava. 1995. "Training and Productivity in African Manufacturing Enterprises." Working Paper 15101. World Bank, Washington, DC.

Black, Sandra E., and Lisa M. Lynch. 1996. "Human Capital Strategy and Productivity Outcomes." *American Economic Review Papers and Proceedings* 86(2): 263–67.

———. 2001. "How to Compete: The Impact of Workplace Practices and Information Technology on Productivity." *Review of Economics and Statistics* 83(3): 434–45.

Bloom, Benjamin S. 1976. *Human Characteristics and School Learning.* New York: McGraw-Hill.

Clark, Damon, and René Fahr. 2001. "The Promise of Workplace Training for Non-College-Bound Youth: Theory and Evidence from German Apprenticeship." IZA Working Paper 378. Institute for the Study of Labor, Bonn, Germany.

Cohen, Suleiman I. 1985. "A Cost-Benefit Analysis of Industrial Training." *Economics of Education Review* 4(4): 327–39.

Dar, Amit, Sudharshan Canagarajah, and Paud Murphy. 2003. "Training Levies: Rationale and Evidence from Evaluations." World Bank, Washington, DC.

Frazis, Harley, and Mark A. Loewenstein. 2005. "Reexamining the Returns to Training: Functional Form, Magnitude, and Interpretation." *Journal of Human Resources* 40(2): 453–76.

Hallberg, Kristin. 2000. "A Market-Oriented Strategy for Small and Medium Scale Enterprises." World Bank, Washington, DC.

Harhoff, Dietmar, and Thomas J. Kane. 1997. "Is the German Apprenticeship System a Panacea for the U.S. Labor Market?" *Journal of Population Economics* 10(2): 171–96.

Heckman, James J., Lance Lochner, and Christopher Taber. 1998. "Explaining Rising Wage Inequality: Explanations with a Dynamic General Equilibrium Model of Earnings with Heterogeneous Agents." *Review of Economic Dynamics* 1(1): 1–58.

Heckman, James J., Jora Stixrud, and Sergio Urzua. 2006. "The Effects of Cognitive and Noncognitive Abilities on Labor Market Outcomes and Social Behavior." National Bureau of Economic Research (NBER) Working Paper 12006. NBER, Cambridge, MA.

Johanson, Richard. 2009. "A Review of National Training Funds." Social Protection Discussion Paper 0922. World Bank, Washington, DC.

Lee, Chingboon. 1985. "Financing Technical Education in LDCs: Implications from a Survey of Training Modes in the Republic of Korea." EDT Discussion Paper 6, Education and Training Department. World Bank, Washington, DC.

Lee, Kye Woo. 2009. "Productivity Increases in SMEs: With Special Emphasis on In-Service Training of Workers in Korea." Social Protection Discussion Paper 0917. World Bank, Washington, DC.

Lee, Wooyoung, Jinsoo Seol, and Jinwoo Kim. 2009. "A BRIDGE Model of University-industry Cooperation to Develop Skills of Practical Engineers for Small-medium Companies." Unpublished paper. Korea University of Technology and Education.

Leuven, Edwin, and Hessel Oosterbeek. 2004. "Evaluating the Effect of Tax Deductions on Training." *Journal of Labor Economics* 22(2): 461–88.

Lillard, Lee A., and Hong W. Tan. 1992. "Private Sector Training: Who Gets It and What Are Its Effects?" *Research in Labor Economics* 13: 1–62.

López-Acevedo, Gladys, and Hong W. Tan. 2005. "Evaluating Training Programs for Small and Medium Enterprises: Lessons from Mexico." Policy Research Working Paper 3760. World Bank, Washington, DC.

————. 2011. *Impact Evaluation of Small and Medium Enterprise Programs in Latin America and the Caribbean*. Washington, DC: World Bank.

López-Acevedo, Gladys, and Monica Tinajero-Bravo. 2010. "Mexico: Impact Evaluation of SME Programs Using Panel Firm Data." Unpublished paper. World Bank, Washington, DC.

Lynch, Lisa M. 1992. "Private-Sector Training and the Earnings of Young Workers." *American Economic Review* 82(1): 299–312.

Middleton, John, Adrian Ziderman, and Arvil Van Adams. 1993. *Skills for Productivity: Vocational Education and Training in Developing Countries*. New York: Oxford University Press.

Moore, Richard, Daniel R. Blake, G. Michael Phillips, Daniel McConaughy. 2003. "Training That Works: Lessons from California's Employment Training Panel Program." W. E. Upjohn Institute for Employment Research, Kalamazoo, MI.

Phillips, David, and William Steel. 2003. "Evaluating the Development Impact of Demand-Side Interventions for BDS Markets: Kenya Voucher Program." *Small Enterprise Development* 14(4): 1–11.

Pierre, Gaëlle, and Stefano Scarpetta. 2004. "Employment Regulations through the Eyes of Employers: Do They Matter and How Do Firms Respond to Them?" Policy Research Paper 3463. World Bank, Washington, DC.

Ra, Young-Sun, and Kyung Woo Shim. 2009. "The Korean Case Study: Past Experience and New Trends in Training Policies." Social Protection Discussion Paper 0931. World Bank, Washington, DC.

Riley, Thyra, and William Steel. 2000. "Voucher Program for Training and Business Development Services: Kenya Micro and Small Enterprise Training and Technology Project." International Labour Organization, Geneva.

Rosholm, Michael, Helena Skyt Nielsen, and Andrew Dabalen. 2007. "Evaluation of Training in African Enterprises." *Journal of Development Economics* 84(1): 310–29.

Soskice, David. 1994. "The German Training System: Reconciling Markets and Institutions." In Lisa Lynch, ed., *International Comparisons of Private Sector Training*. University of Chicago Press, NBER Conference Volume.

Tan, Hong W. 2001. "Malaysia's HRDF: An Evaluation of Its Effects on Training and Productivity." World Bank, Washington, DC.

Tan, Hong W., Yevgeniya Savchenko, Vladimir Gimpelson, Rostislav Kapelyushnikov, and Anna Lukyanova. 2007. "Skills Shortages and Training in Russian Enterprises." IZA Discussion Paper 2751. Institute for the Study of Labor, Bonn, Germany.

Winkelmann, Rainer. 1996. "Employment Prospects and Skill Acquisition of Apprenticeship Trained Workers in Germany." *Industrial and Labor Relations Review* 49(4): 658–72.

World Bank. 2010. *Impact Evaluation of SME Programs in Latin America and Caribbean*. Washington, DC: World Bank.

Ziderman, Adrian. 2003. *Financing Vocational Training in Sub-Saharan Africa*. African Region Human Development Series. Washington, DC: World Bank.

5

Training Programs for the Unemployed, Low-Income, and Low-Skilled Workers

*Jochen Kluve, Friederike Rother, and
María Laura Sánchez Puerta*

In countries around the world, several groups of workers are challenged with finding and keeping jobs or are employed in low-productivity or low-quality jobs. Many find themselves outside the systems of formal education and technical and vocational education and training (TVET) and do not have access to on-the-job training. Some may not fulfill the academic requirements to enter or continue with formal education, while others may be working in informal sector jobs. Yet others may be unemployed or inactive and in critical need of upgrading their skills and improving their employability.

To assist these population groups, several countries have invested in a strategy of training-related active labor market programs (ALMPs) to reduce the risk of unemployment and increase workers' employability and earnings. These programs generally consist of classroom training complemented by subsidies, assistance to find internships or jobs, and counseling for trainees.

The programs can target a diverse set of skilled and unskilled workers and may take many forms. This heterogeneity reflects, in part, the different needs of these groups of workers, as well as the particular labor market challenges that each country faces. This chapter focuses on three core groups:

- *Low-skilled and unskilled workers.* They often work in the informal sector either as self-employed, or wage earners in microenterprises or small formal enterprises. Few are unemployed or transiting between jobs.
- *Skilled youth transitioning from school to work.* These individuals have recently obtained a degree from a university or vocational training program and are searching for a job—often for the first time. Some of them might also be considering opening a business.
- *Skilled workers in transition between jobs.* This third group is composed of workers transitioning between jobs because of idiosyncratic unemployment or major reallocations of labor and capital between sectors or subsectors. Because they are skilled, often the jobs they have left are formal sector jobs.

The objective of this chapter is to take stock of training-related ALMPs for these three groups. The chapter analyzes the rationale for the programs given the main constraints that individuals face with access to training, and it discusses issues regarding design and implementation. The chapter draws from experiences with particular programs and from the small number of overview studies and impact evaluations covering training worldwide. Clearly, these recommendations need to be interpreted with caution given issues of replicability and scalability of particular interventions.

The remainder of the chapter is organized as follows. The first section discusses the main market failures likely affecting the three groups of workers outlined above. The second and third sections review training-related ALMPs worldwide and propose options that could be considered to address the various market failures. The fourth section translates this discussion into a blueprint for designing training systems for disadvantaged workers, focusing on administrative and institutional issues. The last section concludes with a summary of recommendations.

A Typology of Target Populations for Training Programs

As previously discussed, training-related ALMPs can be important to improve the employability of three types of workers: low-skilled or unskilled workers, skilled youth transitioning from school to work, and skilled adult workers transitioning between jobs. This section discusses key characteristics of these groups and their prevalence in labor markets across regions.

Low-Skilled or Unskilled Workers

This target group consists of workers who were early dropouts from the school system, often before having completed secondary education. Despite major improvements in access to education (in a majority of countries enrollment rates in primary education are above 90 percent), large segments of the labor force have less than primary education. In countries like India and Nepal, for instance, 50 percent or more of workers in the labor force do not have a primary education (see figure 5.1).

Regardless of age, most of these workers usually lack sufficient skills to find and keep jobs or to engage in higher-productivity activities. The problem tends to be more severe among younger workers who lack both skills and work experience. In 2008, for instance, youth were nearly three times more likely to be unemployed than adults, resulting in a global average ratio of youth-to-adult unemployment of 2.8 in most regions. In Southeast Asia and the Pacific, the ratio was 4.6 (ILO 2010). The situation is complicated by demographics. African economies, for example, will need to absorb as many as 7 million to 10 million new entrants into the labor force each year over the next decade as a consequence of rapid population growth.[1] Despite improvements in access to education, most of them will continue to be unskilled workers. In fact, recent projections for South Asia show that the share of low-skilled workers in the labor force will drop very slowly even under optimistic scenarios. Figure 5.2 shows decompositions and projections of the labor force by level of education from 2005 to 2030 for India, Bangladesh, Pakistan, and Nepal.[2]

Figure 5.1 Level of Education of the Labor Force by GDP per Capita

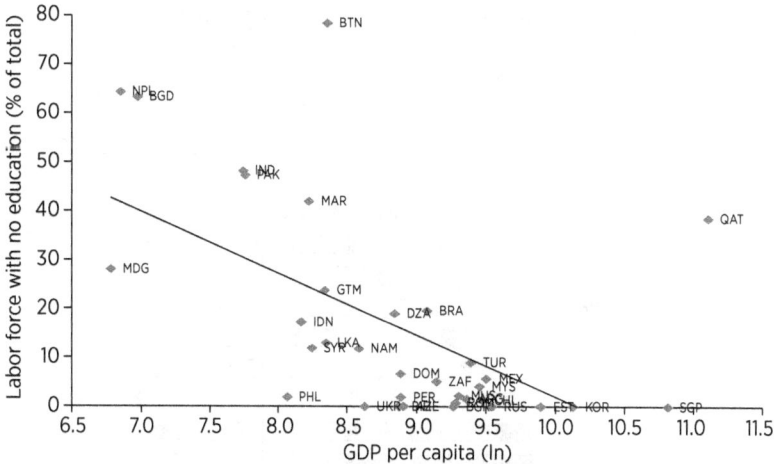

Source: Robalino, Rother, and Newhouse (2011).

Note: ARG = Argentina; AZE = Azerbaijan; BGD = Bangladesh; BGR = Bulgaria; BIH = Bosnia and Herzegovina; BRA = Brazil; BTN = Bhutan; CHL = Chile; DOM = Dominican Republic; DZA = Algeria; EST = Estonia; GTM = Guatemala; IDN = Indonesia; IND = India; KOR = Republic of Korea; LKA = Sri Lanka; MAR = Morocco; MDG = Madagascar; MEX = Mexico; MUS = Mauritius; MYS = Malaysia; NAM = Namibia; NPL = Nepal; PAK = Pakistan; PER = Peru; PHL = Philippines; QAT = Qatar; ROM = Romania; RUS = Russian Federation; SGP = Singapore; SYR = Syrian Arab Republic; TUR = Turkey; UKR = Ukraine; ZAF = South Africa

Figure 5.2 Decompositions and Projections of the Labor Force by Level of Education

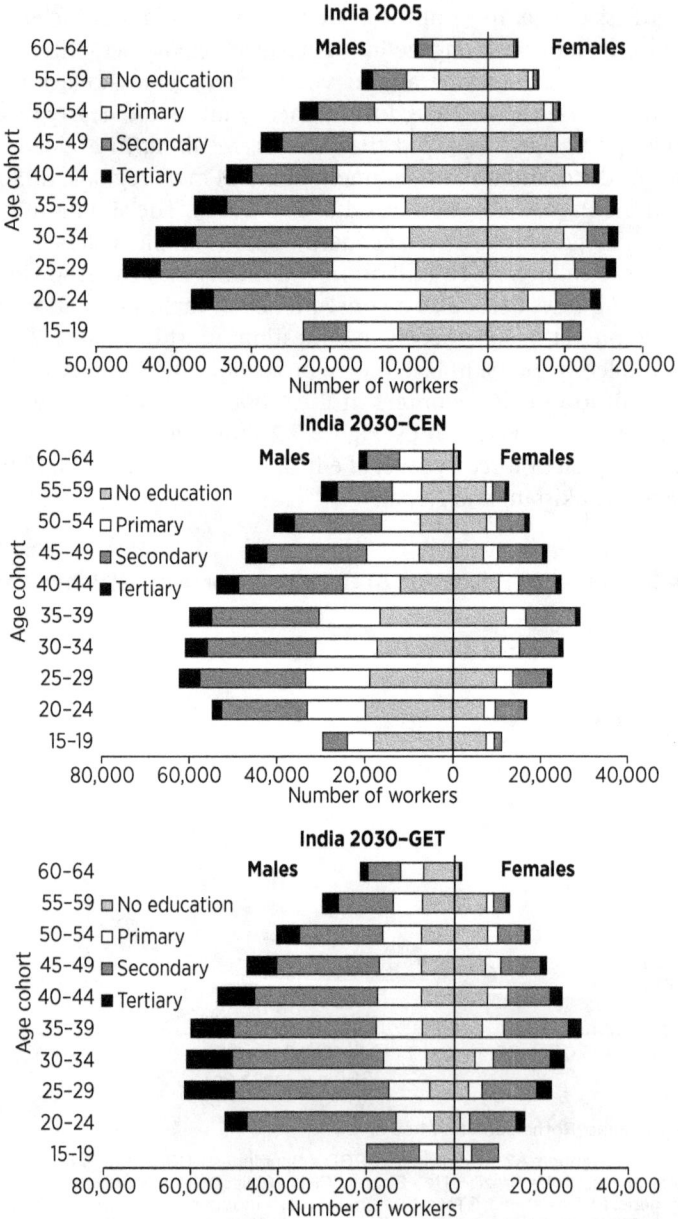

India 2005

India 2030–CEN

India 2030–GET

(Figure continues on next page)

Figure 5.2 *(continued)*

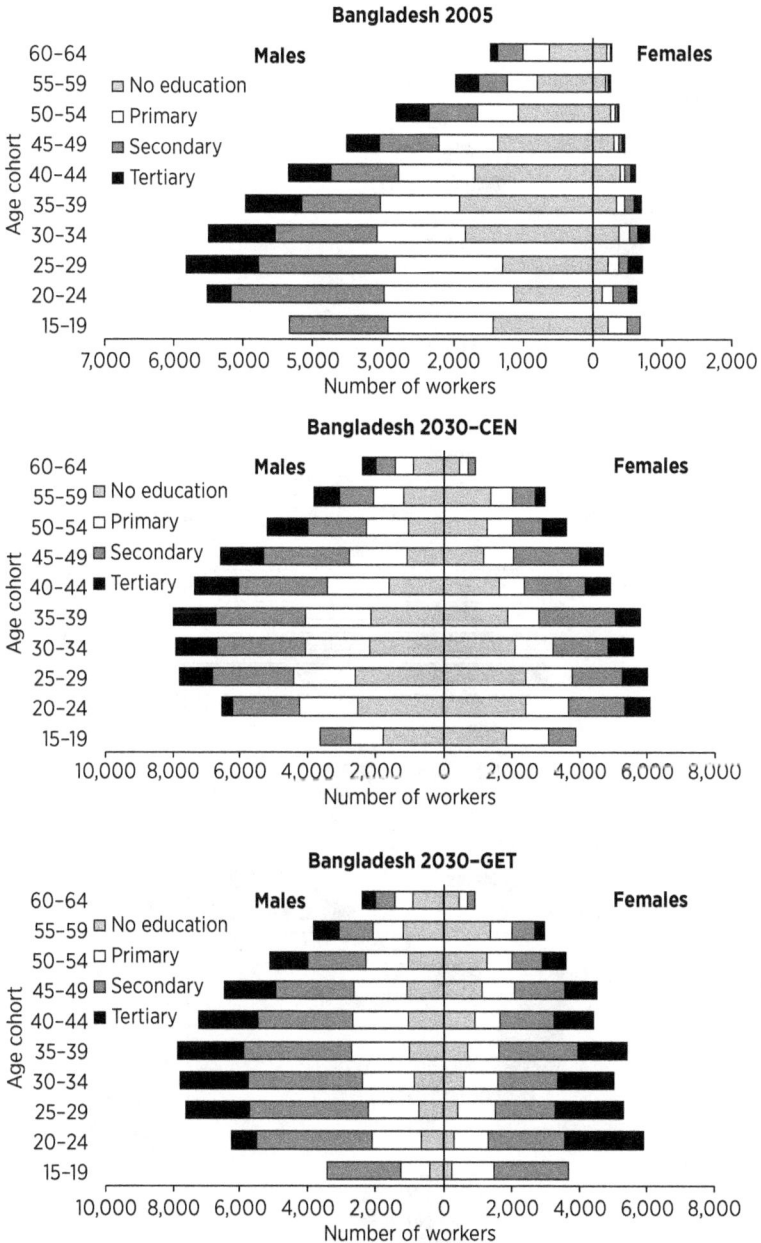

Bangladesh 2005

Males   **Females**

- ☐ No education
- ☐ Primary
- ▨ Secondary
- ■ Tertiary

Age cohort: 60–64, 55–59, 50–54, 45–49, 40–44, 35–39, 30–34, 25–29, 20–24, 15–19

Number of workers: 7,000 6,000 5,000 5,000 3,000 2,000 1,000 0 1,000 2,000

Bangladesh 2030–CEN

Males   **Females**

- ☐ No education
- ☐ Primary
- ▨ Secondary
- ■ Tertiary

Age cohort: 60–64, 55–59, 50–54, 45–49, 40–44, 35–39, 30–34, 25–29, 20–24, 15–19

Number of workers: 10,000 8,000 6,000 4,000 2,000 0 2,000 4,000 6,000 8,000

Bangladesh 2030–GET

Males   **Females**

- ☐ No education
- ☐ Primary
- ▨ Secondary
- ■ Tertiary

Age cohort: 60–64, 55–59, 50–54, 45–49, 40–44, 35–39, 30–34, 25–29, 20–24, 15–19

Number of workers: 10,000 8,000 6,000 4,000 2,000 0 2,000 4,000 6,000 8,000

(Figure continues on next page)

Figure 5.2 *(continued)*

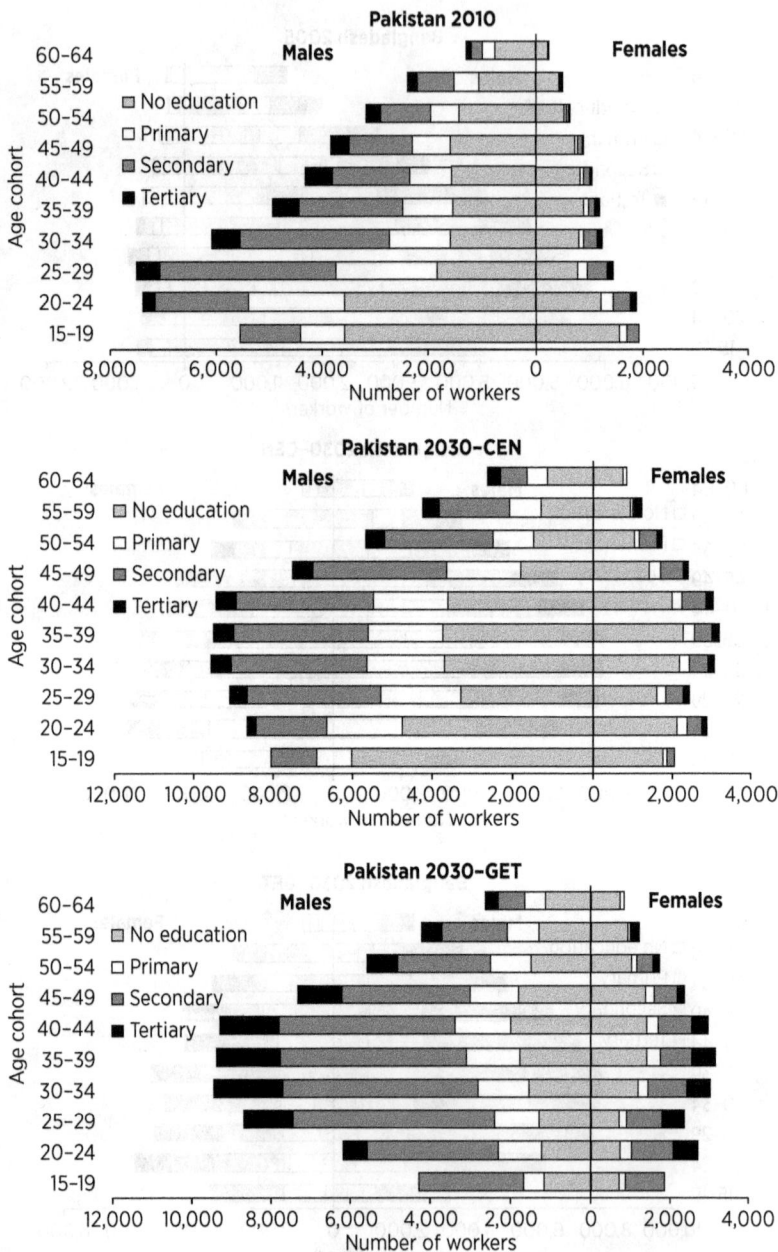

Pakistan 2010

Pakistan 2030–CEN

Pakistan 2030–GET

(Figure continues on next page)

Figure 5.2 (continued)

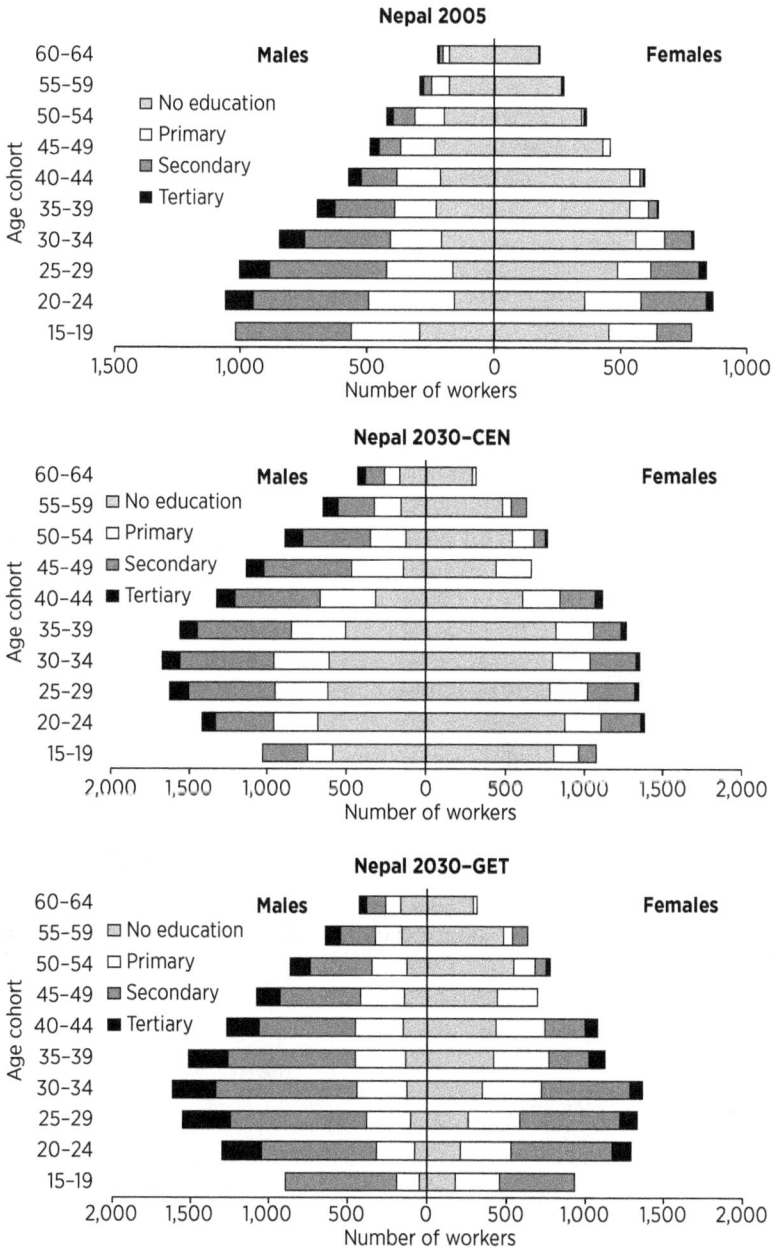

Nepal 2005

Nepal 2030–CEN

Nepal 2030–GET

Source: Di Filippo et al. (2012).

Note: CEN = constant enrollment number; GET = global education trend.

The main market failures affecting unskilled and low-skilled workers are likely to include liquidity constraints, which constitute an almost insurmountable obstacle because these workers hardly have access to financing for any type of investment in training. Coordination failures in the form of low-productivity traps are also a serious threat, because many workers in this group end up working in sectors that rely heavily on unskilled labor. Unskilled and low-skilled workers also typically lack crucial knowledge on the return to investment on skills development and also have little information on where and how to find training opportunities.

Youth Transitioning from School to Work

This group consists of young individuals who have graduated from universities or technical vocational centers but are failing to transition successfully and sustainably into employment. Though skilled in principle, this group frequently experiences high unemployment and long transitions into stable jobs in lower-middle-income countries (see table 5.1). Often, these workers enter the labor market through the informal sector, accepting low-productivity jobs or taking several jobs of short duration.[3] In the case of Latin America, for instance, there is evidence that higher unemployment rates among youth are explained not by longer unemployment spells but by high turnover rates between jobs (see Ribe, Robalino, and Walker 2010).

Skill mismatches can be a factor here, if too many graduates acquire diplomas or specializations for which there is little demand. In Tunisia, for

Table 5.1 Unemployment Rates by Level of Education, Regional Aggregates

	Primary-level education or less (%)	Secondary-level education (%)	Tertiary-level education (%)	Countries in data
Developed economies and EU	10.7	5.7	3.5	32
Central and Southeastern Europe (non-EU) and CIS	11.6	10.1	8.7	13
Asia and Pacific	4.0	6.2	6.1	9
Latin America and the Caribbean	8.6	9.3	5.0	15
Middle East and North Africa	12.1	15.9	13.4	8
Sub-Saharan Africa	27.4	23.2	8.4	3

Source: ILO (2010).

Note: EU = European Union; CIS = Commonwealth of Independent States. Table entries are unweighted averages of those countries for which data by education level are available. Gender and age groups are combined. Values are from the most recent year available, typically 2007.

instance, a growing number of graduates, mainly in business, economics, and finance, are confronted with an insufficient number of salaried jobs. The number of new job seekers with higher education had risen to a total of around 50,000 in 2007, while the absolute number of new salaried jobs for higher education graduates is 20,000 to 30,000 a year. According to a tracer survey by the Tunisian Ministry for the Employment and the Professional Insertion of the Youth, graduates in law, economics, and finance are the least successful in the labor market (World Bank 2009a). In Macedonia, a recent firm survey found that despite high unemployment, it is hard to find workers with the right skills. The most important skills (cognitive and noncongnitive) that employers expect job applicants to possess are a work ethic, overall literacy, and communication skills (World Bank 2010). There are other countries where evidence points to a lack of noncognitive skills of graduates. See Blom and Saeki (2011) for an assessment of employability and the skill set of newly graduated engineers in India.

Such skill mismatches can be caused by various government failures discussed in chapters 2 and 3. In particular, public universities and vocational training centers often lack the incentives or the means to respond to the needs of students and employers.

What factors can preclude access to additional training for this group, if such training can help them find jobs (assuming jobs that pay their reservation wages exist)? Although no data are available to answer this question, it is likely that many of these workers have low expectations about the benefits of additional training. In many cases, they may not even be aware of labor market demands, the skill gaps they have, or the reasons they fail in job interviews. Those who have identified the need for additional training may also face difficulties in identifying the right training provider and financing the training. To a certain extent, this group may also be affected by innovation failures. Workers do not invest sufficiently in training because firms do not innovate and pay higher wages, whereas firms do not innovate because there are not enough skilled workers with the right skills. Finally, in many settings, there simply might not be enough salaried jobs for university or TVET graduates. Self-employment or the creation of small enterprises would be alternatives, but these pursuits also require special skills that are usually not part of the academic curricula. Incentives to invest in training for entrepreneurship will be low if there are barriers to creating successful startups, including difficult access to credit or complicated procedures to open and register a business.

Skilled Workers in Transition between Jobs

In this group we refer mainly to adults who have stable jobs in the formal or informal sector (for example, self-employed workers) and skills that allow them to earn average or below-average wages (namely, middle-class workers). These workers can become unemployed because of idiosyncratic or covariate risks—a recession that can involve sectoral reallocations of capital and labor. Contrary to what one can expect, both of these types of transitions are relatively frequent. In Brazil, for instance, the risk of unemployment among formal and informal employees ranges between 5 and 15 percent per month (figure 5.3). Workers in informal activities seem to face even higher unemployment risks—probably because informal production units are smaller and less able to accommodate a fall in demand and/or because they are not affected by unions and labor regulations.

In developed economies, higher education levels are typically strongly correlated with a lower risk of unemployment and shorter unemployment spells. However, such a correlation is not necessarily found in low- and middle-income countries. In Latin America and the Caribbean, for instance, in all countries but five—Argentina, Costa Rica, El Salvador, Uruguay, and the República Bolivariana de Venezuela—unemployment rates are higher for those with medium levels of education than for those with low levels. In half the countries, unemployment rates for workers with higher education are also higher than those for unskilled workers (Ribe, Robalino, and Walker 2012). In addition, for educated workers in Latin America and the

Figure 5.3 Unemployment Risks for Formal and Informal Sector Workers in Brazil

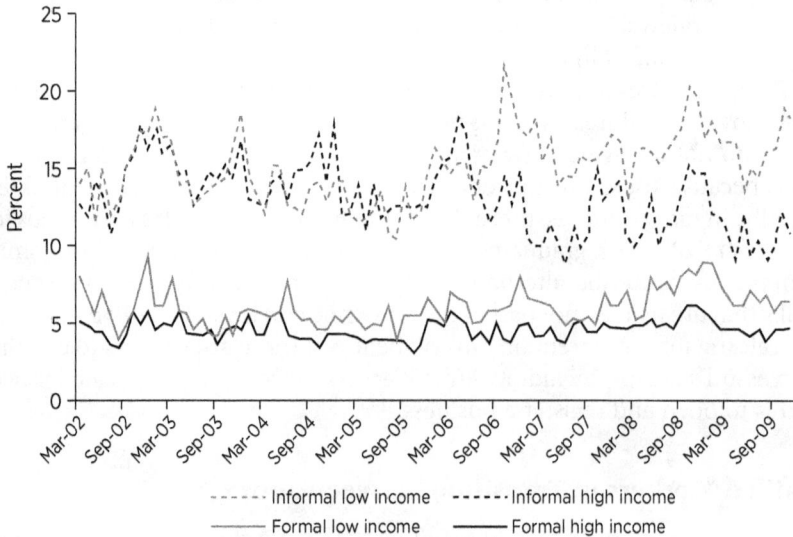

Source: Based on Ribe, Robalino, and Walker (2012, chapter 2).

Caribbean, longer unemployment durations go hand-in-hand with higher unemployment rates. Long durations can be explained by a lower ratio of vacancies relative to the stock of unemployed workers, but also by the (in)efficiency of the matching process. In the case of skilled workers, in particular, longer durations can be the result of skill mismatches and high reservation wages.

Because these workers are not low-income individuals and have skills and work experience—those in the formal sector can even receive unemployment benefits or severance pay—one would expect them to understand and finance training needs while in transition between jobs. They might seek such training if unemployment spells are short and the training consists of a few hours spent learning an upgraded version of a given software program or interviewing techniques. In this case, the role of the government could be limited to ensuring that there is enough information about the quality of different training providers. However, as previously seen, unemployment spells can be long, particularly during recessions, and training needs may be more demanding, including learning new skills. Workers in this situation may also start to face liquidity constraints as unemployment benefits and savings run out. They may also experience a depreciation of their skills. Displaced workers may lack information about available retraining programs and the skills that are in demand in the labor market.

Many countries that are members of the Organisation for Economic Co-operation and Development (OECD) have thus adopted strategies of immediate activation of unemployed workers through job-search assistance, counseling, and monitoring. However, when activation does not lead skilled adults back into employment, this group is targeted by training interventions (often short term) to avoid depreciation of skills and facilitate lifelong learning.

Table 5.2 presents an overview of the training market failures that each group faces, along with suggested interventions for them, which will then be discussed in further detail.

Training-Related Active Labor Market Policies around the World

Many studies have highlighted the worldwide popularity and importance of training programs relative to other ALMPs.[4] Most training interventions target unskilled and low-skilled workers. Table 5.3 is based on a recent inventory of evaluations of such programs (Fares and Puerto 2009) and shows the distribution of training programs by target group.[5] The first part of the table shows the number of programs specifically targeting one of the three previously defined groups. Note that among programs for low-skilled

Table 5.2 Suggested Policy Interventions by Target Group and Training Market Failures

Target group	Training market failure	Suggested intervention
Low-skilled and unskilled workers	• Imperfection in capital markets: credit constraints • Coordination failures: low-productivity trap • Limited information on returns to training and training provision	• Training subsidies, possibly taking the form of vouchers • Large-scale training programs in particular sectors • Counseling services and job-search assistance
Skilled youth in school-to-work transition	• Imperfection in capital markets: credit constraints • Coordination failures: innovation externalities • Low expected rates of return for investments in skills useful for self-employment • Limited information on labor market demands and the quality of training providers	• Access to credit or student loans • Large-scale training programs focused on high value–added sectors • Counseling services and job-search assistance • Access to retraining and self-employment training
Skilled workers in job-to-job transition	• Imperfection in capital markets: credit constraints • Limited information on training provision and demand for skills	• Credit • Counseling services and job-search assistance • Access to retraining and self-employment training

Source: World Bank.

Table 5.3 Incidence of Evaluations of Training Programs by Target Group

Programs serving one target population	Number of programs	% of total
(i) Unskilled or low-skilled workers	199	0.59
among which: specifically youths	176	0.53
among which: specifically adults	18	
(ii) Youths in transition school-work	33	0.10
(iii) Workers in transition job-to-job	50	0.15
Programs targeted across groups		
(i) + (ii) Youths across skill groups	42	0.13
(i) + (iii) Adults across skill groups	6	0.02
(ii) + (iii) Skilled youths and adults	5	0.01
Total	335	

Source: Fares and Puerto (2009).

Note: The data originally comprised 345 evaluations of training interventions, of which 335 could be classified according to the target groups defined here.

workers, the majority are designed to assist disadvantaged youth, the group most strongly in need of effective skill development strategies. The bottom part of the table indicates that several training programs exist that are more broadly designed and cover more than one of the target groups. For instance, many training interventions target both unskilled and skilled youth ("Youths across skill groups"), indicating that the more comprehensively targeted programs also focus on youth training.

Figure 5.4 displays the corresponding breakdown of evaluated training programs by region for the group of low-skilled workers. Several interesting patterns emerge. First, and not surprisingly, the inventory database is biased toward OECD countries.[6] Second, all regions—with the exception of the Middle East and North Africa—have training programs for unskilled or low-skilled workers. Latin America, in particular, has substantial experience with training programs targeting this group. Also, within regions, coverage is broad. Programs range, for instance, from training low-skilled adults in Poland, to increasing skill development opportunities for dropout youth in Albania, to promoting girls' education and employment in Togo.

Figure 5.4 Regional Breakdown of Evaluations of Training Programs for Low-Skilled and Unskilled Workers

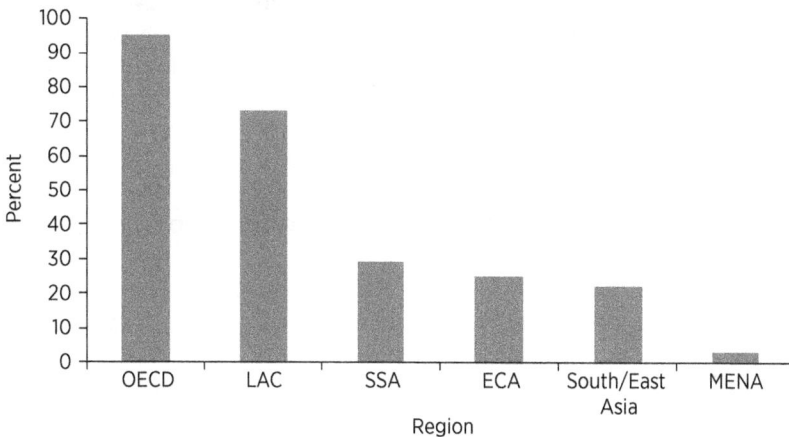

Source: Fares and Puerto (2009).

Note: The figure shows the number of program evaluations in the Fares and Puerto (2009) inventory. The distribution covers a total of 249 training program evaluations. It includes 199 interventions specifically for low-skilled workers, as well as 42 youth programs and 6 adult programs covering all skill groups.

OECD = Organisation for Economic Co-operation and Development; LAC = Latin America and the Caribbean; SSA = Sub-Saharan Africa; ECA = Europe and Central Asia; MENA = Middle East and North Africa.

The training evaluations inventory suggests that training for low-skilled and unskilled workers seems to play a minor role in Middle Eastern and North African countries, but in fact there are many training programs in the region. However, these programs are very recent, and most have not been evaluated (see Angel-Urdinola, Semlali, and Brodmann 2010 and the discussion in the next section). Hence, the existing body of evidence on training—in particular for youth transitioning from school to work—needs to be augmented substantially over the next few years with experiences from the Middle East and North Africa.

The evidence for training programs targeted at the other two groups—youth transitioning from school to work and workers in transition between jobs—comes mostly from OECD countries, in particular North America and Western Europe. Experiences from Eastern European and Central Asian countries include several entrepreneurship training programs for educated youth in Turkey and a workplace internship program for recent Romanian graduates.[7] Although training programs in Sub-Saharan Africa almost exclusively target unskilled and low-skilled youth, training programs for self-employment among the small group of educated youth exist in the Central African Republic, Rwanda, and Senegal (Brewer 2004; World Bank 1999).

For skilled adults in involuntary job-to-job transitions, most countries in Eastern Europe and Central Asia—including Bulgaria, the Czech Republic, Romania, the Russian Federation, and the Slovak Republic—have implemented retraining programs during the restructuring of their economies in the past two decades (Benus et al. 2004). Similarly, training programs for workers affected by mass layoffs because of sectoral restructuring were implemented in East Asia and Latin America.

Addressing Market Failures in the Provision of Training

The following subsections discuss core features of how training can be designed and promoted for each of the three target groups. In each case, the focus is on lower-middle-income countries. The discussion builds on a review of international experiences with the design and implementation of training programs and corresponding impact evaluations.

Training for Unskilled or Low-Skilled Workers

Training programs for unskilled workers generally focus on providing cognitive and behavioral skills in addition to relevant technical skills. International experiences suggest that these programs should have three main complementary components: (i) subsidies to finance all or part of the training costs, (ii) counseling, and (iii) job-search assistance or support for self-employment. Subsidies address credit constraints and information problems by providing incentives to acquire skills given potentially high discount rates or expected low rates of returns to training. In light of the characteristics of the group, full subsidies rather than credit arrangements such as lending schemes are likely more appropriate.

The other two components also play a crucial role in designing training for this vulnerable group. Counseling workers adds value by providing information about the potential benefits from training and the specific types of training that best suit individual capacities. Such counseling expands the information available to workers and can increase their expected rates of return to training. This effort is also accomplished through job-search assistance and support for self-employment, which essentially link workers to jobs that will actually use the skills acquired. Subsidies may also be needed to overcome low-productivity traps for this group of workers. Indeed, jobs using more skilled labor may not be available (support for job-search assistance alone would not work). But jobs could follow if there is a critical mass of skilled labor. As previously discussed, the government can help to address this coordination failure.

Three types of training programs can be considered given the specific needs and market failures facing unskilled and low-skilled workers. These programs include demand-driven training programs, composed of subsidies and employment services (such as counseling and job-search assistance) and training and self-employment support, both mostly targeted at youth, as well as training programs for beneficiaries of public works.

Training systems incorporating wage subsidies and employment services

Several countries have implemented comprehensive training programs that offer a package of services for low-skilled youth including counseling, training, job-search assistance, and workplace internships. A core feature of such a training system is that it relies on market signals: qualified private firms, nongovernmental organizations (NGOs), and public institutions provide training and other services on a competitive basis. To be eligible for funds, providers are required to line up internships and identify the types of skills that are needed. Although the current programs have focused on youth, they could also target unskilled and low-income adults. These programs can be designed to respond to specific demands from workers or public-private partnerships to train a given group of young people to work in a given sector.

Most of the programs implemented so far are in Latin America and the Caribbean and are known as the *Jóvenes* programs. Countries include Argentina *(Proyecto Joven)*, Chile *(Chile Joven)*, Colombia *(Jóvenes en Acción)*, the Dominican Republic *(Juventud y Empleo)*, Panama *(ProCaJoven)*, and

Peru *(ProJoven)*. The *Jóvenes* programs have been typically accompanied by impact evaluations assessing their effectiveness (see box 5.1). In general, the programs have had positive effects on employment and earnings and

---

BOX 5.1

Benefits and Costs of the *Jóvenes* Training Programs for Unskilled Youths in Latin America

Impact evaluations of the *Jóvenes* programs have generally produced positive results for program participants in at least two variables of interest: the beneficiaries' chances of job placement and the quality of their jobs as measured by salary, benefits, and type of contract. Table B5.1.1 summarizes these results.

Table B5.1.1 Impact and Cost-Benefit Analysis of the *Jóvenes* Programs in Latin America

Country	Increase in employment	Increase in earnings	Cost-benefit analysis
Argentina: *Proyecto Joven*	10% (women)	10% (monthly wages)	NPV > 0 if 12 years of positive benefits (DR = 5%)
Chile: *Chile Joven*	21% (individuals younger than 21 years old, women)	26%	—
Colombia: *Jóvenes en Acción*	5% (women)	18% (men), 35% (women)	IRR = 4.5% (men), 13.5% (women)
Dominican Republic: *Juventud y Empleo*	Not significant	10%	NPV > 0 if 2 years of positive benefits (DR = inflation)
Peru: *ProJoven*	6%	18% (hourly)	NPV > 0 if 7 years of positive benefits (DR = 5%) IRR > 4%
Panama: *ProCaJoven*	10–12% (women and Panama City residents)	Not significant	NPV > 0 if 1 year of positive benefits (IR = DR)

Sources: Card et al. 2010; Ibarraran and Rosas 2009; Jaramillo 2006; Puerto 2007.
Note: — = not available; DR: discount rate; IR: interest rate; IRR: internal rate of return; NPV = net present value.

(Box continues on next page)

BOX 5.1 *(continued)*

The evaluations have shown that women and younger beneficiaries have higher rates of return from participating in these programs than do men and older cohorts. Given their low cost per trainee and their positive effect on employment and earnings, nearly all such programs have a positive ratio of benefits to costs, even without considering any positive externalities such as reduced risky behavior.

Estimates of unit cost for the *Jóvenes* programs range from the upper US$600s to about US$2,000 per participant served. Active private sector participation represents significant savings to the government when firms cover the costs of on-the-job training. Likewise, the bidding mechanism to select training institutions has shown to be an efficient instrument to set competitive training prices, ensuring high quality and low cost. *ProJoven* in Peru is one of the few ongoing programs that has had continuously measured costs and benefits since its implementation in 1996. Direct costs are nearly two-thirds of total costs, as can be shown by breaking total expenses into training, financial incentives, and beneficiaries' opportunity cost.[a] Across *Jóvenes* programs, *Proyecto Joven* in Argentina reported relatively high costs, which became barely affordable for the government, hampering its sustainability.[b]

Source: World Bank.
Note: a. Direct costs (per beneficiary) are US$316.20 for training and US$118.00 for stipend and insurance. Opportunity costs (per beneficiary) are US$96.50 during the training phase (three months) and US$160.70 during the internship phase (three months) and consist of the average monthly salaries before and after training, respectively. b. The program ended in 2001 and was replaced by smaller programs (such as *Programa Capacitar*), which inherited the demand-driven model but were implemented on a much smaller scale.

are cost-effective. The specific programs vary, but most of them follow a model first piloted in Chile. Disadvantaged young people are identified using, for example, out-of-work statistics, socioeconomic data, and poverty mapping. The main criteria in targeting are income levels, education, gender, and regional coverage (within countries), and participants are poor youth with low levels of education—high school at most—who are unemployed or underemployed.[8]

There is anecdotal evidence that the main factors for success for these types of interventions are (i) competition for providers and (ii) internships that help to map the demand for skills. Beyond technical skills, the programs provide life-skill training focusing mainly on problem-solving skills, correct workplace behavior, conflict management, job-search techniques, and building of self-esteem.

Training and support for self-employment

Entrepreneurship programs for unskilled or low-skilled youth consist of training that targets those workers inclined to become self-employed. Successful programs package technical training with training in business skills (for example, mentoring or bookkeeping); literacy; and life skills (including counseling to improve risk behavior). They can also be linked to other business services, including access to credit. In lower-middle-income countries with very large informal sectors, the training may be targeted to craftworkers and their apprentices, and the focus may be on using improved production techniques that are better adapted to market demands. This type of entrepreneurship program for unskilled youth has several advantages: it provides trainees with flexible and demand-driven skills, it is self-regulating, it is typically inexpensive, and it does not require many skills or previous experience from the apprentice. The concept, however, is broader and can also apply to middle-income countries. The general goal is to help first-time job seekers transit into self-employment and self-employed workers to increase their productivity or to diversify into higher-value-added activities.

Several programs of this type have been implemented in Africa.[9] For example, the Benin Support Project concentrates on the development of on-the-job vocational training (see box 5.2). This program focuses on the informal sector, which employs 41 percent of the labor force in Benin, and combines several additional innovative features. For instance, the project has facilitated the institutional development of a marketplace for training

---

BOX 5.2

Benin Support Project for the Development of On-the-Job Vocational Training

The Benin Support Project for the development of on-the-job vocational training focused on the informal sector. The program was specifically designed to address the shortage of qualified labor caused by low educational attainment and limited access to vocational training outside the formal education system. The importance of this objective is highlighted by the fact that 66 percent of adults in Benin are illiterate, whereas on-the-job vocational training programs are rare (less than 1 percent of the labor force currently receives on-the-job training). The program aimed at increasing the availability, quality, and cost-effectiveness of labor force training to people working in the informal sector,

(Box continues on next page)

BOX 5.2 *(continued)*

including women, and relied on several innovative elements, including a strong demand focus in which the government refrained from prescribing the content of training courses. Moreover, the program supported the development and implementation of a monitoring and evaluation system in the public sector, combined with a private sector capacity-building dimension to strengthen the organizational, managerial, and strategic aspects of program management and training delivery.

Over five years, the training program reached 20,000 beneficiaries, mostly informal sector workers and women. In the agricultural sector, training components aimed at increasing the competitiveness of small producers and improving their purchasing power. For craftworkers and their apprentices, training components focused on (i) strengthening productivity of microenterprises, including enhancing capacity for the adoption of improved production technology to better respond to market demand, while encouraging a transition to the modern sector; (ii) improving employment stability; and (iii) increasing workers' revenues. About 40 percent of the project financing (US$2.1 million) was dedicated to capacity building for the institutions involved in the project.

Evaluation of the program by the World Bank (2006) aimed at estimating net effects via a control group approach and covered four dimensions: placement rates, effect on earnings, effect on employment, and responsiveness to market changes. The evidence suggested that the Benin project resulted in enhanced availability, quality, and cost-effectiveness of vocational training and that it was successful in targeting the informal sector and women. The estimates showed that training had a positive effect on earnings, living conditions, and employment of participants. Graduates of the program were contacted annually to follow up on their job status and history, earnings, and acquisition and application of skills (tracer study). To ensure consistency of project objectives with labor market needs over time, researchers used annual reports that consolidated all relevant information on Benin's labor market and, in particular, on the types of skills that were identified as critical for the high-growth sectors, to guide decisions on the allocation of financing and on specific training components.

Source: World Bank (2006).

---

proposals, leading to a more competitive selection process. In addition, it analyzes specific training needs and skill mismatches in selected areas, leading to more targeted training curricula so that participants completing the program better match the demand and supply in the labor market. Finally, constant supervision of the effects of the program's different subcomponents has helped policy makers select the right portfolio of interventions and adjust them when needed.

Many other programs for unskilled youth combine training with business skills or other services, addressing the needs of the target population. For example, the Adolescent Girls Initiative project (a World Bank–led initiative covering Afghanistan, Liberia, Nigeria, Rwanda, and South Africa) combines skill training with job-placement assistance or with business development services and microcredits targeting young female entrepreneurs (see World Bank 2010). Typically, the skill development component is comprehensive, comprising technical and life skills as well as providing entrepreneurial support through credits and mentoring. Some programs even include psychological counseling and empowerment (see World Bank 2008).

Combining training with public works

Many of the unskilled adults are long-term recipients of welfare or unemployment assistance. Recently, some countries have been linking these transfers to training programs that help beneficiaries improve their employability and eventually graduate from social assistance. Access to the transfers can be linked to other conditions, such as saving part of the earnings and eventually obtaining credit to begin an activity.

One example of this type of program is Argentina's *Jefes y Jefas*, which required participants to work or participate in training or education activities for 4 to 6 hours a day (no less than 20 hours a week) in exchange for payment (see box 5.3). Similarly, the Rural Maintenance Program in Bangladesh targets women and requires program participants to attend training to help them generate income and learn skills (World Bank 2005). In addition, these women must save part of their wages on a regular basis (participants are paid Tk 51—approximately US$0.70—per day with a forced savings of Tk 10). The strategy is to create new microentrepreneurs with adequate skill training and seed capital from the forced savings (Hashemi and Rosenberg 2006). The program provides year-round employment to approximately 42,000 destitute rural women for a period of up to four years. Their task is to maintain 84,000 kilometers of earthen, rural roads around their village.

The Expanded Public Works Program in South Africa provides training opportunities beyond the skills acquired on the job to prepare participants for possible longer-term employment, self-employment, and further education or training (del Ninno, Subbarao, and Milazzo 2009). This program targets adult workers as well as youth. For example, youth employed as manual laborers on a labor-intensive road project may be offered training in unrelated building skills such as bricklaying, if there is demand for such skills in the labor market. The average number of training days varies from 10 days in the environmental sector to 30 days for those participating in

---

BOX 5.3

Training and Public Works in Argentina and El Salvador

Argentina's main social policy response to the severe economic crisis of 2002 was the program *Jefes y Jefas* (Heads of Household Program). The program aimed to provide direct income support for families with dependents whose heads of household had become unemployed because of the crisis, combined with a training component. Rigorous impact evaluations for the period from 2002 to 2003 used counterfactual comparisons based on a matched subset of applicants not yet receiving the program and on panel data spanning the crisis. Researchers found that the program reduced aggregate unemployment, though it attracted as many people into the workforce from inactivity as it did people who would have been otherwise unemployed. Although there was substantial leakage to formally ineligible families and incomplete coverage of those eligible, the program did partially compensate many of those affected by the crisis. The program prevented 10 percent of the beneficiaries from falling into extreme poverty, and long-term benefits for participants included the acquisition of useful skills and better job prospects.

Among the most recent of these types of programs, the Temporary Income Support Program of El Salvador emphasizes the provision of "soft" skills in addition to technical skills. This program, also known as PATI (*Programa del Apoyo Temporal al Ingreso*), looks to guarantee a minimum level of income to extremely poor urban families, as well as provide a labor market experience at the municipal level. Unlike traditional income support programs, PATI includes an innovative training component that aims to enhance beneficiaries' technical skills and soft skills useful in the labor market. The government expects to preferentially target female household heads, as well as young individuals between 16 and 24 years old living in urban areas.[a] An impact evaluation is being designed to closely assess the effects of the program on beneficiaries' welfare and employability as well as the effects of the life skills training component.

Sources: Galasso and Ravallion (2004); World Bank (2009b).
Note: a. Similar programs in other countries are specifically targeted to youth, such as the World Bank youth projects in Kenya and Papua New Guinea.

---

social activities. To the extent possible, all training must result in some type of accredited certification. This important training design feature will be explained in the blueprint later in this chapter.

Training for Youth Transitioning from School to Work

The programs that have been implemented to support this group usually center around three main components: (i) assessment of acquired competencies, (ii) provision of information and counseling on where to find jobs (including as a self-employed worker) and what skills are required, and (iii) training or retraining to transfer those skills. An important difference with these programs is that they are targeted to a group of workers with presumably higher reservation wages who are looking for jobs of higher value added than those sought by unskilled workers. Because they are graduates of universities or vocational training centers, these youth have skill gaps that can be more difficult to identify. For instance, in Tunisia, many graduates in economics have difficulty finding jobs. Is it because there are not enough jobs for economists, in which case individuals would need to start a new career that perhaps involves a shorter training period? Or is it because graduates may lack some behavioral skills (including those needed to succeed in interviews), even if there are jobs? Or is it because graduates failed to acquire the core skills economists are supposed to have (for example, modeling skills and a good mastery of econometrics)? Addressing the last problem could be difficult. It could involve learning specific technical skills linked to the main profession that will depend on the more general skills of the graduates, such as mathematics and calculus.

A training system is conceivable in which the majority of these interventions are handled by employment service offices (public or private), a core design component in the training system blueprint (described later in this chapter). These employment offices would assess workers' skills and aptitudes, identify work opportunities, and advise on training needs—including preparing a business plan and obtaining other skills to facilitate transition into self-employment. As is the case with training for low-skilled workers, training for this group can be provided through private or public institutions that arrange internships with employers or prepare participants for self-employment. An important difference for this group, however, is that part of the financing of the program could come from the young graduates themselves, who internalize most of the benefits from training. Governments can, for instance, open credit lines to finance the cost of training, workplace internship, or start-up credit, which participants later repay once they start to receive salaries or make profits with their businesses. To address innovation failures (see chapter 2), the government can also consider training for large groups of graduates in certain professions to work in particular sectors. This training would be designed with strong involvement from the private sector.

High unemployment rates among university graduates in many countries have raised concerns about whether it is realistic to rely on wage employment to absorb all the youth transitioning from school to work. Even with the right set of skills (and no public sector distortions to cue for jobs), not enough jobs may be available. As a result, several countries have focused on training programs to facilitate transitions from school into self-employment.[10] Although not every skilled young person is suited for self-employment, many can benefit from these programs.

One approach to training for self-employment is the corporate mentoring of students in universities and vocational training centers. This type of training takes place at an early stage, provides students with basic business skills and information on private sector skill requirements, and may even establish contacts between entrepreneurs and graduates for potential future collaboration. Similar interventions can be implemented during the final years of university education. A common approach is to provide training to support the preparation of a business plan. The best business plans can then be rewarded by further assistance—through financing, mentoring, and training—during the actual incubation of the business project.

An example of this type of program is Turkey's Entrepreneurship for Youth project. The program offers eight months of entrepreneurship training, at the end of which graduates draft their own business plans. The most feasible business plans then receive funding from the Entrepreneurship Board. A similar program is the Youth Enterprise and Capacity Building program in Senegal, although the training period to prepare the business plan is much shorter (just two weeks). Selected participants are then eligible for a small loan of up to US$900 from the YMCA (Young Men's Christian Association), the Micro Lending Agency, and other organizations. The program follows up on projects and continues to offer participants advice after incubation of their business. Similar programs have been implemented in the Middle East and North Africa. In summary, these programs try to build self-employment capacity among graduates and to generate better matches of graduates and private sector needs. Qualitative evaluations have shown positive results (see box 5.4).

Training for Skilled Workers in Transition between Jobs

As previously discussed, workers in this group may benefit from training to prevent the depreciation of their skills, to upgrade their skills in a given field (that is, by learning to use the latest technologies), and to switch career paths. Governments would intervene mainly to address liquidity constraints and to provide information about skill requirements and training providers. The resulting programs would be quite similar to the ones for skilled youth and would include assessing workers' existing skills, providing information and counseling on where to find jobs and what new skills are required, and training to upgrade their skills.

BOX 5.4

Promoting Self-Employment Training in the Middle East and North Africa

The *Injaz al-Arab* program aims at bridging the gap between educational outcomes and private sector needs in Middle Eastern and North African countries. Its objective is to enhance the skills of youth entering the job market as employees or entrepreneurs. The program proceeds by creating a public-private partnership—typically between the country's ministry of education and leading companies from the private sector—and bringing private sector mentors into public schools and universities to provide students with practical business-related skills. *Injaz al-Arab* first started in 2004 and operates in 12 countries in the Middle East and North Africa. The training consists of work readiness, entrepreneurship, and financial literacy. Over six semesters, one hour per week, students learn skills such as managing budgets, following stocks in the newspaper, and writing business plans.

This in-classroom training is integrated into regular school hours. Activities include setting up community projects and learning business basics, such as competition, marketing, and support from the banking sector for businesses and industries. The program is comprehensive, targeting male and female youth from grade 7 to university level. It includes urban and rural youth of all income groups.

Because the mentors are corporate volunteers, the intervention is inexpensive. It has achieved sizable coverage. Since 2004, more than 500,000 students across 12 countries have attended the program, and about 10,000 volunteers were engaged. An external impact evaluation found that, whereas there is heterogeneity by course type and country, participants consistently reported that *Injaz al-Arab* played a significant role in their lives. They also strongly gained in their confidence in their own abilities. Moreover, *Injaz al-Arab* students had up to 50 percent more subject-matter knowledge than students in a comparison group.

A similar type of intervention is Turning Theses into Enterprises, a program recently introduced in Tunisia for university graduates. The program aims to foster entrepreneurship among this group and better align graduates' skills with private sector needs. The objective of the program is to lower unemployment among graduates. Under the program, final-year university students can write their theses on an enterprise project—essentially a business plan—and participate in a business plan competition. Students receive feedback on the business plan from external coaches as well as two weeks' training on enterprise start-up by the Tunisian Agency of Labor and Self-Employment. At the end of

(Box continues on next page)

BOX 5.4 *(continued)*

the year, an external jury ranks the finalized theses—which are detailed business plans—and the top 50 receive a monetary reward along with further external coaching for actual project incubation. The program was implemented during the academic year 2009/10 by the World Bank, the Ministry of Labor, and the Ministry of Economy. A total of 1,920 students across Tunisia registered for the program (approximately 10 percent of final-year university students in the country), and an impact evaluation based on a randomized controlled trial is under way.

Sources: Angel-Urdinola, Semlali, and Brodmann (2010); World Bank (2009a). See also the *Injaz al-Arab* website at http://www.injazalarab.org.

Skills retraining

The significance of skill retraining interventions can be noted in case studies in Eastern Europe and Central Asia. In that region, most countries experienced a process of structural change, with important reallocations of capital and labor across sectors. Thus, they placed much emphasis on retraining during the 1990s, even though use of such policies has generally declined since (see box 5.5). An overview of the experiences with training during the transition across countries indicates that the majority of interventions were important and effective (Betcherman, Olivas, and Dar 2004; Card, Kluve, and Weber 2010).

BOX 5.5

Training and Retraining for Displaced Workers in Romania

Some Central and Eastern European countries underwent the transition process from centrally planned economy to market economy in less than a decade—notably the Czech Republic, Estonia, and Poland. However, transition has been slow in Romania. Other countries in the region—Albania, Bulgaria, Moldova, and Ukraine—also share the slow pace of transition along with characteristics such as high poverty levels and the importance of the rural sector. In the 1990s, open unemployment reached about 10 percent in Romania, though this figure likely

(Box continues on next page)

BOX 5.5 *(continued)*

understates the real problem with displaced workers. A policy approach of limiting job destruction by adjusting real wages, combined with various early retirement programs, pushed workers out of the labor force and into low-productivity jobs, primarily in subsistence agriculture and the urban informal sector. Between 1989 and 2001, the share of agricultural employment relative to total employment grew from 28 to 42 percent.

Against this background, in 1997 the Romanian government launched a set of ALMPs on a significant scale, facilitated by a loan agreement with the World Bank. Training and retraining programs for displaced workers were offered, along with self-employment assistance, public employment programs, and job-search assistance. Public employment agencies handled program design and implementation, and the actual service provision was contracted out to public and private service providers. The training programs consisted of vocational training, general education and literacy, and skill building. The program targeted displaced workers who lacked these skills or needed to learn new, marketable ones. The maximum duration was nine months, and service providers had to agree to a negotiated job-placement rate of at least 60 percent.

An impact evaluation of the program covers participants enrolling in 1999 and shows that training had positive effects. It increased the earnings of participants and reduced the likelihood that they would receive unemployment benefits. The self-employment assistance and job-search assistance programs also proved effective, though the effects of the training program were larger. Targeting of the program worked well, as the population served was indeed displaced workers. Training participants had an average of 22 years of previous work experience at the time of enrollment, 94 percent had at least a secondary school degree, and 30 percent had a higher degree. Until 2001, 2,892 clients were served with training, of which 1,197 (41.39 percent) were subsequently placed. Although unit placement costs were somewhat higher for training than for the other successful programs (about US$130 relative to US$100 for self-employment assistance and US$60 for job search assistance), the training placement rate was more than twice as high.

Source: Rodríguez-Planas and Benus (2010).

Similarly, training programs for workers affected by mass layoffs because of sectoral restructuring were implemented in China and Hong Kong SAR, China (Bidani, Goh, and O'Leary 2002; Chan and Suen 2000). In Latin America and the Caribbean, Mexico's Job-Training Program for Unemployed Workers (*Programa de Becas de Capacitación para Trabajadores Desempleados,* or Probecat), started in 1984, is likely the most prominent example. Probecat comprises short-term, demand-driven courses, which are complemented by internships that emphasize on-the-job training. Private firms offer both the courses and the internships. Subsequent to the Mexican experience, variants of Probecat have been implemented in El Salvador and Honduras.

Generally, training programs for workers in job-to-job transition can be incorporated into the broader context of activation policies for the unemployed, as has increasingly been done in OECD countries (OECD 2007). These policies share several core components, such as early intervention during the unemployment spell by the employment services (which are typically public), frequent contact between job seekers and employment services, regular reporting and monitoring of job-search activity, establishment of individual action plans, and referral to training programs (or other ALMPs) to prevent depreciation of skills and increase employability. Service delivery of these components has typically been integrated into one-stop centers. One of the best examples of this policy is the United Kingdom's New Deal for Young People (box 5.6).

BOX 5.6

The New Deal for Young People in the United Kingdom

In 1998, the U.K. government launched the New Deal for Young People (NDYP) as a key element of its welfare-to-work strategy. The objective is to help unemployed youth find work and increase their employability. Participation is mandatory for all 18- to 24-year-olds who have been receiving unemployment benefits (the jobseeker's allowance) for six months or more. Within the NDYP program, youth first go through a period of job-search assistance before being offered training or alternative programs. Initially, individuals enter a gateway stage during which they are assigned personal advisers who give them extensive assistance with their job searches. If the unemployed youth are unable to find unsubsidized jobs and remain on benefit receipt at the end of the gateway (at most four months), one of four New Deal options follows: (i) full-time education and training, (ii) job subsidy ("employers' option"), (iii) public employment ("environmental task force"), or (iv) voluntary work. All options last up to six months, with the exception of

(Box continues on next page)

BOX 5.6 *(continued)*

the full-time education and training option, which can last up to 12 months. With all other options, employers are obliged to offer education and training at least one day a week, which should also lead to the achievement of a formal education. The final (third) stage is follow-through with continuing advice and assistance to those remaining in the NDYP program after completing their options.

Evaluation results suggest that a significant increase in outflows to employment can be attributed to the NDYP and that social benefits outweigh the costs. Unemployed young men are about 20 percent more likely to get jobs as a result of the policy. Much of this effect is likely due to the employer wage subsidy option, but at least a fifth of the effect is due to enhanced job search. The role of the more intensive and longer-lasting education and training option cannot be fully assessed, because long-term follow-up data have not yet been evaluated. However, intensive human capital investments are likely to yield returns specifically in the long run, and the NYDP training option is a more intensive program than the other options. Because the job-search assistance element of the program is more cost-effective than the other ALMP options, the NYDP stands as the least costly comprehensive intervention for youth in OECD countries. The cost per beneficiary served ranges from US$734 to US$1,277 (in 1999 values). In addition, the cost per job created is under US$6,500, given an average placement rate of 17,250 participants per year.

The NYDP has been accompanied by key reforms in service delivery. Since 2001, the new Jobcentre Plus brings together the services of the previous Employment Service and the Benefits Agency, thus providing a single point of service for jobs, benefits advice, and support. Its objective is to improve the assessment and delivery of benefits so that clients receive efficient and needs-tailored service. The evaluation of the Jobcentre Plus showed that it succeeded in raising the number of job entries among the target groups.

Sources: Corkett et al. (2005); Dorsett (2006); Van Reenen (2003).

Accreditation as a signaling device

For workers participating in retraining programs, receiving accreditation is important—especially because upgrading skills may be comprehensive in terms of course contents or time spent in training. While retrained workers are particularly in need of skill accreditation, this issue does arise for all training participants discussed in this chapter. Skills provided in training programs—and in particular in skill retraining—accompanied by corresponding certification have shown positive effects in the labor market.

The *ChileCalifica* Lifelong Learning and Training project, for instance, targets different types of beneficiaries corresponding to different stages of the working career over the life cycle (and thus also different skill levels): (i) youth and adults without TVET, (ii) economically active workers with low skills, and (iii) skilled workers in need of skill accreditation and further training. Regarding the latter group, *ChileCalifica* uses a set of tools, including a qualification and skill award system, technical and vocational pathways, skill training, quality assurance of technical and vocational education, and information systems for education and training supply. The system is regulated under the Chilean quality assurance standard and contains a catalog of some 1,000 competencies for 315 occupational profiles in 12 sectors of the economy. Since 2003, more than 29,000 workers have been certified according to these competency standards, and with the National System for Certification of Labor Competences, an institutional umbrella was established for the different types of education (academic, vocational, and technical) and training modalities (formal, informal, pre-employment, and enterprise based).

An impact evaluation carried out in 2009 found that the labor competency program had a positive and significant effect on labor income for workers age 40, highlighting the importance of accreditation and certification as part of training programs (Santiago Consultores 2009). This finding is supported by evaluations of similar programs in other countries. For example, German retraining programs leading to complete, certified vocational degrees are typically the most successful at increasing participants' employability and earnings (see Kluve et al. 2010; Lechner, Miquel, and Wunsch 2011). An accredited certificate or degree received when participants complete a program thus increases the external value of the program, while likely also increasing the subjective value for the participants and the probability that they will actually complete the course.

Toward a Blueprint for Training-Related ALMPs

One of the main observations from the review of training programs in this chapter is that they have common design features. In all cases, subsidies, credit, counseling, and intermediation services are important complements to the training itself. The importance of the various services and the content of the training, of course, respond to the specific needs of the targeted group. The implication is that it is possible to outline a set of core principles for the design of training-related ALMPs. Implementation would then be adapted to specific local conditions and institutional realities. The ideal structure would be a system that operates through one-stop shops, which can be public or private service providers. As previously discussed, this type of service delivery is now common in many OECD countries.

The one-stop centers would constitute the interface between potential program participants—that is, the three categories of target groups previously discussed—and training providers. Depending on the target group and a given country's support system, either side can play a more or less active role in this interaction: adult workers in registered unemployment would likely actively ask for services, whereas in the case of unskilled, low-income youth, employment office agents would be expected to develop outreach activities to bring targeted individuals into the programs.

A key factor in the service delivery is to identify the needs of a target population and correspondingly assign individuals to programs (see figure 5.5). Regardless of the mechanism used to register individuals, the process ideally starts by assigning a counselor to the worker. The counselor assesses the worker's competencies and aptitudes. The counselor then discusses potential job prospects and training needs with the worker. An initial stage of the process may focus on increased job-search assistance, including that for self-employment, for several weeks or months. If the job-search assistance stage has not been successful, or if the counselor has already identified training needs, he or she may refer the worker to training providers. These providers are selected on a competitive basis and offer training packages that respond to different needs: they can be either short term,

Figure 5.5 An Integrated Training System for Unemployed, Low-Income, and Low-Skilled Workers

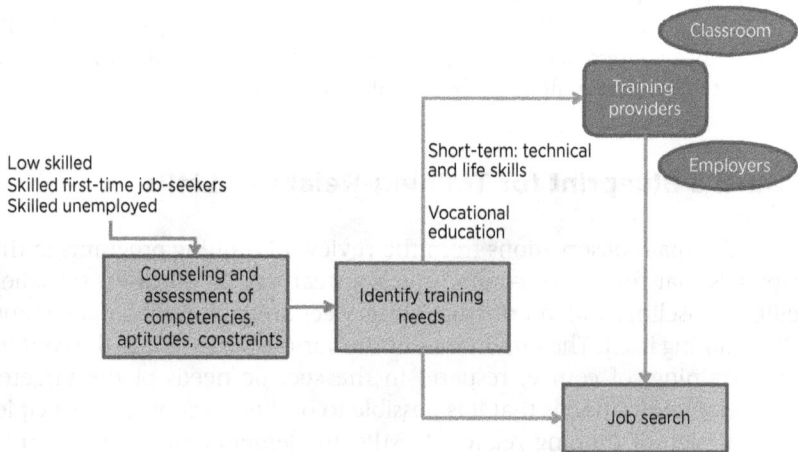

Source: World Bank.

focusing on basic technical and life skills geared toward unskilled workers (including vulnerable youth), or medium term (one to two years), focusing on vocational training to help skilled workers change careers. Longer programs focusing on vocational training should lead to an accredited degree, as emphasized by the Chilean and German experiences. Training programs should also be linked to credit facilities and advisory services to entrepreneurs.

In all cases, a successful system of training-related ALMPs needs to pay attention to issues related to governance, financing mechanisms, administration, and monitoring and evaluation systems.

Governance

In terms of governance, it is important to balance decision making at the centralized and local levels. Although general strategic guidelines are useful for multisite programs, local employment offices and caseworkers need discretion in managing their programs. Implementation should be outsourced to public and private companies through contracts that reward performance. Private companies should meet clearly defined standards regarding staff qualifications, particularly those of counselors, and adhere to certain protocols regarding methods used to assess competencies and aptitudes, provide career advice, and identify training needs.

Financing

The assumption has usually been that training-related ALMPs are to be financed exclusively through government subsidies. Although this assumption is often true in the case of low-skilled, low-income workers, it does not have to be the case for all workers. On the contrary, to be able to expand these programs and improve their outcomes, policy makers must expect individuals with savings capacity to finance part of the costs. There are two modalities that could be considered: (i) social security contributions (not mandatory for employers) and (ii) credit lines. The first would apply to workers in the formal sector who already make contributions for different social security benefits. These workers would have training accounts where contributions (notional or funded) accumulate to finance training and employment services. Depending on the level of subsidy (that is, the level of the government's matching contributions), a given dollar amount in the account would be equivalent to a certain number of hours of training and counseling. The second system would be geared to informal sector workers and first-time job seekers and would involve credit to be repaid once individuals are productively employed or self-employed.

Administration

The administrative complexity of well-designed training-related ALMPs should not be underestimated, in particular if programs are aligned with individual groups' needs. Key processes include registering applicants, contracting employment offices and training providers, setting up tariffs, managing individual contributions or credit lines, and reimbursing providers. It is thus indispensable to build institutional capacity within the employment agencies in charge of managing the system at the central and local levels. Strengthening institutional coordination and the ability to manage multiservice programs can be important for reducing operational costs.

Monitoring and Evaluation

Finally, improving data collection, monitoring, and evaluation systems is critical for better planning and decision making. Programs need to be adjusted and optimized continuously, which can be done only if real-time data are available to managers about their operations and performance. Evaluation efforts that accompany the program from the very first stage of its conception are particularly important. Besides the evident need to properly assess the program's effects, including cost estimates for a complete appraisal of the program is also important.

Conclusion

Training-related ALMPs are the most commonly used strategy worldwide to reduce the risk of unemployment and increase the employability and earnings capacity of workers who are unskilled, transitioning from school to work, or simply transitioning through a period of unemployment. Unfortunately, these programs are often designed and implemented without a full understanding of the market failures they are trying to solve. Implementing these programs simply because policy makers consider that targeted groups do not have the right skills—even if this conclusion was reached on the basis of proper statistical instruments (see chapter 1)—is not sufficient. Policy makers must also understand why workers on their own will not invest in the right types of training. This chapter has shown that in many cases, the programs can have a role in overcoming market failures such as credit constraints, coordination failures, and limited or biased information. These market failures clearly affect disadvantaged workers in the labor market. Nonetheless, a more systematic approach is needed to establish their relative importance in the case of different groups.

A possible blueprint for designing training systems emphasizes identifying the needs of a target population and correspondingly assigning individuals to programs as a key first step. An ideal system for service delivery would therefore consist of one-stop centers where individuals can search for assistance. Governments can also mobilize these centers to implement large-scale training programs. The centers would need to have the right human resources and technologies to understand the training needs that workers have, and they should couple the training providers with providers of complementary services, such as credit, entrepreneurial advice, and intermediation. Understanding the right institutional setting for the system requires further research and policy analysis. The evidence so far emphasizes the importance of governance, administrative, and financing arrangements to ensure that program managers at all levels have the right incentives to respond to the needs of workers and employers. In particular, service providers, including those for training, should compete for their clients and be accountable for the services they deliver.

As an increasing number of lower-middle-income countries are implementing training-related ALMPs for vulnerable groups, further evidence is needed on the effectiveness and mode of operation of these programs. To date, the evaluation of programs in the developing world is rare. Even when a program has been evaluated and shows positive results, it is often difficult to extrapolate and understand the reasons behind its success. Can the program be successful for other population groups in different settings? What are the necessary conditions in terms of institutional design? Would alternative and cheaper interventions deliver the same results? Addressing these questions will require mobilizing more efforts and resources to better measure skill gaps, understand the market failures or constraints that cause them, and identify the right interventions to correct them. Improving program monitoring and data collection and conducting rigorous evaluations of current programs are crucial in this process.

Notes

1. For example, each year 500,000 new entrants enter the labor market in Kenya, and 700,000 in Tanzania. These large cohorts will continue to add pressure to the labor market in the region (Garcia and Fares 2008).
2. The figures in terms of number of people with each degree were derived by assuming constant relative participation rates and using the ILO's projections about growth in labor force participation, linearly projected for the 10 years beyond the ILO's 2020 final date for the projections. The CEN (constant enrollment number) graph can be considered a worst-case scenario, as it assumes

zero expansion of schooling. Therefore, in each country, the number of students in each cohort (by gender) passing onto the next educational level at the given age remains constant over time. That implies that the relative share of education levels may increase and decrease depending on changes in cohort size. The GET (global education trend) graph assumes that investments are sufficient to allow a country's educational expansion to converge to an expansion trajectory based on the country-specific historical global trend.

3. For information on the Arab Republic of Egypt, see Angel-Urdinola and Semlali (2010); for information on Sierra Leone, see Peeters et al. (2009).
4. Betcherman, Olivas, and Dar (2004) build an inventory of ALMP evaluations worldwide, in which 52 percent (45 out of 87) of evaluation studies analyze training programs. Kluve (2010) conducts a meta-analysis of ALMP evaluations in Europe. There, the share of training programs is 51 percent (70 out of 137). Similarly, in the Youth Employment Inventory, which collects data on youth employment programs worldwide, 38 percent (111 out of 289) of the studies focus on training (Betcherman et al. 2007).
5. The inventory does not focus on training programs per se, but rather on evaluations of training programs. The data cover 345 training evaluations, of which 129 are evaluations using a treatment-control design.
6. This bias occurs because (i) the database comprises programs since the 1960s, and although most OECD countries have had several decades of experience with training programs, the incidence of training in lower-middle-income countries is relatively recent; and (ii) the inventory comprises documented, evaluated training programs, and the practice of program evaluation has been emphasized more strongly in higher-middle-income countries.
7. In Turkey, the program is the Young Entrepreneur Development Programme (OECD 2010); for Romania, see IRIS (2005).
8. One of the most recent skill training programs for youth is *Entra 21*. This initiative was developed in 2002 by the International Youth Foundation to improve employability of disadvantaged youth by providing training in information and communications technology. No rigorous impact evaluations of this program have been conducted. However, initial evaluations for Bolivia, Brazil, Colombia, the Dominican Republic, El Salvador, Panama, Paraguay, and Peru indicate that the program has improved participants' chances of getting a job, and the quality of jobs found is higher (Pezzullo 2005).
9. For more information on skill programs in Africa, see Garcia and Fares (2008), Johanson and Adams (2004), and Rother (2007).
10. See, for example, the recent inventory of programs compiled by Angel-Urdinola, Semlali, and Brodmann (2010).

References

Angel-Urdinola, Diego F., and Amina Semlali. 2010. "Labor Markets and School-to-Work Transition in Egypt: Diagnostics, Constraints, and Policy Framework." MPRA Paper 27674. Munich Personal RePEc Archive, Munich, Germany.

Angel-Urdinola, Diego F., Amina Semlali, and Stefanie Brodmann. 2010. "Non-public Provision of Active Labor Market Programs in Arab Countries: An Inventory of Youth Programs." Social Protection Discussion Paper 1005. World Bank, Washington, DC.

Benus, Jacob, Raluca C. Brinza, Vasilica Cuica, and Marina Kartseva. 2004. "Retraining Programs in Russia and Romania: Impact Evaluation Study." CEFIR Working Paper. Centre for Economic and Financial Research, Moscow.

Betcherman, Gordon, Martin Godfrey, Olga Susana Puerto, Friederike Rother, and Antoneta Stavreska. 2007. "Global Inventory of Interventions to Support Young Workers: Synthesis Report." Social Protection Discussion Paper 0715. World Bank, Washington, DC.

Betcherman, Gordon, Karina Olivas, and Amit Dar. 2004. "Impacts of Active Labor Market Programs: New Evidence from Evaluations with Particular Attention to Developing and Transition Countries." Social Protection Discussion Paper 0402. World Bank, Washington, DC.

Bidani, Benu, Chorching Goh, and Christopher J. O'Leary. 2002. "Has Training Helped Employ Xiagang in China? A Tale from Two Cities." World Bank, Washington, DC.

Blom, Andreas, and Hiroshi Saeki. 2011. "Employability and Skill Set of Newly Graduated Engineers in India." Policy Research Working Paper 5640. World Bank, Washington, DC.

Brewer, Laura. 2004. "Youth at Risk: The Role of Skills Development in Facilitating the Transition to Work." EMP/SKILLS Working Paper 19. InFocus Programme on Skills, Knowledge, and Employability, International Labour Organization, Geneva.

Card, David, Jochen Kluve, and Andrea Weber. 2010. "Active Labor Market Policy Evaluations: A Meta-analysis." *Economic Journal* 120(548): F452–77.

Chan, William, and Wing Suen. 2000. "An Evaluation of the Hong Kong Employees Retraining Programme." *Asian Economic Journal* 14(3): 255 81.

Corkett, Jo, Stuart Bennett, John Stafford, Mari Frogner, and Kim Shrapnell. 2005. "Jobcentre Plus Evaluation: Summary of Evidence." Research Report 252. Department for Work and Pensions, London.

Del Ninno, Carlo, Kalanidhi Subbarao, and Annamaria Milazzo. 2009. "How to Make Public Works Work: A Review of the Experiences." Social Protection Discussion Paper 0905. World Bank, Washington, DC.

Di Filippo, Mario, Tanja Lohmann, David Margolis, and David Robalino, with inputs from Tenzin Chhoeda, Amit Dar, and Hong Tan. 2012. "Skills Toward Employment and Productivity." World Bank, Washington, DC.

Dorsett, Richard. 2006. "The New Deal for Young People: Effect on the Labour Market Status of Young Men." *Labour Economics* 13(3): 405–22.

Fares, Jean, and Olga Susana Puerto. 2009. "Towards Comprehensive Training." Social Protection Discussion Paper 924. World Bank, Washington, DC.

Galasso, Emanuela, and Martin Ravallion. 2004. "Social Protection in a Crisis: Argentina's Plan Jefes y Jefas." *World Bank Economic Review* 18(3): 367–99.

Garcia, Marito, and Jean Fares, eds. 2008. *Youth in Africa's Labor Market.* Washington, DC: World Bank.

Hashemi, Syed, and Richard Rosenberg. 2006. "Graduating the Poorest into Microfinance: Linking Safety Nets and Financial Services." Focus Note 34. Consultative Group to Assist the Poor, Washington, DC.

Ibarraran, Pablo, and David Rosas. 2009. "Evaluating the Impact of Job Training Programmes in Latin America: Evidence from IDB Funded Operations." *Journal of Development Effectiveness* 1(2): 195–216.

Institute for Regional Innovation and Social Research (IRIS). 2005. *Thematic Study on Policy Measures Concerning Disadvantaged Youth.* Tübingen, Germany: IRIS.

International Labour Organization (ILO). 2010. *Key Indicators of the Labour Market.* Sixth Edition. Geneva: ILO.

Jaramillo, Miguel. 2006. "Youth at Risk in Latin America and the Caribbean: Supporting Youth Facing Labor Market Risks." Draft Policy Note. World Bank, Washington, DC.

Johanson, Richard K., and Arvil V. Adams. 2004. *Skills Development in Sub-Saharan Africa.* Washington, DC: World Bank.

Kluve, Jochen. 2010. "The Effectiveness of European Active Labor Market Programs." *Labour Economics* 17(6): 904–18.

Kluve, Jochen, Hilmar Schneider, Arne Uhlendorff, and Zhong Zhao. 2010. "Evaluating Continuous Training Programs Using the Generalized Propensity Score." Revised version of IZA Discussion Paper 3255. Institute for the Study of Labor, Bonn, Germany.

Lechner, Michael, Ruth Miquel, and Conny Wunsch. 2011. "Long-Run Effects of Public Sector Sponsored Training in West Germany." *Journal of the European Economic Association* 9(4): 742–84.

Organisation for Economic Co-operation and Development (OECD). 2007. *OECD Employment Outlook 2007.* Paris: OECD.

———. 2010. *OECD Studies on SMEs, Entrepreneurship, and Innovation.* Paris: OECD. Available at: http://www.oecd-ilibrary.org/industry-and-services/oecd-studies-on-smes-and-entrepreneurship_20780990.

Peeters, Pia, Wendy Cunningham, Gayatri Acharya, and Arvil Adams. 2009. *Youth Employment in Sierra Leone: Sustainable Livelihood Opportunities in a Post-conflict Setting.* Washington, DC: World Bank.

Pezzullo, Susana. 2005. *Project Effectiveness and Impact: Youth Employability and Job Placement.* Baltimore, MD: International Youth Foundation.

Puerto, Olga Susana. 2007. "Learning from International Experiences: The Youth Employment Inventory." Background paper for the Sierra Leone Youth and Employment ESW. World Bank, Washington, DC.

Ribe, Helena, David A. Robalino, and Ian Walker. 2012. *From Right to Reality: Incentives, Labor Markets, and the Challenge of Universal Social Protection in Latin America and the Caribbean.* Washington, DC: World Bank.

Robalino, David A., Friederike Rother, and David Newhouse. 2011. "Labor Markets in the Aftermath of the Crisis." Social Protection and Labor Brief. World Bank, Washington, DC.

Rodríguez-Planas, Núria, and Jacob Benus. 2010. "Evaluating Active Labor Markets in Romania." *Empirical Economics* 38(1): 65–84.

Rother, Friederike. 2007. "Interventions to Support Young Workers in Sub-Saharan Africa." Regional Report for the Youth Employment Inventory. World Bank, Washington, DC.

Santiago Consultores. 2009. "Evaluación en Profundidad Programa Chilecalifica." Santiago Consultores, Santiago.

Van Reenen, John. 2003. "Active Labor Market Policies and the British New Deal for the Young Unemployed in Context." National Bureau of Economic Research (NBER) Working Paper 9576. NBER, Cambridge, MA.

World Bank. 1999. "Central African Republic: Agricultural Services Development Project." Implementation Completion Report 19556. World Bank, Washington, DC.

———. 2005. "Social Safety Nets in Bangladesh: An Assessment." South Asia Region Report 33411-BD, Human Development Unit. World Bank, Washington, DC.

———. 2006. "Implementation Completion Report on a Credit in the Amount of US$5.0 Million to the Republic of Benin for a Labor Force Development Project." Report 34601. World Bank, Washington, DC.

———. 2008. "Northern Uganda Social Action Fund Youth Opportunities Program." World Bank, Washington, DC.

———. 2009a. "Turning Theses into Enterprises: A (Randomized) Experiment in Tunisia." Middle East and North Africa, Social and Human Development Group. World Bank, Washington, DC.

———. 2009b. "Republic of El Salvador: Income Support and Employability Project Appraisal Document." Human Development Network Report AB5112. World Bank, Washington, DC.

———. 2010. "The Adolescent Girls Initiative: An Alliance for Economic Empowerment." Gender and Development Group, Poverty Reduction and Economic Management Network. World Bank, Washington, DC.

———. 2011. *More and Better Jobs in South Asia*. South Asia Development Matters. Washington, DC: World Bank.

Komar, Richard, a. 2007. "Expectations to Shift your World Toward...Learn More." Technical Report for Youth Employment Inventory. World Bank, Washington, DC.

Santiago Consulting. 2009. "Evaluacion de Programas de Capacitación." Santiago Consulting, Santiago.

U.S. Bears, John, and J. "Active Labor Market Policies in the United States: Jobs for the Working Poor or Disguised Unemployment in Economy Reform." NBER Working Paper 15790. NBER, Cambridge, MA.

World Bank. 1998. "Literal Social Republic Agricultural Service Development Project: Implementation Completion Report 16578." World Bank, Washington, DC.

———. 2005. Social Safety Nets in Bangladesh: An Assessment. Study 9 of Report 38021 BD, Human Development Unit, World Bank, Washington, DC.

———. 2006. "Implementation Completion Report on an Amount in the Amount of US$76 Million to the Republic of Brazil for a Labor Force Development Project." Report 36076. World Bank, Washington, DC.

———. 2008a. Southern Sudan Social Action Fund (SSASF). Project Appraisal Document. World Bank, Washington, DC.

———. 2008b. "Turning Threats into Opportunities: A Review of Response to Tonasi." Middle East and North Africa Social and Human Development Group. World Bank, Washington, DC.

———. ———. Conflict Affected Transition Countries. Implementation Report. Project Appraisal Document. Human Development Group. World Bank, Washington, DC.

———. 2010. The Nuts and Bolts of Jubilee: Jobs, Social Cohesion, and Reconstruction and Development. World Bank, Washington, DC.

———. 2011. ... ... (Appraisal Manual). Washington, DC: World Bank.